M000213443

Qualitative Research

Qualitative Research

*A Multi-Methods Approach to Projects
for Doctor of Ministry Theses*

TIM SENSING

WIPF & STOCK · Eugene, Oregon

QUALITATIVE RESEARCH
A Multi-Methods Approach to Projects for Doctor of Ministry Theses

Copyright © 2011 Tim Sensing. All rights reserved. Except for brief quotations in critical publications or reviews, no part of this book may be reproduced in any manner without prior written permission from the publisher. Write: Permissions, Wipf and Stock Publishers, 199 W. 8th Ave., Suite 3, Eugene, OR 97401.

Wipf & Stock
An Imprint of Wipf and Stock Publishers
199 W. 8th Ave., Suite 3
Eugene, OR 97401
www.wipfandstock.com

ISBN 13: 978-1-61097-276-5

Manufactured in the U.S.A.

All scripture quotations, unless otherwise indicated, are taken from the Holy Bible, New International Version®, NIV®. Copyright ©1973, 1978, 1984 by Biblica, Inc.™ Used by permission of Zondervan. All rights reserved worldwide.

To
Laura
my life partner
who day by day demonstrates
the goodness and beauty of love!

Contents

List of Illustrations

Acknowledgments

THE IDEA FOR THIS book emerged from a hallway conversation with Bob Reid at the Christian Scholars Conference, Lipscomb University. Bob noted the experience of a recent student who received scarce help with writing a prospectus. He was right. In the field of qualitative research and the writing of theses, the resources for practical theology generally, and the DMin degree specifically, are negligible. Bob looked me in the eye and spoke slowly, "Tim, you are the one to write that book." Bob's encouragement through several writing projects is a blessing.

Thank you to Laura Beall, my graduate assistant, whose fidelity to the task made my work less tedious. She spent many months doing assignments that make projects like this come together. I valued her insights, trusted her judgments, and depended on her attention to detail.

My colleagues at Abilene Christian University continue to support my work. Frederick Aquino, Mark Hamilton, and James Thompson repeatedly affirm my academic efforts. In countless ways this trio has shaped my professional identity as a professor and writer. Their friendship is without measure.

Finally, Charles Siburt, director of the Graduate School of Theology's DMin program, continues to encourage and promote my ministry, teaching, and scholarship. We have co-taught the project thesis seminar since 1999. My understanding of the design and nature of the degree for professional development is connected deeply to Charles' ethos and vision for ministers and churches. Many of the pages of this book emerged from my class notes. When I first mentioned that I might turn my notes into a book during my sabbatical leave graciously granted by Abilene Christian University, he responded, "Praise the Lord!"

In the end, neither the Lord nor those mentioned above are responsible for the foul balls so often hit out of bounds that populate the following pages, but it is with upmost gratitude that I thank them all.

Introduction

THE DOCTOR OF MINISTRY (DMIN) degree has a mixed reputation. For many ministers in the field, the degree has invigorated their practice, enhanced their professional standing, and advanced their skills. Likewise, congregations that have allowed their ministers to pursue advanced education have received the fruit of the process. The DMin degree has served as the ideal degree for hard-working pastors to extend their education in the midst of their busy schedules. These pastors do not work at locations that could allow them to be fully immersed in advanced academic training (e.g., a PhD). The degree exemplifies what education theorists have long advocated about praxis and contextual education; namely, personal and professional development is enhanced through an action-reflection model.

However, there remains an unpleasant smell in the air. The degree has suffered from an "ugly duckling" syndrome among other academic degrees. Trifling jokes about the "demon" degree are common. I have heard various academics say something like, "The quality is not good. My best MDiv students do better than this." The mixed quality among DMin programs exacerbates the problem. I have read several DMin theses that showed little resemblance to the precision I am suggesting in this text. The final product resembled a glorified term paper or an exercise in only one aspect of the research process. Throughout the country, the approaches to research are varied, often reflecting the background of a particular faculty member who may have had little training in research methodology beyond his or her own research interests, thesis, or dissertation.

Other publics also know the mixed reviews about DMin theses. Not long ago, a publisher responded to a proposal about DMin practices with the following remark:

> Unfortunately, I don't have great news. The group ended up deciding that the book you have in mind wouldn't work for us. Without knowing what specific D.Min. work would be included

in the book, they didn't want to take the risk that there might not be enough high quality material available to create a book that would make a significant difference in pastors' preaching and the life of the congregations they serve. I confess with some embarrassment, given that I have a D.Min. myself, that much of the group's skepticism comes from the so-so quality of the many D.Min. dissertations and theses we've reviewed over the years. We really wish we were more enthused about this body of work, because _____ is potentially a perfect match for an approach that encourages folks to reflect theologically on their "real world" experience. But our fear is that this theory about D.Min.s would not be borne out in reality.

Similarly, some congregations have experienced disappointment with their connections with the DMin process. Some DMin projects and/or students wasted their time or, even worse, abused their trust. From all appearances, the student-pastor used the congregation as a stepping-stone for a better position or an academic appointment. The anecdotal evidence suggests that the number of DMin graduates who change jobs immediately after graduation is staggering. Instead of enhancing the pastor's role at the congregation, the pastor resigned leaving behind empty promises. The elders of one small rural church in the Midwest summed up this feeling when they told a recent candidate, "And while serving here, you will not be allowed to pursue an advanced degree. We have gone down that road before."

Yes, the degree has a mixed reputation. To restore the DMin's fallen crest, I propose to advance a more rigorous approach to the DMin's most basic component, the project thesis.[1] It is the intent of this textbook to guide DMin students in the implementation of their projects and the writing of their theses. It is my intent to offer a guide that will "up the ante," by increasing quality and standardization in the field.

THE PURPOSE OF THE DOCTOR OF MINISTRY DEGREE

The DMin is an advanced program oriented toward ministerial leadership. The purpose of the DMin is to improve the practice of ministry for persons who hold the MDiv degree and have engaged in ministerial leadership for at least three years. The research seminar is designed to

1. The term *dissertation* will not be used because it has a connotation of expanding the fund of knowledge. The project thesis is for the solving of a problem in ministry, theological reflection, and personal growth.

integrate the competencies developed in the DMin curriculum and to create a project appropriate for the student's particular ministry setting. The primary assignment in the seminar is for each student to write the prospectus for her thesis. The purpose of this text is to guide the DMin student as she engages in an action research project and writes the subsequent thesis.[2]

At the heart of DMin programs is the intent that projects serve the church, develop ministerial practice, and be applicable to other practitioners in the field. Charles Conniry argues that DMin education effectively enhances the skills of pastors and leaders. He is convinced that by doing so, DMin education serves the church and its leaders in the actualization of the vision of the degree.[3]

The DMin degree finds residence in the field of practical theology. Theology faculties across the country still suffer from a misinterpretation of Friedrich Schleiermacher's *A Brief Outline on the Study of Theology* (1811). His attempt to reestablish *Wissenschaft* on the one hand and professional education for ministers on the other led to a divide between practical theology and the other disciplines. Additionally, within the discipline and across denominational boundaries, there is no single way to think about or do practical theology. However, Swinton and Mowat note, "Irrespective of the theological and methodological diversity, the common theme that holds Practical Theology together as a discipline is its perspective on, and beginning-point in, human experience and its desire to reflect theologically on that experience."[4] Barbara Horkoff Mutch agrees, seeing DMin education as a means to professional knowing ("knowing-in-action" and "reflection-in-action").[5]

The dialogue between the complex dynamics of a particular location and theology has two key consequents. First, congregations will become places ripe for transformation. As the story of the church converses with the story of God, new visions of what God is doing in and for the world emerge. God's activity through the Holy Spirit can change communities who "with unveiled faces contemplate the Lord's glory, are being transformed into the likeness of Jesus with ever-increasing

2. See Stringer, *Action Research*, and Greenwood and Levin, *Introduction to Action Research*, for a thorough treatment of action research. I define action research in chapter 3.

3. Conniry, "Reducing," 147.

4. Swinton and Mowat, *Practical Theology*, v.

5. Mutch, "Assessing," 87–88.

glory, which comes from the Lord, who is the Spirit" (2 Cor 3:18). Since faith is more than mental acknowledgement but is rather an embodied act of commitment, living experience is the location where the gospel takes effect. Second, those same communities will forge and transform their theology. The local theology of a community is always in flux and, hopefully, in the process of becoming a mature articulation of their understandings of the life of God. Practical theology enhances the critical correlation between experience and theology so that both these activities will occur more often. Although many theological traditions may assume that theology is either applied or revealed from above, the DMin project thesis as described in this book assumes that practical theology is both emergent and dialectical. When the congregational situation, religious experience, and other resources of theology are brought together in a dialogical approach, future discernment, actions, and ultimately transformation are possible.[6]

The experiences of particular situations and the practices surrounding those contexts are key, then, for DMin projects. Swinton and Mowat go on to say, "A key quest asked by the Practical Theologian is: is what *appears* to be going on within this situation what is *actually* going on? Practical Theology approaches particular situations with a hermeneutic of suspicion, fully aware that, when the veil is pulled away, we often discover that what we *think* we are doing is quite different from what we are *actually* doing. Thus through a process of critical reflection on situations, the Practical Theologian seeks to ensure faithful practice and authentic human living in the light of scripture and tradition."[7] I would add practical theologians also embrace a hermeneutic of expectation. Confidence in both God's activity and the congregation's integrity encourages pastors to trust that engagement in the world will foster grace, peace, and love.

My own DMin project thesis came into view as I read homiletical literature that made a decisive turn to the listener. My prior preaching habits addressed my needs for finding the right sermon form, uncovering the accurate analysis of the text, and performing the script in such a way as to teach, delight, and move the audience. Yet, while churches affirmed my preaching ministry, I saw little transformation in the lives of people. As one church leader informed me, "People will do what they

---

6. Tillich, *Systematic Theology*; and Browning, *Practical Theology*.

7. Swinton and Mowat, *Practical Theology*, vi.

want to do no matter what we say." The literature claimed that newer approaches to homiletics would increase listener participation in the sermon process and suggested such involvement would impact their faith and change their way of being in the world. Through my engagement in the DMin project, my preaching changed, and so did the congregation's response to my preaching. More than that, I continued my journey of becoming a reflective practitioner.

And although DMin projects are designed with one particular context (the local church) in mind, the wider field (the catholic church) should be kept in close proximity. The standards for the DMin degree require that projects be public and useable by making a professional contribution to the church. According to the Association of Theological Schools (ATS) standards,

> The purpose of the Doctor of Ministry degree is to enhance the practice of ministry for persons who hold the MDiv degree and have engaged in ministerial leadership. The goals an institution adopts for the DMin should include an advanced understanding of the nature and purposes of ministry, enhanced competencies in pastoral analysis and ministerial skills, the integration of these dimensions into the theologically reflective practice of ministry, new knowledge about the practice of ministry, and continued growth in spiritual maturity. . . . The program shall include the design and completion of a written doctoral-level project that addresses both the nature and the practice of ministry. The project should be of sufficient quality that it contributes to the practice of ministry as judged by professional standards and has the potential for application in other contexts of ministry.[8]

What distinguishes between an "expert" and a "novice"? The literature points to the twin assets of *sapience* and *habitus*.[9] Experts have a shared wisdom and practice that enables others to follow their example. For instance, an expert archaeologist could possibly spend her entire career traveling the well-worn path between library and lecture hall, but I doubt many graduates would emerge from this educational setting alone who would go on to make important discoveries in the field. Rather, lifelong learning happens when the archaeology professor takes her class to the desert and points to a distant horizon exclaiming, "Do you see it?

8. Association of Theological Schools, "Degree Program Standards."
9. Long and Tisdale, *Teaching Preaching*.

Just over the ridge, north of the ravine, is a tell. Under that mound is where we will dig." Additionally, an expert in any field will employ best practices. Best practices are not simply a set of effective actions, but a comprehensive and coherent set of practices that are steeped in context-specific theory. Best practices in practical theology are the result of intentional reflective actions accomplished by excellent performers. They are significant, sustainable, and transferable in the life of the church.

To ensure the possibility of best practices emerging from DMin degrees, the project thesis must be designed, implemented, and completed according to the highest levels of academic standards. Even if improvisation by some DMin Programs is encouraged to meet the changing landscape, the basics of research and the structures of knowledge are still needed to provide validity, reliability, and trustworthiness. A solid foundation comes prior to building a structure. Jazz musicians, the masters at improvisation, know and master the fundamentals of music. Actors on the stage, who enthrall us with their ability to improvise, approach their craft with serious dedication and hard work. Architects may introduce the "wow" factor in their modern designs, but the laws of physics and mechanics are rigidly followed. The practice of pastoral leadership is always evolving and adapting to the emerging culture. And successful pastors have navigated those waters by careful observation, listening, interpreting, and corresponding practice. While some ministers seem to know the practices of being a pastor in their bones, possessing natural giftedness, genius, and inspiration, the rest of us must be shown how through years of preparation and hard work. Pastoral improvisation does not emerge from a vacuum but from the fundamentals of the discipline.

The intent of *A Multi-Methods Approach to Projects for Doctor of Ministry Thesis* is to provide the fundamentals of qualitative research that can lay a foundation for the project thesis. From that foundation, it is my hope to see beautiful structures, artistic stage performances, and inspiring improvisations in churches for the glory of God and for the sake of the world.

THE DOCTOR OF MINISTRY DEGREE
AS A THEOLOGICAL ACT

The severing of theology and practice, the development of discrete disciplines, and the extensive borrowing from secular fields is what Thiemann has named "detheologizing" of the seminary.[10] The DMin

10. Thiemann, "Scholarly Vocation," 86–101. The categories of "communal," "forma-

project thesis contribute to this "detheologizing" problem by relying too heavily on the social sciences for theory, practice, and measures of success. When DMin projects ignore the primary foundations that theological resources provide, "detheologizing" occurs and the reputation of the degree suffers. Therefore, DMin programs must engage students in intentional theological acts.

In the literature, various models and metaphors exist for ministers' theological activity. For example, Bevans identifies six models of contextual theology.[11] While I recognize the interplay that occurs through the porous boundaries of any taxonomy, I identify most with Bevans's "The Praxis Model" or "action-reflection-action" activity that is in process and moving forward. In that model, the DMin student functions as a resident contextual theologian who is initiating a ministry intervention within a particular context in order to address critically a discrete problem so that the community will continue its journey of becoming like Christ for the sake of the world. Dissecting that last sentence leads me to a four-fold paradigm for understanding the theological nature of the DMin degree. The student's involvement in the degree, and particularly the project thesis process, highlights the student's functioning as a resident practical theologian who practices (1) theology as a communal activity—faith relating to others, (2) theology as a formative activity—faith shaping identity, (3) theology as a critical activity—faith seeking understanding in practice, and (4) theology as a public activity—faith expressing itself in the marketplace.

Theology as a Communal Activity

I enjoy my study room in the campus library. It is located at the end of a dark alcove where new and old construction meets. Unless you know where you are going, you will not get there. Students often knock at my office door but rarely tread the dusty hallway to find my carrel. I have easy access to shelves of books and journals that kindly invite me into a private discourse that can last days. Books cradled my calling to the ministry. The library can function as a cathedral for me; an altar for intellectual pursuits. Loving God with my mind becomes my ministry. I am content to do it alone. Being a professor is grand work, except for the students. If the university did not need tuition for its balanced budget,

---

tive," "critical," and "public" were proposed by Thiemann and developed as a paradigm in Sensing, *Pedagogies of Preaching*.

11. Bevans, *Models*.

I would vote to stop recruiting them altogether. Unfortunately, many pastors are tempted to say the same thing about congregants.

DMin projects are not done in isolation. While action research requires fluency with the academic resources of libraries, it is foremost a mutually shared engagement with others. As a communal theological activity, DMin research avails itself to open inquiry with others, utilizing the informed judgment that emerges from various theological resources. The community of faith, following the well-known definition of theology as "faith seeking understanding," seeks to understand itself, its local theology, and its mission in the world. And such theological understanding comes from accessing the collective and multiple resources of the larger community.

Sometimes, only one voice reverberates for the whole community. Such situations are unhealthy and lead to a skewed sense of God and God's ways in the world. The church, however, needs to listen to the many voices that make up Christ's body, and the DMin experience facilitates that opportunity. DMin students have the opportunity to encourage theological conversations that are inclusive of all members. Some ministers might be fearful that including the voices of the laity will lead to a watering down of the gospel or a cacophony of voices. Then again, a diverse inclusion of voices signifies that the church community is engaged, living, and vibrant. Others are fearful that the conversation leads to fragmentation due to diversity. Conversely, if a group locks into its own sub-world of reality and abides by its own standards of judgment, then division, isolation, or implosion will occur because conversation is stifled.

When DMin pastor-students foster collaborative learning styles, problem solving, and consensus making through community discernment, they will enable successful future congregational activities. Practical theology prospers in the arena of community discernment. DMin projects should not be about cultural reproduction or reaffirmation of time-honored beliefs. Instead, the project should foster community development and dialogue. The minister, through the project, sets the stage for dialogue. The interchange needs to include a multiplicity of perspectives and a diversity of voices; otherwise, the conversation will only talk about the same old things in the same old ways.

Neither theology nor the practice of ministry can remain in a laboratory. Ministry is not a solo performance or a spectator sport. Ministry occurs within the social realities of communities and articulates God's dynamic word so that the congregation's collective voice may affirm and confess faith. The dominant point of view in society, the hegemony found in culture, is often what ministry needs to call into question. Faithful ministry seeks to express the voices that have been suppressed and marginalized in order to celebrate community. Research that isolates the minister from people does a great disservice to God's activity in this world.

The communal character of theology is rooted in the nature of a triune God. DMin projects reflect God's triune nature by connecting personal stories with God's story and the congregation's story. The minister's story intersects with the participants' stories, creating an environment of dialogue found in community. Community-oriented learning recognizes that participants and ministers alike are part of the people of God rather than members of an individualistic religion in which each person seeks his or her place. The participants in the DMin project represent a microcosm of the congregation, and as the project is implemented, the church becomes a collective story and a vision of wholeness.

Matthew Lipman describes converting the project team into a community of inquiry "in which [participants] listen to one another with respect, build on unsupported opinions, assist each other in drawing inferences from what has been said, and seek to identify one another's assumptions."[12] This kind of learning community is established not just to ensure dialogical processes, but also to provide community crucial to the formation and nurture of the participants' identities. DMin pastor-students will want to develop a community of inquiry that knows and respects every participant who comes through the door. As the church engages in supportive and meaningful dialogue, needs and interests are met. Such a community fosters cooperation and collaboration, values diversity, and creates an inclusive and supportive climate. Treating participants as individuals requires recognition of the different presuppositions each participant brings to the process. The researcher needs to appreciate participants' different backgrounds, be receptive of their varying contributions to the project, and be empathetic with whatever disadvantages have hindered them in the past. In this environment, participants feel freer to risk, discover, and experiment with their own voices in the life of the church. DMin students who engage heterogeneous and cross-cultural projects consisting of groups mixed in terms of gender,

12. Lipman, "Thinking in Education," 261.

marital status, denominational allegiance, race, economic background, and cultural representation will cultivate God's character within the life of the church.

Although each participant in the project is an individual, each new task force or future project is also a group with its own dynamic. A participant in one intervention may respond differently in another context or in another group. Each project will develop its own personality. Therefore, pastor-students cannot let the activities of one project, previous task forces, committees, or experiences of other churches influence how they see this group. By allowing the group to ponder, inquire, test alternatives, and synthesize responses, peer learning takes place. Through synergy, the collective mind influences individual development, for humans were created to be communal beings. A researcher's awareness, flexibility, and openness to these ever-shifting possibilities will invigorate the project and the congregation.

The DMin degree is designed to foster pastoral leadership. The DMin student shares her personal journey by becoming a mentor, facilitator, and fellow struggler who converses with congregants who are presently experiencing their own journeys. Members are encouraged to follow their journeys of imitation and experience as they forge their own personal theology and story within community. The researcher becomes a catalyst to co-author the community's story for at least a chapter or two. Subsequently, the faith community in turn co-authors the pastor's story especially as the pages of the life of the project is lived out during their mutual interaction. In this way, the members of the project team join the researcher as a collective discourse community.

The dialogic nature of a practical theology research project allows the participants to co-author their future stories. Qualitative research involves being reflexive and autobiographical; therefore, when the researcher shares some of his story, the community will have a sense of where he is coming from, where his heart is, and what the influencing factors are for him. Some of a project's participants have been involved in church life a long time while others have not. Engagement in the project will facilitate a forging of their Christian identities into the larger Christian community and story of God.

How is the DMin pastor-student supposed to foster communal activities? Pastoral practice has always relied upon models and mentors.[13]

13. Edwards and Schlafer, "Learning to Preach," 2.

Congregants and project participants both begin to "figure out" the process by watching ways in which it is done (models) by different ministry artists (mentors). Ornstein recognizes the value of exemplars who model not only good practice but also attitudes, feelings, values, and virtues. How ministers care, reach out, build trust and mutual respect, and encourage their participants to reach their maximum potential is teaching more than facts, skills, and techniques.[14] Likewise, it is reaching beyond the mere completion of a project and is accomplishing weightier goals and achieving eternal glory.

The DMin researcher who desires to exercise pastoral leadership will want to facilitate and catalyze the situation so participants can become what God has called them to be. Practical theology is a communal activity—the faith of a minister inter-relating with project participants in the midst of the church for the sake of the world.

Theology as a Transformative Activity

A formative activity is a reflective and cognitive engagement for transforming religious identity. When theology is separated from the community, identity will not form. Each society must reflect upon its ritual practices and forms that have religious and moral dimensions. If structures and languages are adopted due to a former generation's adherence to them, the gap between what is believed and what is practiced will widen. Therefore, it is essential to begin with community, the previous category, in order to progress to the next category of formation.

I do not like change. If I have a few extra hours in a day, I usually do the same old things. However, I am part of the Baby Boom generation that has a reputation for wanting to change everything. Sometimes that change was healthy; sometimes not. Unhealthy change emerged in the form of idolatry when preacher's exhorted churches to change into their image. Churches were shamed, divided, or discarded because they would not adapt or accommodate to the preacher's own vision of the future. I am hopeful about the current generation of religious leaders. I sense that the attitude that pervades their approach is, "I desire to serve the church and help these people to be shaped into the image of Christ in this location." Communal formation, for them, is a healthy process that begins with the congregation's faith response to God.

---

14. Ornstein, "Teacher Effectiveness."

To understand ministry theologically is to understand ministry as a medium that facilitates relationship between God and God's people and not as a platform to communicate objective information or to explain ideas.[15] Theology is a relational language. Community takes precedence over the individual throughout a theological discourse. Although biblical texts and Christian tradition address individual transformation into the image of Christ, predominately those theological resources emphasize the communal nature of Christian formation. Therefore, it must be remembered, even when talking about the minister's development or a particular team member's maturation, the individual parts are all contributing to the building up of the whole body of Christ.

Teaching a student to exercise pastoral ministry within the life of the church is like teaching an artist to paint. The minister is tempted at times to dwell on the externals of the art of ministry or the techniques of practice and neglect the internals of the ministry of prayer and other spiritual disciplines. Good pastoral practice, however, will create an alloy of art and craft. Ministry is an art with an aesthetic aspect, incorporating the nature, charisma, and gifts that each DMin pastor-student brings to the practice of ministry. Great art, though, hides the technical ability of the artist and draws little attention to itself. Craft and character are woven together. Style is rooted in personality. Authentic ministry, having integrity in pastoral ministry, is rooted in who one is. A fundamental relationship exists between a minister's devotional life, character development, and identity formation. Time and attention must be given to spiritual matters so that all participants have opportunity to personally witness an incarnational relationship with Jesus. So as DMin pastor-students engage the project as an exercise in pastoral leadership, their own maturation as Christian leaders must be nurtured.

The DMin project provides the student a focused opportunity not only to paint, but also to show others how to paint. As the student engages in the DMin project, she will mold the participants' giftedness by mixing in some craft along the way. She will guide, encourage, and allow participants to continue the process of becoming who they are and to reflect the incarnate Word within the larger community. The student's pastoral leadership will foster participants to become distinct voices within community, witnessing to their experiences of the gospel and their maturation in Christ.

15. Wilson, *Practice of Ministry*.

The DMin researcher must remember to treat participants in the project with care and respect. Each participant starts somewhere. If the participant begins with the ABC's, the next step is D, not XYZ. The researcher in DMin projects is not an outsider who remains neutral and objective (a myth of a positivist perspective); rather she helps participants begin the journey of becoming all that they are called to be. No matter how shallow or deep a participant's roots are, the pastor-student needs to nurture growth. That task is not accomplished by forcing participants into a preset mold. Instead, engagement in the project's process activates the pastor-student's knowledge and experiences to move the conversation to broader and deeper stages of development. An invitation is offered to participants to interact so that new possibilities are open to them. This is not imposing one person's views upon the group, but is instead a facilitation that helps them compose their own views. Often this is done by questions rather than answers. In this encounter, the pastor-student must maintain the attitude of flexibility in the midst of contingency as well as openness to the possibility of change.

In this way, participants grow in their passion, conviction, and character. This is not done overnight or through a set of classes arranged in the curriculum. Even the project process is not sufficient to carry the weight of their maturation in Christ. It began a long time ago with the parents in the home and has continued in collaboration with the Christian community, the church. But through leadership, the pastor-student will contribute to this particular time and place to their growth by encouraging them to develop spiritual disciplines and practices utilized by this project that will mold them into people of character. Consequently, the DMin researcher exercising pastoral leadership functions as a midwife, facilitating the process of congregants' transformation into the image of Jesus.

Pastoral leadership does not stop with a diploma. The habit of engaging in research, exploration, and innovation within a changing culture needs to be cultivated. The life-long journey of becoming a minister is always an unfinished work that requires continued construction. Pastoral leadership will likewise continue to be exercised long after the project's conclusion. If the DMin process is successful, the graduate will become a catalyst for life-long learning and transformation. Like a midwife, a pastor is not fully responsible for the process, but she is as close to the process of Christ being formed within the congregation as possible. By being present, she can play a role by prompting and promoting maturity. She will seek to get the formative process started, keep it going, and keep it on target (activation, maintenance, and direction). An enthusiasm for learning can be shared when she believes and demonstrates that pastoral activities similar to DMin projects have value and make a formative difference in the life of the church and in society. The faith of a pastoral leader desires to fan into flames the faith of the participants in the project, and subsequently, the faith of the entire church.

Theology as a Critical Activity

I played saxophone in high school. Technically, I could keep up with most of my peers. As a freshman, I became first chair in the senior band. But somewhere along the line, technical skill did not translate into art. It could be said, "He plays all the notes in all the right places but it's just not working." My inability to make the instrument sing emerged when I joined the jazz band. Improvisation is an art that is founded upon technical ability, but blossoms only where talent resides. To an uncritical ear, I played music. However, to those with more discerning taste who knew both the art and craft, I blurted and bleated, honked and squeaked.

As DMin researchers engage in ministry, they should critically reflect on what they do and why they do it. Arbitrary engagement in the ministerial craft leads to banal and ineffective service at best and only occasionally stumbles upon healthy acts. Therefore, the standards according to which DMin researchers make their inquiries into ministerial practice must be articulated. Ministry is a professional discipline containing practices, tools, and techniques. The basics of hermeneutics, theology, rhetoric, and ministry skills can be taught, and analysis of past practices and understandings can function to mold their recognition of why they do what they do in the future.

For some ministers, the church is the primary and only source of application in the field, and a behaviorist model is employed to teach methods and techniques, formulas and paradigms. For ministers using the behavioral model, good ministry is seen when the pastoral leader successfully demonstrates skills and communicates content. These ministers rely on learning skills from other disciplines that may or may not involve theological reflection (e.g., communications, counseling, management, supervision, ethnography, and other social sciences). Blind acceptance of any practice should be frowned upon no matter how time-honored.

Older paradigms often reflect a modernist mind-set that has dominated western philosophy since the seventeenth century. Knowledge is acquired passively as the minister writes on the clean slate of the laity's mind. Inquiry follows the scientific method of careful observation of facts. Ministerial practice in such environments has two principal aims: to transmit all of the important knowledge that has been acquired by those who have preceded and to make sure that the congregants' minds remain accurately aimed and receptive of the orthodox tradition. Ministry is functionally seen as a form of technology rather than as a relational theology between people and God and the relational concern between people and neighbors.

Ministerial leadership as defined by the DMin degree is more than details of techniques. Hermeneutics, theology, rhetoric, and ministerial skills—the nuts and bolts of these disciplines, the how-to-do-it methods seen in traditional manuals of ministry, which all ministers need to know—can be taught. But there is something more imitative and creative about practical theology. An action reflection model of qualitative research relies on models and mentors and leads to experimentation, discovery, and adventure. While technical approaches may give competence, DMin projects open opportunities for the fostering of presence, talent, and even genius.[16]

The DMin degree is a process more than product. How churches think and relate takes precedence over performance. Ministerial leadership is seen in terms of dialogue, listening, and interacting with others. Due to the relationship with the laity, a transaction occurs. Participants are recognized as part of a community more so than as autonomous individuals. Participants do not naturally assimilate the various areas of study that include biblical theology, exegesis, hermeneutics, rhetoric, social analysis, ecclesiology, virtue formation, and speech communication. Likewise, those members who become part of the DMin project most likely do not have training in pastoral leadership. Most participants need help thinking about these classical areas of the church's catechesis and ministerial practices in order to become what God has called them to be and fully realize in their lives the wholeness of the body of Christ.

The DMin project, however, is not a lecture, an examination, or a debate. N. Frye states,

16. Edwards and Schlafer, "Learning to Preach," 5. See also Poulakos, "Toward a Sophistic Definition."

> The [minister], as has been recognized at least since Plato's Meno, is not primarily someone who knows instructing someone who does not know. He [or she] is rather someone who attempts to re-create the subject in the [participant's] mind, and his [or her] strategy in doing this is first of all to get the [participant] to recognize what he [or she] already potentially knows, which includes breaking up the powers of repression in his [or her] mind that keep him [or her] from knowing what he [or she] knows. That is why it is the [minister], rather than the [participant], who asks most of the questions.[17]

The project becomes an opportunity for dialogical inquiry that follows a question wherever it may go. Allen calls this process "critical correlation." The minister correlates the gospel to the contemporary experiences of the congregation in a mutual and critical manner to foster a more honest encounter with God. Conversation that creates critical correlation allows for the possibility of change.[18]

Good DMin researchers will encourage exploration and adventure. The art, skills, and models are brought into relationship with one another as participants experiment and explore their own styles and try out their own leadership wings. They adapt, assimilate, modify, grow, and see their own potential and future. The DMin project allows such adventure within a safe environment. Data is gathered and analyzed in a controlled and disciplined setting so that informed modifications in the congregation's practices, beliefs, and attitudes can be navigated with care.

Participants need to become active inquirers, co-researchers, and contributors to the emerging theology of the congregation. The active inquirer will consistently consider any belief and/or fact in light of both the grounds that support it and the consequences to which it leads. Therefore, participants need to be encouraged to be self-reflective, self-directive, and self-corrective in their practice. Mature reflection is the ability to analyze activities and practices from multiple perspectives so that implicit knowledge is translated into new practices even under new and varying contexts. Reflection can be stimulated in projects through field notes, informal dialogue with the participants, and peer interaction teams. Analysis of documents, transcripts, questionnaires, and other

17. Frye, *The Great Code*, xv.

18. Allen, "Why Preach." See excerpts from the writings of Matthew Lipman in Reed and Johnson as he compares the older and newer paradigms in education. See my critical correlation model for theological reflection in chapter 8.

qualitative methods increases critical activities in a disciplined way. Throughout a critical reflective process, participants learn to make their own theories. DMin pastor-students will foster intellectual freedom in the church, awakening participants to the realities of a world that has a possibility of becoming other than it is. Participants will be empowered to think, to share meanings with others, to creatively conceptualize new realities and possibilities, and to make sense of the world.

The project's design should foster a climate that allows participants to utilize different ways of knowing in the learning process. As DMin students interact with their co-participants in these projects, the diversity of the participants can be appreciated and utilized. Learning has cognitive, affective, visual, mechanical, intuitive, aesthetic, ethical, and logical characteristics.[19] No approach is dogmatically held as superior to another. The participants are asked to stretch, experiment, and risk in order to experience, to become, and to develop their potential. The minister joins them on the journey. Theological process takes precedence over product.

By engaging in guided research, both the DMin student and the project's participants will assimilate knowledge into existing structures and accommodate new structures of meaning. The student-pastor enters the church with a concrete orientation of reality, often dualistic in its dynamic. The process of theological reflection that the minister participates in throughout the project encourages another perspective; it creates a third alternative that will cause disorientation to the status quo. As the student-pastor resolves and/or accepts the tension, a new orientation has the potential to emerge. This cycle of orientation, disorientation, reorientation will be evident in the life of the DMin student who engages in the project thesis process. As an act of pastoral leadership, the minister will lead the project participants to engage the critical process as well. In other words, a deconstruction sometimes is necessary to allow an individual to reconstruct identity, theory, and practice. If such a process occurs within the project, then the potential exists for the process to be duplicated in the life of the church.

The research process enables DMin students and participants to claim their unique gifts and foster new possibilities for the church. Ministers help participants cultivate and harvest what God has planted

---

19. This is similar to how Lazear has summarized Howard Gardener's seven ways of knowing as verbal linguistic, logical/mathematical, visual/spatial, body/kinesthetic, music/rhythmic, interpersonal, and intrapersonal. See Lazear, *Seven Ways.*

in them through genetic inheritance, personality, life experience, the Holy Spirit, and church background. Participants do not come to the church as blank slates who need to be taught how to be Christian as if they know nothing about it and have no equipment for it. Rather, they already know much of what they need. Participants come to the church as whole persons with innate abilities, thoughts, feelings, experiences, doubts, hopes, anxieties, expectations, and histories. They know about ministry through their previous lived experiences. They will continue to learn about ministry as they hear their own voices articulate their understanding of the gospel in the midst of the project. They have already blended their stories with tradition, community, and God's story. Now they engage the project with valued and holy gifts useful for the achievement of the project's purpose. Ministers who respect the identities of their participants will not begin the research process by setting a standard pattern of the ultimate product before the participants have had the opportunity to contribute and influence the outcome.

Since there are diverse ways to view the world and knowledge, a pluralistic approach to research is necessary. The minister should employ different ways of learning to allow understanding and application to occur. Declarative, procedural, conceptual, analogical, and logical knowledge are identified and explored with cognitive processes. Four related reflective strategies are the following: talking, displaying, coaching, and arranging the intervention environment in such a way that the critical reflective contributions of all are facilitated.[20] Each particular participant must be considered when determining how that participant best contributes. Subsequently, a constructivist approach that fosters interaction between a participant's personal knowledge and the subject matter is best suited for the basis of designing and implementing projects. A constructivist approach will respect what participants bring to the table.

Ministerial leadership gives participants new and varied experiences and creates environments in which participants are encouraged to build their own theories and contribute to constructing the congregation's theology. Ministerial leadership is a continual process of assisting people in the reconstruction of their experiences in the life of the church and in the world. Successful projects will enable participants to think about thinking by engaging them in thinking, writing, and speaking that demonstrate cognitive strategies such as summarizing, classifying,

20. Farnham-Diggory, "Paradigms of Knowledge."

comparing, contrasting, and analyzing. In this way, participants become sense-makers. Therefore, the DMin project is an opportunity to facilitate critical inquiry of the whole body of Christ.

Continuing education, like the DMin degree, is not only a formative process but also a critical endeavor that supplies skills and concepts to facilitate further learning. The DMin project provides a pathway for that same process to occur in the lives of the laity. The DMin project should, therefore, enable participants to become independent learners who are able to discover knowledge for themselves. Equipping others to lead will be a skill that enables the participants to rise to heights beyond those the minister or the participants can presently envision. As participants gain conceptual understanding and theological wisdom, they will begin to apply, synthesize, and evaluate information and experiences in new and exciting ways.

As pastoral leaders, DMin students learn to help participants be eclectic and critical thinkers. The information age has overwhelmed not only academic studies but the realm of theology as well. A minister is expected to be a gifted communicator, administrator, master of ceremonies, public relations expert, counselor, and all-round expert on every field. In this information glut, participants also need guidance to choose the essential. They need to learn to understand, cope with, and positively influence the world in which they find themselves. They need to bridge the gap between theory and practice. The expectation to be both competent and relevant requires the minister to stay current in the academic disciplines and be prepared to utilize qualitative research as a pastoral practice routinely in the future. The minister-student should also expose participants to resources, help them experience learning, and enable them to begin processing and applying the knowledge gained. In other words, the minister-student can help participants experience learning so that they can translate what they encounter into their framework of being. To repeat a familiar theme, the pastor-student becomes a timely and critical resource for their stories during the duration of the project.

Practical theology utilizes reason to engage tradition, experience, and culture. The process of growth continually reshapes understanding and identity. Theology is a critical activity, a faith that seeks understanding in practice.

We have examined (gazed) at the communal, transformative, and critical aspects of theology. At this point, a shift from gaze to voice is essential.

Theology as a Public Activity

Ministers are called to influence the common public reality of the church because their private attitudes and actions will have civic, social, and political consequence. When the public is not being affected for the good as anticipated, an examination of private commitments is in order. The minister's private world is shaped by theology. As ministers assess theology on behalf of the congregation (and particularly in the engagement of a DMin project), identity formation occurs and private lives are transformed. As pastoral leaders increase the intelligibility and accessibility of theology in the public arena, an impact will occur for the cause of Christ. For this reason, a sound DMin program will advocate a theology of praxis.

DMin pastor-students strive to develop a practical theology that enables participants to know their own sense of identity, the community's identity, and a sense of God's presence. If one's understanding of God, self, and community does not make a difference in the community of faith, if it does not hold up on the street, then the practitioner needs to reevaluate. Similarly, if a DMin project does not have a life beyond graduation, then the director of the program or the primary advisor needs to help the student reevaluate. The DMin project is not merely an academic exercise. It must have public consequence for the glory of God.

If the minister desires the participant to master skills and acquire factual knowledge, then the theology in the church will be reflected in demonstrations of techniques, lectures on facts, and practice labs. The participants will be indoctrinated with the history and theology of ministry and inculcated with an understanding of the basic techniques of Christian practice. However, if the minister is more concerned with values, character development, integration of principles, and other fundamental aspects of identity, the church environment will foster a lifetime of learning, seen in a climate of mutual respect, trust, support, affirmation, nurture, and celebration.[21] Subsequently, the work of the DMin pastor-student will have a life beyond the parking lot and will bring godly influence to bear in both the home and the marketplace.

If the DMin degree achieves its purpose, pastors will stand before congregations and claim realities about God and provide leadership for God that is theologically informed. Likewise, their identities outside the

---

21. Wardlaw, ed., *Learning Ministry*.

four walls of the sanctuary will reflect coherence with their identities within the midst of the people of God. The theological, sociological, and pedagogical aspects of their development will be integrated into one cohesive and holistic way. The theology of ministry is a public activity. The congregations where they serve will also mirror their pastor's example by being God's missional people. God has called us all to a public ministry for the sake of the world. Together, a communal, formative, and critical theology of ministry engenders a faithful public witness.

While the DMin degree has a mixed reputation, those ministers who engage theology as a communal, formative, critical, and public activity will not only improve the degree's reputation, but will, more importantly, augment their ministry, honor the people they serve, and glorify God.

1

Beginnings

I RARELY TELL THIS story. I walked into my dissertation defense full of high hopes. The many anxious months of researching and writing had finally reached a satisfying denouement. I prepared a thirty-minute presentation and knew I was ready for any question. However, before I sat down, I was asked to leave. "Please stand in the hall while we deliberate." After an hour in the hall, I was asked to return. Due to the time, my presentation was nixed. The questions from three of the committee members addressed my research in expected ways. The fourth member of the committee, however, critically addressed my methodology chapter. He asked several questions about options that I did not choose. When he finally concluded, I was asked to leave again. My primary advisor gave me the news. "Three of us have signed your dissertation. Here are some minor changes. When these are completed, Dr. [Smith] will sign it and you will graduate. Congratulations." She later explained that the hour I spent in the hall was to give her an opportunity to argue on my behalf. She told me, "I too was blindsided. One of the committee members thought you should have taken a different approach and wanted you to go back and redo months of work." I learned that the issue was about political infighting between Dr. [Smith] (who was the department chair), and my advisor (who was a faculty member in a different department). My advisor won the argument that day because all four committee persons signed my prospectus. My thesis fulfilled my end of the contract with the university by following my methodology exactly the way it was outlined in the prospectus. The prospectus saved me. My primary defended me. After a few trivial changes in the dissertation, I received the fourth signature and graduated on time. Anxious moments come with the territory.

Anxiety. No other word describes the tension that gnaws the inside of students when they hear the word *thesis*. Writing is not the issue. Many ministers write a bulletin article, blog post, sermon, and a classroom lesson or more each week. The DMin project does not intimidate ministers either. They are eager to engage in meaningful projects that serve their congregations. However, the thesis is another animal. Horror stories abound about the non-graduates who finished their course work yet bogged down at the thesis stage. The letters that follow your name in the realm of specialist have significant meaning. DMin, PhD, MSW, CPA, MD, RN, etc. all represent people's professional identities. In the academic world, "ABD," unless temporarily assigned, are embarrassing initials. The daunting task of writing a substantial document like a thesis causes angst. Term papers might overtake a student's life for a month, but rumors about losing a year or more of one's life are disheartening. The cost to families and ministries is often high. For most students, this will be the first time they have tackled such an enterprise. A thesis requires work, but managed appropriately, can be accomplished. I have written two theses and a dissertation. I know from experience, and my theological convictions confirm, that hope conquers anxiety.

BEGINNING AT THE END: A RETROSPECTUS

The standards of a DMin degree state, "the program shall include the design and completion of a written doctoral-level project that addresses both the nature and the practice of ministry. The project should be of sufficient quality that it contributes to the practice of ministry as judged by professional standards and has the potential for application in other contexts of ministry."[1] Throughout this text, I will refer to the *written doctoral-level project* as a *project thesis*, or simply the *project* or the *thesis* depending on which aspect is being emphasized. Before beginning the project thesis, DMin programs will require a proposal paper or a prospectus. It is written in the future tense describing what the DMin researcher plans to accomplish in the project thesis. The thesis is a retrospectus. It is written (except for parts of the last chapter of the thesis) in the past tense. It describes what actually took place in the project and the subsequent conclusions and interpretations that emerged from the project.

---

1. Association of Theological Schools, "Degree Program Standards."

In my experience, DMin students fall into one of two categories. The first group is interested in advancing their academic training by extending their knowledge first gained in the MDiv. They want to engage in a descriptive research project that hones their skills in the exegetical, historical, and critical craft. They want to do a "mini" PhD. They see the endless days of sitting in a dusty library as a retreat that will refresh their soul and invigorate their teaching and preaching ministries. The second group rarely identifies with the first group. They are activists. They want to do and accomplish tasks. They see their future assignments as engaging the field full-throttle. They have little time to explore theological rationales, ethnographic listening, or critical reflections. They do not discount academic work; they are MDiv graduates, and they respect the foundations the academy provides. They simply want to engage in ministry that "works." They want to do good. However, both groups see little value in and are often bored with a class on research methodologies.

Although I am painting with a broad and biased brush, it is true that most DMin students have little background or training in conducting social-science research. Their MDiv degrees, ministry models, and pastoral mentors have done little to highlight the value of social-science research. I am not saying that DMin students are defenseless. Their skills in historical-critical research will serve them well but are insufficient for the task that is presently facing them. Likewise, being admitted to a DMin program affirms that these students have demonstrated professional competence in the field. Some MDiv graduates have had training in ethnography, cross-cultural anthropology, and other social-science activities, but, even then, rarely have these students taken a research methodologies course. Unlike the PhD, where students may take multiple research courses to supplement their areas of interest, DMin programs do not have the financial resources or the personnel to manage the demand that requirement would put on the academic system.[2] In response, DMin programs usually implement a one-size-fits-all course in research methodologies designed to prepare the students for the project thesis. Although fewer in number, some programs will have courses throughout the curriculum that incorporate appropriate assignments to introduce students to various tools. *Qualitative Research: A Multi-*

2. This last statement may not apply to PhD studies in the classical canons of religious studies because New Testament, Old Testament, history, philosophy, theology and the like rely upon the same descriptive research methods students have been trained in during their MA work.

Methods Approach to Projects for Doctor of Ministry Theses is a text designed to mediate the gap by providing a description of the necessary tools most often used and an approach to critical thinking necessary for the implementation of those tools. The book is designed to help DMin researchers to know that qualitative research is possible.

Writing a thesis intimidates even the best students. Just mentioning to students that I have written two theses and one dissertation draws quizzical looks about my sanity. Although some poor souls have completed theses, dissertations, and books on topics that do not interest them, I have found that when this happens to my DMin students, they often do not finish the degree. Students have different motives for pursuing higher education. From the desire to receive recognition and prestige of the degree, or the overwhelming sense of duty and obligation, to the sheer love of learning, students enter educational programs with various goals. The same is true for choosing their topics for writing. The three reasons I hear most often are: "I have discerned that this problem is the congregation's most pressing concern." "My professor (or mentor, church board, associate, etc.) advised me that I needed to write about this topic." Or, "This idea really floats my boat." A topic that emerges from the congregational context fulfills the intent of the DMin degree. More than that, being pastorally sensitive to your context in order to facilitate transformation of the community into the image of Christ is the primary reason for being in ministry in the first place. Reason # 1 is vital. Likewise, reason # 2 helps keeps you in the current conversation within the community of scholars. Asking for advice and help also increases the probability that your project will have significance beyond your graduation ceremony. Furthermore, asking members of the congregation for help increases their role as participants in the research. While all three reasons are valid and compelling, unless your topic energizes and intrigues you ("floats your boat"), you will be less likely to finish. My congregational context in Washington, Indiana, contained many pressing issues that a DMin project could address. Every church is susceptible to a wide variety of issues. Churches do not have natural immunity, and few vaccines exist to ward off all the possible infections. However, the question of how to make my preaching more effective burned in my soul. That question still drives my passion and subsequently my career.

While engaged in the process of writing your thesis, read. Read good writing. Experience good writing while you are in the process of writing yourself. Although you have read many good books and articles in the past, during the thesis writing process, you can lose your way; therefore, continue to read. Additionally, read key books about writing and research. Books that assisted me on my journey (yet not responsible for my misapplication of their principles) include Patricia T. O'Conner's two books *Woe Is I* and *Words Fail Me*, Joan Bolker's *Writing Your Dissertation in Fifteen Minutes a Day*, and the classic work of Wayne C. Booth, Gregory G. Colomb, and Joseph M. Williams, *The Craft of Research*. A book specifically designed to address qualitative research is Harry Wolcott's *Writing Up Qualitative Research*.[3]

Your voice should be evident throughout the writing process. Reid describes voice as the "assumptions" of the preachers' stances, personas, and "implied identities" that shape their "effects" and reveal their cultural consciousness.[4] Aristotle argues that a person's character as communicated in the speech is the single most important ingredient to persuasion.[5] Aristotle elaborated, "There are three reasons why speakers themselves are persuasive; for these are three things we trust other than logical demonstrations. These are practical wisdom [*phronesis*] and virtue [*arête*] and good will [*eunoia*]."[6] Reid summarizes the three canons of persuasion as follows, "Congregants come to trust wise counsel (*logos*) from the preacher who seems to possess good character (*ethos*), who becomes appropriately passionate (*pathos*) about matters that the community views as central to their corporate shared identity."[7] Although all three—*logos*, *ethos*, and *pathos*—contribute to the preacher's credibility and authenticity, *ethos* is primary. Embrace your voice and consistently express it throughout the thesis.

Keep the picture of your audience before you throughout the writing process. The primary audience of your DMin thesis is the DMin committee. Your primary advisor will guide you as to what she deems

3. O'Conner, *Woe Is I* and *Words Fail Me*. Bolker, *Writing Your Dissertation*. Booth, Colomb, and Williams, *The Craft of Research*. Wolcott, *Writing Up*. Additionally, Murphy, *Reasoning and Rhetoric,* is invaluable.

4. Reid, *Four Voices*, 12. Reid describes his map as a "Matrix of Contemporary Christian Voices rather than merely a matrix of preaching voices." His use of "voice" then differs from Cicero's classical canons of rhetoric where voice is discussed under "delivery."

5. Aristotle, *On Rhetoric*, 1.2.4. (2.1.5).

6. Ibid., 2.1.5.

7. Reid, *Four Voices*, 17.

the best approach, but usually theses and dissertations are thought about as a distinct genre. They are not textbooks, novels, or handbooks. The conventions of the thesis genre may seem awkward at times, but as in any genre, ignoring those conventions risks disorienting your reader and going against their expectations. However, you also must bear in mind that your congregation or your project's participants will likely read your thesis. Make sure you have maintained confidentiality as well as a non-offensive tone. Most DMin students will likely want to maintain their employment as well as expand their future ministries with the research site.

Throughout the process, keep writing. Don't just take notes; engage your reading with summaries, questions, interpretations, and critiques. If you do not know where to start, you can always begin by describing an event, process, or people's words and actions. Writing clarifies thinking. If I am not able to explain a subject, then maybe I do not yet understand it myself. But through the writing process, my understanding of the subject not only clarifies but also increases. Connections, associations, and conclusions are drawn that otherwise were simply rambling in my head. Drawing diagrams and drafting charts works for me because it connects to the way I process information. The way you think may require other techniques, but writing as you go will boost your morale and propel you to completion.

The thesis is a retrospectus. While the prospectus was written in the future tense intending towards potential actions and results, the thesis is looking back. As you write, maintain a constant point of view. Point of view begins with a point of entry. Whether it is a chapter, subsection, or a paragraph, once you enter the discussion, keep the sequence of the episodes, the time perspective, and the location of the reader in mind. Keep in mind the social location of the research, the intent of the project, and the details of how the study was conducted. In the thesis, you are writing about past action. Only in the final chapter will you consider future implications or next steps.

A thesis is a different genre than a novel. Often readers come to a thesis and only read the pertinent chapter relating to their questions. Rarely is a thesis read from beginning to end. The first and last paragraph of each chapter function as an *inclusio*. The opening paragraph of a chapter should connect it to the thesis as a whole, transition the reader from the previous chapter, and clearly describe the way forward. The concluding paragraph should remind the reader what ground was just covered and prepare the reader for the next chapter. In the midst of the chapter, each subheading should be anticipated with a prior explanation of its place in the argument.

Start with what you know, laying out the macrostructure of the whole thesis before you begin. If your prospectus is done well, it will provide an accurate outline of each of the major components of the thesis. Along the way, you may need to rearrange, add, or discard sections depending on where your research takes you, but your basic outline will safely guide you through the crooks and turns in the road. Furthermore, write up your notes as you go and recognize gaps of what you do not yet understand while time allows for fuller inquiry.

If the reader is to understand and evaluate the conclusions you draw, the report must provide accurate and complete supporting data. Be clear about your methodology. Be intentional. If someone disagrees, then they can argue with the method or your interpretation, but not with your clarity about the what and why of your research. To insure credibility, many will include the raw data along with interpretations, giving readers a chance to make their own interpretations. If the raw data is determined to be too lengthy, your primary advisor may ask you to include only a sampling of your raw data in an appendix. Answering the question, "How much data is enough?" Miller-McLemore and Myers write,

> Sometimes you may need to gather additional data to replicate, triangulate, or validate key observations. A criterion about gathering data is: Is the material useful? For who? Additional data can be used to test emerging theory or discount alternative explanations. When the generation of data fails to produce new or significant themes beyond those already generated, the DMin student has reached the conclusion of the data collection period. As a project draws to a close, the evaluator is increasingly concerned with validity of data and less concerned with the generation of new data.[8]

Van Manen summarizes the value of writing as an interpretive act essential for the research process. He describes writing under the provocative headings: "Writing Mediates Reflection and Action," "To Write is to Measure Our Thoughtfulness," "Writing Exercises the Ability to

---

8. Miller-McLemore and Myers, "Doctorate of Ministry," 19.

See," "To Write is to Show Something," and "To Write is to Rewrite."[9] The process of action, reflection, interpretation, and subsequent action is a difficult path to substantiate into practice. Van Manen notes how writing functions to facilitate the process under the following categories: "Writing separates us from what we know and yet it unites us more closely with what we know." "Writing distances us from the lifeworld yet it also draws us more closely to the lifeworld." "Writing decontexualizes thought from practice and yet it returns thought to praxis." "Writing abstracts our experience of the world, yet it also concretizes our understanding of the world." "Writing objectifies thought into print and yet it subjectifies our understanding of something that truly engages us."[10] Writing of research becomes part of the action that you take as a pastor-student. Action flows from thought that is deepened through writing. Writing encourages you to speak and act with greater awareness in your future ministry.

DMin programs are best organized when students have opportunities to take course work after the completion of their prospectus. With the guidance of the primary advisor, a paper can be written as a course assignment that will also contribute to one of the chapters in the thesis. For example, my DMin thesis on assessing Buttrick's methodology on preaching parables from Matthew 13 required that I do research relating to Buttrick and an exegesis of Matthew 13. Following the writing of the prospectus, I took a class in advanced preaching strategies, where I wrote a paper on Buttrick's methodology. Subsequently, I also was afforded the opportunity to take an advanced exegetical seminar on the Gospel of Matthew. These papers contributed greatly to the first draft of my thesis.

BEGINNING AT THE BEGINNING: A PROSPECTUS

A detailed prospectus of the Project thesis will be expected from each student before any work on the project begins.[11] The purposes of the prospectus are several:

---

9. Van Manen, *Researching Lived Experience*, 124–33.

10. Ibid., 127–9.

11. In writing the prospectus, use the same style manual that you will use in writing the thesis. Although your particular institution may have its own thesis style guide or recommend MLA or APA, the most common style guides used in religious studies are Turabian, SBL, and Chicago.

- To refine, delimit, and focus the ministry project

- To substantiate the need for such an applied research project

- To indicate adequate awareness of the resources necessary to complete the project

- To lay out the organizational structure and timetable for the completed project thesis

- To provide the students' thesis committee and DMin director with sufficient material to effectively supervise the project thesis to completion

Writing the prospectus usually happens as an assignment in a research methodology course or immediately following such a course. It is the purpose of such courses to help students identify their topic, problem, purpose, and methodology. However, the primary advisor will guide the theological and theoretical sections of the prospectus and the thesis' final format.[12]

A prospectus is the proposal for the research strategy or design of the study intended in the project. "In effect, during the design stage, you, the investigator, sketch out the entire research project in an effort to foresee any possible glitches that might arise. If you locate a problem now, while the project is still on the drafting board, there is no harm done. After the project has begun, if you find that concepts have been poorly conceived, that the wrong research questions have been asked, or that the data collected are inappropriate, the project may be ruined."[13] The following questions outline the components of research design.

---

12. The remainder of this book is designed to help the student develop and utilize the tools of qualitative research. While some of the tools are utilized when gathering an understanding of the ministry context (an ethnographic use), the primary purpose of this text is to help students accomplish the tasks necessary for implementing the evaluation of their project and navigating chapters 3–5 of the DMin thesis.

13. Berg, *Qualitative Research Methods*, 27.

- Where are we now?
  - ⊙ Setting, congregational context.
    - ⬠ At ACU, congregational context projects that provide initial demographic research usable in chapter 1 of the thesis are assigned in the student's second course of the program.
  - ⊙ Analysis—needs-based assessment problem/need/rationale. From the analysis, questions emerge. From the questions, a problem statement is formulated.
- Where are we going?
  - ⊙ Intended purpose, goals
  - ⊙ Theological rationale
- How are we going to get there?
  - ⊙ Intervention—a plan of action that emerges from a theological foundation.
  - ⊙ Strategy—program/project
- How will we know when we get there?
  - ⊙ Data Collection—What will the data look like?
  - ⊙ Findings—How will the data be organized?
  - ⊙ Assessment
    - ⬠ Assess the effectiveness
    - ⬠ Assess the change
  - ⊙ Evaluation—interpretation
- Now that we are there, what have we learned?
  - ⊙ Interpretations
  - ⊙ Significance and Implications
  - ⊙ Future actions

A primary advisor should be invited or assigned as soon as possible. The selection of the primary advisor should involve a dialectical process between the student, DMin office, and the faculty member to ensure a good fit between all involved. Additionally, it is always good to have had at least one course with your primary advisor prior to the commencement of a project thesis. If issues emerge between you and your primary advisor, the DMin office can mediate the dispute. All parties involved should be reticent to make changes. However, exceptions are possible. For example, when writing my methodology chapter for my PhD, I changed my theoretical construct. My primary advisor confessed that he was unfamiliar with my approach and suggested I ask a colleague from a different department. Since I knew the professor he suggested, and I had a good relationship with her, I negotiated with the department for the change.

Instructions for Writing the DMin Project Thesis Prospectus[14]

In developing the prospectus, the student should use precise language to state a clear ministry need, what she plans to do to address that need, how she plans to do it, what her schedule is for completing the project thesis, and how the thesis document will be organized. If done well, substantial portions of the prospectus will likely be included in the thesis itself. Once the prospectus is accepted and signed by the appropriate persons at your institution, it then functions as a "learning contract" or "covenant agreement" between you and the institution. The following sections should be included in the prospectus:

TYPICAL PROSPECTUS OUTLINE

1. Introduction
    a. Title
    b. Ministry Context
    c. Problem and Purpose
    d. Basic Assumptions
    e. Definitions, Delimitations, and Limitations
2. Conceptual Framework
    a. Theological Foundations
    b. Theoretical Foundations

14. The following outline emerged from several editions of a handout used by Harding Graduate School of Religion in Memphis, TN, and the Graduate School of Theology at Abilene Christian University. Although I do not know all the fingerprints that have edited this document through the years, primary authors and editors include Jack Reese, Evertt Huffard, Charles Siburt, and Tim Sensing.

3. Methodology
   a. Intervention
   b. Evaluation
      1. Procedures for data collection
      2. Procedures for data analysis

4. Results
   a. Description of what you think you will find
   b. Description of how you intend to report your findings

5. Conclusion
   a. Description of how you intend to interpret your findings
   b. Description of how you will discuss implications and significance

6. Resources
   a. Time: Schedules and calendars
   b. Finances and Materials: Preliminary budget (only if costs exceed routine operating expenses)
   c. Facilities: Availability, costs, suitability, and clean-up
   d. Human: Availability of staff, independent experts, participants, and outside consultants

7. Thesis Outline

Title

The title is a descriptive designation of the content of the ministry project. It should be brief, clear, and relevant to the purposes of the project. It should not be cute, wordy, filled with technical jargon, or overly complex. Specifically, the title should enable readers to understand at a glance what the study is about and should invite their attention to the content of the thesis. The best time to write a title is immediately after you have formulated your problem and purpose statements. Although your findings and conclusions might alter your final title, having a clearly stated title at the outset will help focus your work.

Ministry Context

DMin projects are an exercise in contextual theology. Practical theologians believe context matters. The same project implemented in a different setting will look and feel different. The incarnation helps us understand how God in an embodied way entered into the messiness and complexity of our lives. God becoming human, dwelling in our midst, enabled people to know God's glory (John 1:1–17). The incarnation was an act of contextual theology. DMin projects are likewise incarnational in nature. As fieldwork, DMin projects take seriously the concrete places where God encounters God's people. DMin projects will effectively engender transformation in the lives of congregants when they engage them in particular and concrete ways rather than abstract and generalized approaches. Additionally, pastoral practices are incarnational in nature. Nieman states these practices are "tangible actions that are socially embedded, meaningful for users, offering strategies for right use while seeking an intended purpose."[15] He goes on to state that such practices will be occasional and timely, situational and grounded, social and personal, cultural and symbolic.[16]

Describing the ministry context is an ethnographic process of gathering information about the participants' experiences and perspectives. It has the dual function of locating the problem and purpose of your project so that it makes sense to the community in their own language and worldview (see next section). In action research, describing the context, defining your problem, and stating your purpose, are communally and mutually derived. Although common practice, it is not wise to impose your personal agenda upon the congregation or para-church organization. The DMin degree is not designed in our image, but is intended for the service of the community. Key informants, gatekeepers, and stakeholders are resource people who guide you in the process of describing the ministry context in a way that the community would recognize themselves when reading it.[17] Subsequently, participants will invest time and energy and will work with you to find viable solutions.

15. Nieman, *Knowing the Context*, 9.

16. Ibid., 9–13. See also, Tisdale, *Preaching as Local Theology*, as an application of contextual theology to preaching.

17. Key Informants: A local person who is a resident expert who provides important background or current information about the community. Key informants assist the researcher to understand the people and the context of the project. They also can facilitate the researcher's access to resources, organizations, gatekeepers, and others who might not otherwise be available. Finally, key informants can facilitate wise decisions in many areas of the project (e.g., participant selection, problem analysis, interpretation of data, etc.). Gatekeepers: A person whose position in the community affords him or

While the methodology section of this book will present a multi-method approach to undertaking a ministry intervention, the particular ministry context must be described prior to the beginning of your project. The tools and techniques may be similar, but the project thesis is not a full-scale congregational study.[18] The context has a full and rich history, complex dynamics, and layers of meaning. Every context will have activities (rituals and rites, education, fellowship, functional operations, and ministries), artifacts (buildings, art, emblems, and furnishings), and stories (language, history, worldviews, symbols, and theologies).[19] As such, the context is too large for a single project to analyze. The problem and purpose statements of the study narrow the field and delimit the conversation. Ammerman offers further refinement by asking key questions:

- "Which rituals are most predictable and central to the congregation's culture?

- Which other activities are most instrumental in shaping the people who participate and in influencing what this group thinks of itself?

- What symbols best describe who they are? What objects, people, and events carry meanings linking them to the ideals of this group?

- Which routine practices and styles of relationship best capture what this congregation values most?

- What stories are the essential myths of this people?

- What beliefs and ideas best describe what they think a practicing member ought to be like?"[20]

---

her formal or informal access to the power to make decisions, open doors, or facilitate processes necessary for the researcher to complete her work. Examples include community leaders, church board members, pastors, treasurers, teachers, committee chairs, donors, founders, and other respected and influential members. The gatekeeper may or may not be the same person as the key informant. Stakeholders: A person who has a vested interest in the project or ministry context. The stakeholder's position accrues that person with power and influence that can be wielded for either good or bad.

18. See resources like Moschella, *Ethnography*, for an in-depth look at studying your context through ethnography, or Ammerman et al., *Studying Congregations*, for an introduction to the field of congregational analysis.

19. Ammerman et al., *Studying Congregations*, 84–100.

20. Ibid., 101.

As stated above, a full ethnographic study of the context is beyond the scope of a DMin project. The section describing the congregational context is only an ethnographic snapshot that orients the reader's attention to the occasion and situation that surrounds the project thesis' problem and purpose. Although there are a variety of ways to describe the context of the project, a narrative account that focuses on the particular aspects of your topic is common.

In the descriptions of the ministry context, include the social characteristics of the people involved in your investigation. Is it a congregation, several congregations, or some other ministry context? Give any geographical, historical, and demographic information that would be helpful in defining the group. What is your relationship with the group? What historical or traditional events of this group are associated with your particular project? What activities occurring regularly connect to your research? What resources are available in terms of finances, people, time, and influence?

The task in this section is to offer a beginning analysis of your ministry context and to provide some parameters for your study. Most DMin programs will have a beginning course in congregational studies or ethnography that will include a project that can be adapted for this section. The various methods described in the methodology chapter may also be employed to study the context of the project. Above all else, listen to people's experiences, stories, and perspectives.

Problem and Purpose

The most important section of the prospectus is the statement of the problem. The more clearly the problem is defined, the more focused the project will be. The problem the project addresses emerges from the ministry context previously described. When you examine any organization, process, or system, multiple needs, issues, and changes will call for your attention. When you listen to the concerns of the community, some issues will emerge as immediate and rise in priority. Problems that are communally discerned and mutually agreed upon will garner support and enthusiasm for your project.

Merriam notes that a problem is anything that "perplexes and challenges the mind."[21] She lists four common locations for finding emerging problems: in everyday practice, in the literature, questioning whether a particular theory can be sustained in practice, and from current social

---

21. Merriam, *Qualitative Research*, 56.

and political issues.[22] Her first category of everyday practice corresponds with the intent of the DMin degree. Everyday practice, obviously, is located in the field. An action research project not only "challenges the mind," but calls for intervention and change. If your imagination needs a spark, access *Research in Ministry (RIM)*. RIM contains online indexes and abstracts of project reports and theses from more than fifty Doctor of Ministry and Doctor of Missiology programs accredited by the Association of Theological Schools in the United States and Canada.[23]

Stringer reminds everyone who engages in organizational or communal research,

> Problems do not exist in isolation but are part of a complex network of events, activities, perceptions, beliefs, values, routines, and rules—a cultural system maintained through the life of the group, organization, or community. As people reveal relevant details of their situation, they see more clearly the ways in which the research problem or focus is linked to features of their organizational, professional, and/or community lives. This disclosure leads people past their taken-for-granted perspectives and promotes more satisfying, sophisticated, and complete descriptions of their situation.[24]

The problem statement is a concise description of a need within the congregational system that can be addressed by a ministry intervention and is both researchable and manageable. Defining the problem and purpose statement means narrowing the topic. Wolcott's mantra should be typed in bold letters and taped to the screen of your laptop: *do less, more thoroughly.*[25] All those other needs, issues, and desired changes can be addressed after you are a doctor. If you want to graduate, selectively narrow your focus.

22. Ibid., 56–57.

23. See American Theological Library Association, "ATLA Catalog."

24. Stringer, *Action Research*, 67.

25. Wolcott, *Writing Up*, 63.

The Problem & Purpose of
the Study

Figure 1: Discerning the Topic

The literature offers two distinct ways to talk about problems. On the one hand, Mason's *Qualitative Researching* describes four intellectual puzzles that need solving.[26] The developmental puzzle asks, "How did this come to be?" The mechanical puzzle asks, "How does this work (this way)?" The comparative puzzle asks, "How does this compare to that?" And the causal or predictive puzzle asks, "How does this impact that?" On the other hand, Ammerman, et al., *Studying Congregations* utilizes the concept of frames that help the researcher see what is happening within congregations.[27] The ecological frame understands the church within a larger social context. The church is but one organization within the larger social, political, and religious community. The cultural frame examines the church's unique way of being that gives it a definable identity. Within the cultural frame, items like group rituals, symbols, practices, and theology are examined. The resources frame describes the potential social or financial "capital" or influence the church has to wield power. Finally, the process frame "calls attention to the underlying flow and dynamics" that explores how things work within congregational life. These frames and puzzles are not mutually exclusive. They have permeable walls. To assume one position without recognizing the influence

26. Mason, *Qualitative Researching*, 16–17.

27. Ammerman et al., *Studying Congregations*, 13–16. Nieman, *Knowing the Context*, 26–28, describes cultural frames as borders providing perspectives about people. Within the cultural frame, he includes identity issues related to ethnicity, class, beliefs, generation, region, gender, ableness, or sexual orientation. Furthermore, he describes structural frames that provide support for how a congregation operates. He includes the categories of resources like skills, finances, property, and people, political connections and the processes of power, and symbolic significance of items like story, ritual, and art.

of another would lead to an anemic analysis. However, the models of frames or puzzles do give the researcher handles with which to describe congregational life. While there is not a one-to-one correspondence between the two models, the following relationships might prove helpful.

Intellectual Puzzles	Frames
Developmental Puzzle	Cultural Frame—The connection here is the most tenuous, but understanding how a congregation's identity came into being also contributes to the researcher's comprehension of the tacit set of shared attitudes, values, goals, and practices that characterizes the community.
Mechanical Puzzle	Process Frame—Both categories describe how and why systems operate the way they do. The Process Frame emphasizes operations over time.
Comparative Puzzle	Ecological Frame—The Comparative Puzzle often compares the church in a particular respect with some other institution or organization. However, if the comparison is localized, the Cultural Frame may be preferred.
Causal/Predictive Puzzle	Resources Frame—When examining the cause and effect of a congregation's way of being or organization in reference to possible future ramifications those actions or thoughts might have on its own members and those outside the membership, then the various resources the church accesses to act will be a key component suitable for analysis.

In the ministry context described in the earlier section, what specific problem or need emerged? State it in a clear and concise manner. "The problem of the project is . . ." Avoid informal language and jargon (i.e., don't be chummy). Most contexts have several identifiable needs. List the various needs and identify possible relationships between them. More than likely, one problem is basic and the others are derivative.

The statement of the problem clarifies and focuses the project and justifies its implementation on behalf of the people. It gives direction to the study and unifies all sections of the thesis. This section should culminate in a positive statement of the purpose of the project thesis. The purpose statement specifically reflects and connects to the problem statement and should suggest why you want to do the study and what significance this project has for your ministry context. The action of the project, the intervention, results from the purpose statement. The purpose statement closely parallels the problem statement, often repeating the same wording. "The purpose of the project is . . ."

Subsequently, research questions and objectives will emerge that will guide the researcher in the selection of appropriate methodological procedures, the choice of theoretical and theological foundations, and the range of options possible for the final interpretations and implications of the thesis. Research questions make your theoretical assumptions and conceptual frameworks explicit. Research questions also delineate what you want to know most and first.[28] Not all advisors will ask you to make your research questions and objective explicit. If you choose to write research questions to clarify your problem statement or delineate research objectives to focus your purpose statement, be sure they converge into how one pastoral intervention fulfills the project's purpose in order to address the project's problem. The evaluation methodology will produce the data to answer the questions and fulfill the objectives.

Once the problem and purpose statement has been written, the standard for coherence becomes set. All other sections of the thesis flow from these two sentences. If you were to read the thesis backwards, then the interpretations and implications in the conclusion should cohere with the methodology and evaluation sections. The methodology and evaluation chapter would correlate with the theological and theoretical foundations. Finally, the theological and theoretical constructs should appropriately arise from the congregational context. The problem and purpose statement can adjudicate the contribution and significance of each section. My common practice when reading theses for the first time is to read the problem and purpose statement first. Then I proceed to the last chapter and work my way backwards. I ask questions like: "What kind of data prompts these interpretations and implications?" "These data sets and artifacts are produced from what kinds of methods?" "What theoretical and theological constructs are necessary to support this methodology?" And, "What are the social locations and circumstances that necessitate these foundations?" Through this backward reading, the problem and purpose statement remains the final arbiter as to whether the argument of the thesis is to be believed.

---

28. Miles and Huberman, *Qualitative Data Analysis*, 22. Mason, *Qualitative Researching*, 16–17, offers advice about crafting research questions.

Basic Assumptions

What is your place of beginning? What things are necessary to your study that you will assume (i.e., which you will not set out to prove)? What assumptions have you made regarding the nature of the behavior you are investigating, the underlying theory behind your methodology, the conditions in which your study occurs, the significance or value of the ministry in which you are engaged, or the relationship of this study to other situations or people? These assumptions should be stated concisely and listed in a meaningful order.

Definitions, Delimitations, and Limitations

In this section, define key terms or concepts so that a reader will know not only what you are studying but also what you are not. The research may have concepts, words, and phrases that have unusual or restricted meanings. When possible, concretize the intended meaning of conceptual and operational definitions. Operational (stipulative) definitions are restricted to meanings specified by you and used consistently throughout the study. "Do not define the terms in everyday language; instead, use accepted language available in the research literature."[29] Your reader might not agree with your definition. "As long as they understand what you mean by certain concepts, they can appraise how effectively the concept works in your study."[30] If there are no ambiguous terms, you may omit definitions.

Your research cannot cover every conceivable angle or investigate every single interesting or pertinent idea. It must be keenly focused. Delimitations arbitrarily narrow the scope of your project. You delimit the project when you focus only on selected aspects, certain areas of interest, a restricted range of subjects, and level of sophistication. Define your scope by setting boundaries. Let the reader know what you consider to have direct bearing on your project. Establish the bounds of your research so you are not caught in pursuit of endless points. A sharp focus will result in higher quality research and improve the reporting of your findings. Delimitations help you avoid over generalizing your conclusions. Any broader applications of your findings are always tentative and should be noted cautiously.

Your study may have limitations as well as delimitations. There may be limitations surrounding your study and within which conclusions

29. Cresswell, *Research Design*, 145.
30. Berg, *Qualitative Research Methods*, 25.

must be confined. Limitations may exist in your methods of approach due to sampling restrictions, uncontrolled variables, faulty instrumentation, and other compromises to external validity. At the proposal stage, it may be difficult to identify weaknesses in the study. However, you still need to anticipate potential weaknesses. All research strategies of data collection and analysis have inherent limitations.[31] These limitations should not be confused with delimitations of your study.

For example, in my three narrative research projects interviewing preachers, the literature identified a common limitation in the method. Carter suspects that stories told by experts tend to be "autobiographical, self-serving, and grounded in ego."[32] Carter finds the stories told to researchers are often told for affect and may not represent the discourse openly. A primary weakness that results from using qualitative methods with perceived experts centers on the nature of who they are as advocates in the field. They have a stake in presenting their congregation or their identity from a certain perspective. Researchers need to exercise caution when analyzing the data because they may only be hearing a rehearsed script. Finding the deeper levels of their theory and practice may be subsequently hindered. For example, one of the preachers I interviewed told his narrative on various occasions. The performance was so rehearsed that the cues for tears, the trembling voice, the hand gestures, and other scripted aspects were replicated even a decade later. The adaptation of his story for the stage overshadowed my research agenda.

Similarly, another limitation in qualitative studies is connected to the relationship that is established between the researcher and the participants. Grumet cautions the researcher who takes the role of friend.[33] A story, an explanation, or response told to a researcher differs from what is told to friends. Although friendship may lead to openness, it creates risks, for some stories should remain just between friends. Therefore, Ornstein endorses stories told to researchers.[34] He sees that the distance that exists between subject and investigator enhances the reliability of the responses. In the research context, the subjects have a modified character that strips away some of the original meaning and vitality; however, the order and patterns brought about by the researcher garner trustworthiness.

31. Cresswell, *Research Design*, 148.
32. Carter, "Place of Story," 7.
33. Thomas, "Putting Nature."
34. Ornstein, "Teacher Effectiveness."

Theological and Theoretical Constructs

Your work is not being done in a vacuum. When you take the keyboard into hand and begin writing, you enter a dialogue with other scholars. Similar research has been done in similar contexts. Your contribution to what others have previously said obligates you to know the history and current state of your discipline. You will fulfill this obligation when you write chapter 2 on the theology that shapes your research project.[35]

This section is most commonly called a "Literature Review" or "Related Literature." I often call this section the "Conceptual Framework." DMin projects often access theoretical constructs from the social sciences on the topics of leadership, counseling, sociology, psychology, and many more.[36] When this happens, the DMin thesis will need to integrate or correlate its theoretical construct into the larger conceptual framework of the project. Since the DMin degree is primarily a theological degree, engagement with a theological construct is the orientation of the framework.

The theology chapter is the backbone of the peer review process that forms the quality control mechanism of your field; in this chapter you acknowledge that you are not trying to "reinvent the wheel" through repeating the work of others. Knowing what others have said also helps you refine the form of your research project, helping you better understand the reasons for studying the problem. In addition, a familiarity with the theoretical background of the subject helps you state why the problem should be studied and the future implications of the findings that address the "so what" question. In other words, you will be able to answer the question, "Is my problem still worth pursuing in the form I am posing it?" A familiarity with the works of others presents an avenue to answer these questions in the scholarly community.

35. The thesis is subject to copyright laws. Failure to comply with these laws may subject the student to financial and other penalties that courts apply. US copyright law governs the protections and limitations in sections 107 through 118 of the Copyright Act (title 17, U.S. Code). Information on copyright and "fair use" may be found at: U.S. Copyright Office, "Fair Use."

36. Although there exist many ways to classify the theoretical traditions that fund research, Patton, *Qualitative Research*, 132–3, lists sixteen perspectives, their disciplinary roots, and the central questions that guide them. These are ethnography, autoethnography, reality testing: positivist and realist approaches, constructionism/constructivism, phenomenology, heuristic inquiry, ethnomethodology, symbolic interaction, semiotics, hermeneutics, narratology/narrative analysis, ecological psychology, systems theory, chaos theory: nonlinear dynamics, grounded theory, and orientational: feminist inquiry, critical theory, queer theory, among others.

Your project should grow out of theological principles. Do not "read back" into theology from your assumptions, rather allow your theology to be the foundation from which your ministry intervention flows. For example, introducing a small groups program for the enhancement of fellowship within the congregation might be rooted into the doctrine of the Trinity. Or, a social justice intervention might choose as an appropriate rationale an incarnational theology. What are the theological or philosophical principles that undergird this specific project? How does the project flow out of your understanding of biblical, historical, practical, or systematic theology? How does it fit within your overall theology of ministry? This discussion will provide the theological rationale for your research and should help you steer your study into appropriate and effective channels.

However, a review of literature (theology, theory, methodology) is not a cursory laundry list of works consulted in the style of an annotated bibliography, abstracts, or book reviews. Nor is a survey of the literature a synthesis or summary of the theological or theoretical field. You have reached an academic level that does not require every thought to be footnoted. State your thesis and argue your case.

1. Do not include everything a book says, but only that which contributes to your project's purpose and the argument you are making. To avoid redundancy, many important but similar contributors can be listed in a footnote.

2. Original sources are weightier than secondary sources. Critical works and refereed journals are weightier than popular literature.

3. State your opinion and interpret your sources as you engage in a dialogue with them.

4. Allow your problem statement to control what you include and omit. Every paragraph must contribute to the ongoing discussion of your project.

5. Avoid the pitfall of writing a Bible study. Although your theology will inform your public teaching, the theology portion of a thesis is not written for Sunday School. It is an attentive and rigorous theological argument that is comparable to peer-reviewed academic journals.

The literature more than likely will fall into several categories. These ought to be discussed in subsections, logically arranged and located throughout the thesis. Theological underpinnings or primary theoretical constructs for your research will be in chapter 2. Supporting theoretical concepts and models for your ministry context or problem may end up in chapter 1 or chapter 3 depending on whether the material is more connected to the context or the methodology. Relevant applications, common practices in the field, and methodological considerations will be in chapter 3. Finally, the discussion of the findings and the conclusions drawn always interacts with the literature. You will point out what and how the study contributes to the knowledge base of the field and practice by showing how your findings extend, modify, or contradict previous understandings.

Jonathan Camp addressed a common and well-defined problem, declaring, "The problem that this project seeks to address is a generation gap between adult members at White Station."[37] However, not so common or simple is his chapter 2 on theological foundations. He states,

> The theology of intergenerational ridge building is founded upon a critical correlation of contemporary philosopher Kwame Anthony Appiah's notion of "rooted cosmopolitanism" and a New Testament metaphor of the church, God's *oikos* (household). This mutual action between the two poles of contemporary thought and Scripture provides a coherent foundation for bringing together people from distinct communities within White Station. As a theological method, critical correlation was especially useful for this project for two reasons. First, because generational cohorts function as communities with distinct cultures, it is easy for members of different generations to adopt uncritically their common experience as the rule for other generations. Therefore, attending to contemporary thought, especially that which addresses cultural diversity, frees us from intellectual enslavement to our present context or community. Second, attending to Scripture is necessary because of the mutual forming interplay between church and Scripture throughout history.[38]

The outline below of Camp's chapter 2 demonstrates that he is not simply listing or summarizing resources, supplying background materials, or providing Sunday School lessons. Camp's theological construct is a complicated and articulate argument that funds his project's intervention.

---

37. Camp, "Bridging the Generation Gap," 14.
38. Ibid., 19–20. I omitted Camp's footnotes.

1. A Theology of Cosmopolitanism

    a. Classical Cosmopolitanism

    b. Appiah's Rooted Cosmopolitanism

    c. The Challenge of Generational Diversity

    d. *Oikos* in Ephesians 2: A Metaphor of Cosmopolitanism

2. Necessary Qualities for Constructing God's *Oikos*

    a. Epistemic Humility

    b. Narrative Imagination

3. Conclusion

Bert Reynolds perceives that "teachers of adults are not equipped to facilitate classes on spiritual disciplines."[39] He introduces his theological chapter by saying,

> This project, however, intends to reframe a theology of salvation to reveal how it is better understood as participation in the triune life of God that leads to transformation into the image of Christ beginning now. Spiritual transformation is not only a means to a salvific end but in fact a part of the desired end itself. Also, true participation in the life of God, who by his nature is communal, necessitates communion with God, with his church, and with the rest of his creation. Authentic spiritual formation cannot take place in isolation, but must transpire in, with, and for community. Further, this project intends to reveal that grace is not a substitute for the need for spiritual formation, but is rather a means of formation through participation. In this sense, the people of God intentionally collaborate with the grace of God to enable participation in his life and transformation into his image. Finally, I intend to reveal through this intervention how the individual and corporate practice of spiritual disciplines is a means of collaborating with God in the process of spiritual formation.[40]

While it would have been easy to access popular literature on spiritual disciplines and describe the lesson content for teachers, Reynolds, instead, explored the theological underpinnings of the topic. His outline of chapter 2 is not an exhausted theology of spiritual disciplines. Nor is it a survey of all the literature, related or otherwise, to the field of spiritual

39. Reynolds, "Deep Calls to Deep," 11.
40. Ibid.

disciplines. Reynolds selects and sequences an argument about one key theme, namely, the Trinity. From a trinitarian perspective, his outline is:

1. Participation in the Triune Life of God

   a. Salvation as Participation in the Triune Life of God

   b. Jesus: The Image of Participation in the Life of God

   c. Transformation into the Image of Christ

2. Communal Nature of Participation in the Triune Life of God

   a. The Communal Nature of the Triune God

   b. The Necessity of Communal Connection

3. Grace as a Means of Participation in the Triune Life of God

   a. Sin as an Obstacle to Participation in the Triune Life of God

   b. The Necessity of Collaboration with God to Participate in God's Life

4. The Role of Spiritual Disciplines in Participating in the Triune Life of God

   a. Spiritual Disciplines as a Means of Collaborating and Communing with God

   b. A Theology of Disciplines Practiced in This Series

5. Conclusion

Methodology

The term *methodology* is the overarching paradigm the research utilizes to study a particular problem. It differs from the word *method(s)*, which refers to the individual techniques employed by the researcher for data collection, analysis, and evaluation. The methodology chapter explains the design of the intervention and what individual methods will be employed. How will the stated problem be solved or better understood? How are you going to study the problem? What is your ministry intervention that will address the problem you have stated? Be specific. Include protocols that delineate the details about interviews, planning sessions, sermons, retreats, questionnaires, classes, surveys, data collection, data analysis, evaluation sessions, and/or any other parts of the ministry intervention. Make apparent the ways your methodology addresses your project's problem and flows out of your theological assumptions. Describe how you will evaluate the intervention. Establish the coherence between the ministry context, problem and purpose statements, intervention, evaluation, and results.

Resources

You will utilize various resources in the course of your project. A lack of resources will hamper if not doom your project. You need to specify the management details surrounding time, finances, facilities, and personnel.

Specify your target dates for various parts of the project. When will you have theoretical and theological reflection completed? When will you conduct classes, workshops, and sermons, if any? When will data collection tools be developed, conducted, tabulated, and analyzed? Will you be conducting a pilot study? When do you expect to finish the project? Is your personal or family schedule flexible during the anticipated timeframe? Lay out the schedule by specific dates. Give yourself plenty of cushion.

Many DMin projects will not require funds outside the normal operating budgets of the church or organization. However, if funds are needed for transportation, honorariums, transcribing data, software, etc., then provide a preliminary budget.

You will not be conducting your research in a vacuum. Identify the co-participants in your study, including consultants, independent experts, staff, and members of your intervention team. You should not assume you have access to people's time, knowledge, expertise, or talent. Do you or any of the participants need further training or skill development? Do you have people who can accomplish all the tasks necessary for completing the project? Consider your personal situation. Is your family supportive of your research? Have you adequately prepared for the project?

You should also anticipate any other accessibility issues. Who controls the space you intend to use? Who keeps the schedule and calendar for the organization? Who authorizes or grants permission for key decisions? Do you have access to all necessary equipment?

Outline

Provide an outline, preferably by chapter divisions, of your project thesis. This will help you check for balance and continuity. A "typical" thesis has five chapters. (You need to consult your school's particular thesis guidelines.)

1. Introduction

    a. Introductory paragraph(s)

    b. Description of the ministry context

    c. Statement of the problem

    d. Statement of the purpose (including a description of the intervention)

    e. Basic assumptions

    f. Definitions, delimitations, and limitations

    g. Transitional paragraph

2. Theological and Theoretical Underpinnings: What have others said and done that contributes to and supports your thesis?

    a. Introductory paragraph(s)

    b. Description of theological themes pertaining to the project

    c. Description of theoretical frameworks or models contributing to the project

    d. Application or integration of the theological and theoretical perspectives to the project

    e. Transitional paragraph

3. Methodology: How you have studied the problem?

    a. Introductory paragraph(s)

    b. Format of the project intervention (curriculum, sermon series, model of ministry, training series, etc.)

    c. Description of the participants (how many? how selected? their function in relation to you as the leader of the project)

    d. Description of the project sessions (what kind? how many? how long? session objectives, session content)

    e. Evaluation methodology (what types of evaluation? how will evaluation be administered? how will data be collected? how will results be interpreted?)

    f. Transitional paragraph

4. Findings and Results

    a. Introductory paragraph(s)

    b. Evaluation of findings

        1. A description of the results derived from the three angles of evaluation.[See chapter three under the section on triangulation for a description of the three angles of evaluation]

        2. A description of the conclusions derived from the three angles of evaluation

    c. Transitional paragraph

5. Conclusion and Implications: Why is this study significant?

    a. Introductory paragraph(s)

    b. Interpretations

    c. Trustworthiness

        1. Applicability

        2. Dependability

        3. Credibility

        4. Reflexivity

    d. Significance and Implications

        1. Sustainability

        2. Personal significance: Summary of personal and professional insights gained from the project

        3. Ecclesial significance: Summary of implications for further ministry growth, additional study, or for ministry leaders who may choose to replicate the project in the future

        4. Theological interpretations and significance of the data

     e. Questions still not answered or that warrant further research

     f. Concluding paragraph(s)

6. Bibliography

7. Appendices

Not all theses will follow this outline arrangement. Divide your sections in ways that are most meaningful for your project and according to the direction given to you by your primary advisor.

The process of prospectus, project, and retrospectus is a time-consuming and grinding ordeal. Few students whose master's degree did not require a thesis are prepared for the rigor or scrutiny that a terminal thesis requires. Although there are other, more significant first-tier life events (marriage, children, baptism, etc.), finishing a doctoral level degree does reach into that second-tier category. Greater than a sense of accomplishment is the personal and professional growth that occurs. Churches in every denomination and social agencies in various fields of service all benefit from the enhanced skills and wisdom that come from pastors who successfully navigate the waters of higher education.

Above all else, know that the writing of the thesis is possible. Anxiety, while it might persist, is best navigated with a plan. The prospectus is your plan and your security blanket. Treasure it.

2

Good Practice

I THOUGHT ABOUT BEGINNING this chapter with a case study of ministerial misconduct. I omitted the scenario not because I could not locate a pertinent example, but because the stories are too plentiful. Students who will utilize a book designed for DMin research, sadly, are able to recount a plethora of examples ranging from the naïve pastor who fumbled into gross negligence to the mean-spirited and depraved person who preyed on trusting parishioners. For this reason, the media and Hollywood have portrayed professional ministers in the darkest of ways. While religion should foster ethical behavior throughout humanity, the littering of history with counterexamples dilutes the numerous ways religion has cultivated health in society.

DMin students are ambassadors of God and servants of the gospel of Christ. The gospel calls you to a virtuous life of kindness, compassion, generosity, peace, joy, faithfulness, holiness, gentleness, humility, meekness, longsuffering, and above all else, love. Ethics is the logical consequence of your having died with Christ, being raised with him, and looking forward to being made manifest with him. Your profession and your behavior are integrated into the very fabric of your identity and being. You are the voice that reminds us of the gospel.

As a researcher, you have an ethical obligation to your congregants and participants. You are examining and leading change in the social-religious lives of people. Your role as a minister is a sacred trust. Violations of this trust sometimes happen, and once the damage is done, it may take months or years to repair. Therefore, ethical considerations must be attended to in the research design phase of the project. We all need reminders.

ETHICAL CONSIDERATIONS

"Ethics is concerned with the principles of right and wrong. Questions of morality and what it means to be honorable, to embrace goodness, to perform virtuous acts, to generate goodwill, and to choose justice above injustice constitute the study of ethics."[1] *Professional ethics* deals with relationships between colleagues, intellectual property, fabrication of data, and plagiarism. DMin project/theses represent the religious institutions that graciously agreed to participate. *Research ethics* pertains to the interaction between researchers and participants. Throughout the process of research, remember that the people who participated in the project matter. By telling their stories, recounting the project's intervention, and drawing interpretations and conclusions, the thesis will have public consequences. Engaging in a research project involving others and subsequently representing findings in a thesis is a political act and a wielding of power. Ethics in research is an issue of accountability.[2]

When the researcher explicitly reveals the ethical standards of the project and the appropriate oversight is in place so that the needs and concerns of the participants are addressed, then a basis for trust can be established. Include a brief description of the ethical safeguards you used for the protection of your research participants, highlighting any new ethical issues that emerged in the research process and explaining how you addressed them. Issues include informed consent, intellectual rigor, the sensitive handling of personal information (e.g., how and where you store your data), what is expected of a research participant (including the amount of time likely to be required for participation), expected risks and benefits, confidentiality, anonymity, and the exercise of authorial power.[3] Various organizations have written policy papers on ethics that connect well with DMin research projects.[4]

Four core ethical principles guide research practices. Although these fundamentals may take on various names, the typical list includes non-malfeasance, beneficence, autonomy (or self-determination), and

---

1. Madison, *Critical Ethnography*, 80.

2. Ibid., 5. See also Murphy and Dingwall, "Ethics of Ethnography." Mason, *Qualitative Researching*, is a text that addresses ethical issues in every chapter by directly connecting specific methods and approaches to particular concerns.

3. Moschella, *Ethnography*, 86.

4. American Anthropological Association, "Code of Ethics." American Sociological Association, "Code of Ethics." American Educational Research Association, "Ethical Standards." Social Research Association, "Ethical Guidelines."

justice.[5] Family Health International's publication on qualitative research describes these principles:

#1   *Respect for Persons* requires a commitment to ensuring the autonomy of research participants and where autonomy may be diminished, to protect people from exploitation of their vulnerability. The dignity of all research participants must be respected. Adherence to this principle ensures that people will not be used simply as a means to achieve research objectives.

#2   *Beneficence* requires a commitment to minimizing the risks associated with research, including psychological and social risks, and maximizing the benefits that accrue to research participants. Researchers must articulate specific ways this will be achieved.

#3   *Justice* requires a commitment to ensuring a fair distribution of the risks and benefits resulting from research. Those who take on the burdens of research participation should share in the benefits of the knowledge gained. Or, to put it another way, the people who are expected to benefit from the knowledge should be the ones who are asked to participate.

#4   *Respect for Communities* "confers on the researcher an obligation to respect the values and interests of the community in research and, whenever possible, to protect the community from harm." We believe that this principle is, in fact, fundamental for research when community-wide knowledge, values, and relationships are critical to research success and may in turn be affected by the research process or its outcomes.[6]

Often cited in the literature is Spradley's discussion of research ethics and particular ways those principles are spelled out:[7]

1. Consider Informants First

2. Safeguard Informants' Rights, Interests, and Sensitivities

3. Communicate Research Objectives

4. Protect the Privacy of Informants

5. Don't Exploit Informants

6. Make Reports Available to Informants

5. Murphy and Dingwall, "Ethics of Ethnography," 339.

6. Mack et al., *Qualitative Research Methods*, 9. See the National Commission, "The Belmont Report," and Weijer, Goldsand, and Emanuel, "Protecting Communities in Research."

7. Spradley, *Ethnographic Interview*, 35–39.

At the heart of these ethical concerns is the maxim, "First, do no harm." The well-being of those who have graciously consented to be participants in your project is a primary concern. However, such a simple maxim is difficult to apply in all the complex and diverse places social research is implemented. This is the case, for example, when interviewing people about issues of inclusivity may create doubts about their previously held positions. You did not intend to disorient these participants, and you did not plan to create tensions in their homes when they returned. The act of research itself could also possibly harm someone else. In DMin projects, the likelihood that the interventions will introduce anxiety, fear, ill will, doubt, anger, conflict, and harm is even greater than less intrusive modes of inquiry. The following guidelines are designed to protect people and to embrace the gospel call to serve people.

Informed Consent

Sometimes researchers are convinced their agenda would be advanced if they kept their identities a secret and conducted their projects in secret. Methodologically, certain projects and contexts are inclined to such secrecy. However, two issues preclude secrecy on the part of DMin projects. First, as a DMin researcher, your prior relationship with the setting requires you to maintain openness and trust. Second, since the DMin program receives federal funds, you will be legally required to obtain informed consent. If the project was a class assignment, federal regulations would not require disclosure, but a master's or doctoral thesis will. In most situations, people will adapt quickly to your candor and will often do and say the same things, even knowing you are conducting research. This is true even in news reporting. The person being interviewed, given enough time, will often disclose more than what might be prudent.

Informed consent involves a set of practices designed to give everyone connected to the project the information they need to decide whether to participate in the project. "*Informed consent* means the knowing consent of individuals to participate as an exercise of their choice, free from any element of fraud, deceit, duress, or similar unfair inducement or manipulation."[8] Working with people involves using discretion in order to protect their privacy and dignity. A hallmark principle for research is rooted in the fundamentals of human dignity and echoed by the second greatest command, "Love your neighbor as yourself." Paul told the Philippians, "value others above yourselves, not looking to your

---

8. Berg, *Qualitative Research Methods*, 47.

own interests but each of you to the interests of the others" (Phil 3b–4). Conflicts of interest may arise between the academic institution, the church board, and the individual participants in the project. As a pastor-researcher, the protection of the participants is primary.

Every university or seminary that receives funds from the federal government has an obligation to have a Human Subjects Committee or an Institutional Review Board (IRB) that reviews the research proposal.[9] A secondary consideration for the review is for your legal protection and to safeguard the university.

Informed consent is a mechanism for ensuring that people understand what it means to participate in a particular research study; it ensures *respect for persons*.[10] There are two parts to an informed consent process. Obviously, you are asking the participants to grant their permission to use their words, insights, and actions as part of your project. Additionally, you should inform the participants what the project actually is. You should inform them about why you are doing the research, the methodology involved in the project, indications of any foreseeable risks or benefits to the participants, and what you intend to do with the data you collect (e.g., publication).[11]

Additionally, in the midst of the project, people need to know they have the freedom to refrain from some of the components or the rest of a project. If someone chooses not to participate, accept amiably. No one who chooses not to engage in your research should be pressured or treated unkindly. Similarly, if a participant chooses to pull out of your project, even in the middle of an interview, remember, he is within his rights to do so. For example, there may be a question that the interviewee refrains from answering or an activity that a participant resists joining. The researcher should respect and honor these changes of heart. Sensitivities to such concerns are necessary, especially if the participant feels pressure from the group or other power relationships.

9. See the U.S. Department of Health and Human Services, "Federal Policy," or the American Anthropological Association, "Statement on Ethnography." See an example of an institutional review board policy: Abilene Christian University, "ACU Institutional Review." Moschella, *Ethnography*, 96–97, gives an example of a simple informed consent form (Appendix 1), and on page 112, an example of an IRB application (Appendix 2). Training courses in research ethics are available and may be required by some agencies, churches, or universities. Online options include Family Health International's "Research Ethics Training Curriculum," the U.S. National Institutes of Health, "Educational Materials," and UCLA Health Sciences, "CTRL Training".

10. Mack et al., *Qualitative Research Methods*, 9.

11. Moschella, *Ethnography*, 92.

Sometimes it is not feasible to get an informed consent form from every participant. If you are observing a large group social justice project in the community or a congregation's liturgical activities during Advent, for example, then there are too many people involved. In these cases, informing people of the project is still important. It will help prevent suspicion and engender trust. Announcements, advertisements, information sheets, and bulletin inserts are means to communicate and create understanding. The local church board, para-church leadership, or community organization should be informed and asked to approve the research activities.

Confidentiality and Anonymity

Assuming issues of confidentiality and anonymity only apply to participants in the project underestimates the scope of all those who may have something at stake. Gatekeepers, key informants, staff, board members, ministry leaders, and other congregants also must be protected. As a researcher, you must also understand the congregation as a corporate identity possessing a story, history, and reputation.

Through the course of the research project, personal details about participants and incidents may be disclosed to you. Assuring participants in the project and those persons who are interviewed, respond to questionnaires, join focus groups, etc. that what they say and report will be kept in confidence is vital for earning trust. Only in a trusting environment can you be sure of eliciting good data. The protocol for each method used should outline the procedures for protecting the participants' privacy. Additionally, you should be able to clearly state in a concise way the measures that you are using to protect confidentiality.

In a group setting, the researcher and those connected to the project may pledge confidentiality; while they cannot make that promise for others, they should encourage discretion. For example, in a focus group, it is important to emphasize at the beginning and the ending of the session that everyone should respect each other's privacy and anonymity. Once outside the focus group setting, they should not reveal the identities of other participants or indicate who made specific comments during the discussion.

The usual practices for protecting anonymity are the use of pseudonyms and the alteration of details so that places and persons cannot be identified. However, in DMin contexts, most everyone will know the location, and even when the names have been changed to protect someone's identity, it is not difficult to figure out who is who. When congregants read the thesis, they often will recognize themselves and others. Further measures will need to be taken in order to protect those who willingly participated in the project. For example, inflaming material may need to be recast in broad and generic terms—"Research data suggests that conflicts and ill will still exist within the congregation." The statement does not disclose whether the data came from an interview, observation, or survey. Additionally, the statement does not indicate that a member of the project team still bears a grudge. If the statement is true, congregants will already possess the knowledge. But the finger has not been pointed at any particular person.

Academic Integrity

DMin programs and the institutions they represent often have detailed academic policies. I include the following paragraph in my syllabi:

> Violations of academic integrity and other forms of cheating, as defined in ACU's Academic Integrity Policy, involve the intention to deceive or mislead or misrepresent, and therefore are a form of lying and represent actions contrary to the behavioral norms that flow from the nature of God. Violations will be addressed as described in the Policy. While the university enforces the Policy, the most powerful motive for integrity and truthfulness comes from one's desire to imitate God's nature in our lives. Every member of the faculty, staff, and student body is responsible for protecting the integrity of learning, scholarship, and research.[12]

The section relating to plagiarism and fabrication connect directly to thesis writing.

1.2.4. Plagiarism:

1.2.4.1. Failure to give credit to sources used in a work in an attempt to present the work as one's own.

1.2.4.2. Submitting for credit in whole or in part the work of others.

1.2.4.3. Submission of paper(s) or project(s) obtained from any source, such as a research service or a club paper file, as one's own.

1.2.5. Fabrication:

---

12. The full policy is available for review: Abilene Christian University, "Academic Integrity."

1.2.5.1. Written or oral presentation of falsified materials and facts, including but not limited to the results of interviews, laboratory experiments, and field-based research.

1.2.5.2. Written or oral presentation of the results of research or laboratory experiments without the research or experiment having been performed.[13]

Inclusive Language

Since language informs our perceptions of the world, it is important to use it carefully.[14] As Christians and as participants in the academic world, we want to cultivate an environment that is free from any form of harassment, intimidation, victimization, or discrimination on the grounds of sex, race, color, ethnic or national origin, disability, religion, sexual orientation, age, marital status, language, social origin, political opinion, property, birth, or status. Because we believe all people are created in the image of God and we believe that "one died for all," then all people should be treated with dignity and respect and should be valued for their contributions. Likewise, expansive language that communicates the nature and activity of God should fairly reflect the faith convictions of those involved in the project.

The following guidelines are just that—guidelines. Language is always in flux, so these principles are meant more to raise awareness of responsible use of language rather than provide rules for every circumstance.

Stereotypes: Stereotyping (attributing the same characteristics to all members of one group) denies people's individuality and makes assumptions that may be unfair. This includes language that may be understood as being pejorative of persons when referring to color (e.g., "the presence of evil" rather than "the darkness of evil"; "washed clean" rather than "washed white"; "lies" rather than "white lies"; "discriminated against" or "excluded" rather than "blacklisted" or "blackballed"; "two options" or "yes or no" rather than "black or white." Other common examples include gender and age-related stereotypes (e.g., "Men are more aggressive drivers than women," or "Old people are always complaining about the young.").

Cultural awareness: Thoughtful use of language values a range of cultural experiences. At its simplest, you should avoid terms like "Christian name"—"forename" or "first name" is preferable. At a more

13. Ibid.

14. This guide has been adapted from several sources and primarily from the University of Wales Institute, "UWIC Student Services."

complex level, you will consider the impact your cultural background has upon your academic work and any views you express in it.

Gender-neutral language: Gender related pronouns are sometimes difficult to navigate. It is not just a case of using "chair" or "chairperson" instead of "chairman." It is good practice to alternate the order of the genders (though not mid sentence, as it sounds a bit forced). If the gender of the person is unknown, do not make an assumption, but use "he" or "she" or "they." Regardless, be sure that you maintain consistency in number (e.g., not "A Christian should care; they should always love." Rather, "Christians should care; they should always love." Or, "A Christian should care; she or he should always love." Also, "Give each person a Bible" rather than "Give each person his Bible.")

It is not always possible to avoid gender-specific terms, particularly if one needs to make a precise point. It is useful, however, to get into the habit of using gender-neutral terms such as those included in the list below. Do not forget these are not just replacements for female terms—terms like "head teacher" apply to both sexes and should be used for both.

Words or Phrases to Avoid	Suggested Replacements
Best man for the job	Best person for the job
Businessman/woman	Businessperson, manager, executive
Chairman/woman	Chair, chairperson, convener, head
Charwoman, cleaning lady	Cleaner
Craftsman/woman	Craftsperson, craft worker
Delivery man	Delivery clerk, courier
Dear Sirs	Dear Sir/Madam (or Madam/Sir)
Fireman	Firefighter
Forefathers	Ancestors, forebears
Foreman/woman	Supervisor, head juror
Gentleman's agreement	Unwritten agreement, agreement based on trust
Girls (for adults)	Women
Headmaster/mistress	Head teacher
Housewife	Shopper, consumer, homemaker (depends on context)
Layman	Lay person
Man or mankind	Humanity, humankind, human race, people
Man (used as a verb—e.g., man the desk)	Operate, staff, work at

Man in the street, common man	Average/ordinary/typical citizen/person
Man-hour	Work-hour, labor time
Man-made	Artificial, manufactured, synthetic, hand made
Manpower	Human resources, labor force, staff, personnel, workers, workforce
Miss/Mrs.	Ms. unless a specific preference has been stated—though it's common not to use titles at all these days
Policeman/woman	Police officer
Right-hand man	(Chief) assistant
Salesman/girl/woman	Sales assistant/agent/clerk/representative/staff/worker
Spokesman/woman	Spokesperson, representative
Sportsmanship	Fairness, good humor, sense of fair play
Steward/ess	Airline staff, flight attendant, cabin crew
Tax man	Tax officer/inspector
Waitress	Waiter, server
When you become a man	When you become an adult
Woman doctor (or feminine forms of nouns— e.g., actress, poetess)	Doctor (actor, poet, pastor, etc.)
Working man, working mother/wife	Wage-earner/taxpayer/worker
Workman	Worker/operative/tradesperson
Workmanlike	Efficient/proficient/skillful/thorough

Disability awareness: Avoid pejorative language regarding different physical conditions and abilities of persons. The following examples might be helpful:

WORDS OR PHRASES TO AVOID	SUGGESTED REPLACEMENTS
Wheel-chair bound or confined to a wheelchair (the wheelchair is not the source of the disability)	Wheelchair user
The Blind	Blind or Visually impaired people
The Deaf	Deaf or deaf people
Handicap ('cap in hand' associations)	Disability
Victim or sufferer of. . .	Person who has/experiences . . .
Mentally handicapped	Learning disabled
Mentally ill	Person with mental health issues

One should think carefully, too, about whether the disability has any relevance in a particular situation. Why use it as a way of describing someone if his or her job title, hair color, or strange taste in clothes might be just as descriptive?

Age awareness: Unfortunate associations include old people as being infirm, doddering, or no longer useful and young people as being rash or important only in the future. "Older people" is a much better term than "the elderly," which has connotations of frailty.

Military metaphors and analogies: All metaphors and analogies "must be selected with some sensitivity to how those being described would feel and how intended audiences will respond."[15] Military metaphors include: strategic planning, cutting edge, and rapid reconnaissance (a term used in short-term fieldwork projects).

Sexuality and relationships: The terms "homosexual" and "heterosexual" are to be avoided, if possible. Referring to "same-sex" and "other-sex" relationships is a good option. Terms such as "spouse," "husband," and "wife" make assumptions about relationships and should only be used when you know they are the preferred term. Otherwise, "partner" is more suitable.[16]

THE ROLE OF THE RESEARCHER

No research methodology or data collection method gets the researcher out of the way. "Hermeneutic theory argues that one can only interpret the meaning of something from some perspective, a certain standpoint, a praxis, or a situational context, whether one is reporting on one's own findings or reporting the perspectives of people being studied."[17] Even in the so-called objective fields of quantitative research, the investigators always have to make judgment calls about what goes where. The researcher influences research design, abductive reasoning in hypothesis construction, choice of variables, the coding of data, and the interpretation of data. The role of you, the researcher, as the primary qualitative research tool necessitates the identification of your biases, values, emotions, and agendas. Additionally, your role as a co-participant in the

15. Patton, *Qualitative Research*, 504.

16. For more examples, see the National Council of Teachers of English "Guidelines," and the APA Style Manual, "Supplemental Materials," for further guidelines on how to reduce bias concerning gender, sexual orientation, and disabilities.

17. Patton, *Qualitative Research*, 115.

project requires you to view the context and the people not as objects to be studied, but as people deserving of respect, dignity, and reciprocity.

If DMin research is a communal activity, then Stringer's list describing the role of researcher applies:

1. You are there as a catalyst.

2. Your role is not to impose but to stimulate people to change. This is done by addressing issues that concern them now.

3. The essence of work is process—the way things are done—rather than the result achieved.

4. The key is to enable people to develop their own analysis of their issues.

5. Start where people are, not where someone else thinks they are or ought to be.

6. Help people to analyze their situation, consider findings, plan how to keep what they want, and change what they do not like.

7. Enable people to examine several courses of action and the probable results or consequences of each option. After a plan has been selected, it is the worker's role to assist in implementing the plan by raising issues and possible weaknesses and by helping to locate resources.

8. The worker is not an advocate for the group for which he or she works.

9. The worker does not focus only on solutions to problems but on human development. The responsibility for a project's success lies with the people.[18]

DMin students are pastorally connected to the participants in their projects. At times, these roles are mixed and confused. Your first priority is always to your ministry and to the service of the people in your parish. Similarly, if your project is in a nursing care facility, prison, or other para-church context, you have a moral obligation to the care of people first. Sometimes you will need to proceed "off the record" in order to engage in the pastoral process. If these moments arise, you have the opportunity to either enrich your relationship or break a sacred trust. The

18. Stringer, *Action Research*, 25. Stringer continues on 26–36 to detail a communal working relationship the research facilitator has with the participants under the categories of communication, relationships, participation, and inclusion.

quality of the project may suffer, but your pastoral ministry and leadership will flourish. And isn't that the point of a DMin degree anyway?

Researchers also begin their projects socially and philosophically located. They possess theories, common sense, and presuppositions that predispose them to interpret before they come to grips with the problem and purpose of the project. They already possess convictions and preconceived ideas about God, ecclesiology, and pastoral ministry. Just as the participants are not "blank slates," researchers are not neutral and unbiased. Lincoln and Guba state the following:

> The net that contains the researcher's epistemological, ontological, and methodological premises may be termed a paradigm, or an interpretive framework, a "basic set of beliefs that guides action" (Guba 1990, p. 17). All research is interpretive; it is guided by a set of beliefs and feelings about the world and how it should be understood and studied. Some beliefs may be taken for granted, invisible, only assumed, whereas others are highly problematic and controversial. Each interpretative paradigm makes particular demands on the researcher, including the questions he or she asks and the interpretations the researcher brings to them.[19]

During the research process, investigators will also possess emotions. Recognizing how one's emotions affect the research process is known as *reflexivity*. Reflexivity is defined by Swinton and Mowat as "the process of critical self-reflection carried out by the researcher throughout the research process that enables her to monitor and respond to her contribution to the proceedings."[20] Patton describes reflexivity under the category of voice and perspective.

He states,

> The qualitative analyst owns and is reflective about her or his own voice and perspective; a credible voice conveys authenticity and trustworthiness; complete objectivity being impossible and pure subjectivity undermining credibility, the researcher's focus becomes balance—understanding and depicting the world authentically in all its complexity while being self-analytical, politically aware, and reflexive in consciousness.

19. Lincoln and Guba, "Paradigmatic Controversies," 20.

20. Swinton and Mowat, *Practical Theology*, 59. See 110–6 for a discussion of the hermeneutics of Hans Georg Gadamer. All methods have limitations, for they are embedded in their singular perspectives and angles of vision. "Gadamer's key point here is that we must become aware of our own embeddedness or historical situatedness and constantly reflect on the ways in which this situatedness influences the way that we interpret our world."

Reflexivity reminds the qualitative inquirer to be attentive to and conscious of the cultural, political, social, linguistic, and ideological origins of one's own perspective and voice as well as the perspective and voices of those one interviews and those to whom one reports."[21]

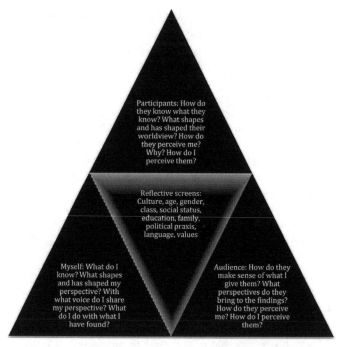

Participants: How do they know what they know? What shapes and has shaped their worldview? How do they perceive me? Why? How do I perceive them?

Reflective screens: Culture, age, gender, class, social status, education, family, political praxis, language, values

Myself: What do I know? What shapes and has shaped my perspective? With what voice do I share my perspective? What do I do with what I have found?

Audience: How do they make sense of what I give them? What perspectives do they bring to the findings? How do they perceive me? How do I perceive them?

Figure 2: Reflexive Questions: Triangulated Inquiry[22]

Reflexivity involves making tacit assumptions explicit by being confessional. As the minister engages in research, she should be clear that the project thesis represents her voice, interpretations, feelings, and emotions. The project thesis is one account—the researcher's—of a particular ministry intervention in a localized setting. Ministers as researchers are highly invested in the context, project, and future of their work. Kleinmann advises, "Examine your emotional reactions to the setting, the study, and the participants. If you do not, your feelings will still shape the research process, but you will not know how."[23] No matter how neutral and objective the researchers want to be during the proj-

21. Patton, *Qualitative Research*, 41, 65.

22. Ibid., 66. Patton's exhibit aids in the self-questioning and self-understanding of *what I know* and *how I know it.*

23. Kleinman, "Field-Workers' Feelings," 184–5.

ect, they influence and are influenced by their projects, sources of data, participants, and other related factors. They cannot remain detached. Although tools will be used to gather data, researchers will become the primary means of engagement during the data analysis and interpretation stages.

So, in the interest of reflexivity, how do researchers handle their emotions? For example, they may be uncomfortable, feel ambivalent, sad, angry, and/or dislike the participants in the project. Some researchers choose to ignore those feelings. The attempt is to remain 'objective' at a distance. Yet, 'subjective' feelings may hinder honest interpretation. Researchers who ignore their feelings may not explore all the possibilities available to them for their interpretation. Ignoring feelings may cause the researcher to ignore significant data.

Kleinman and Copp speak about the two ends of the emotional spectrum in terms of distance (detached concern) and intimacy.[24] Intimacy leads to empathy, closeness, and connectedness with those being researched. Intimacy encourages positive relationships and good will. Researchers do well to maintain a grateful and submissive attitude, for it is the researcher who is the learner. Qualitative research often names the researcher as the primary tool in the data collection and analysis process. Therefore, the ideal of being detached or objective in research is counterproductive and unrealistic.

For Peshkin all researchers (qualitative and quantitative; consciously or not) assume different identity modes based on the research setting, participants involved, and the researcher's feelings about the observations.[25] Some researchers may convince themselves into changing their emotions so that they feel the ways they think they are supposed to feel. This may prove to be a trap that only satisfies the researcher's self-interest. The researcher may be acting deceptively (sometimes self-deceptively). These artificial feelings may lead to cynicism, which is a defense mechanism. The need to identify with the participants may lead a researcher down the path of over-identification.

By acknowledging feelings, biases, and self-interests, the researcher often experiences contradictions. The clash in feelings may lead to the best questions. When researchers recognize their emotions, these feelings can be used as a tool to increase analytical interpretation. All re-

24. Kleinman and Copp, *Emotions and Fieldwork*.
25. Peshkin, "In Search of Subjectivity."

searchers have an agenda. Honesty about that agenda brings objectivity due the ability to bracket those items, or at least an acknowledgment of subjectivity or empathic neutrality.[26] What is not recognized cannot be identified or bracketed. Good analysis is produced by the researcher's interactions with participants, even when the researcher desires to remain distant. Therefore, Kleinman and Copp encourage a practice of recording emotions and reactions that are incorporated in the field notes. Self-awareness helps the researcher bracket personal biases and beliefs systems that otherwise shape the research process. However, the researcher cannot remove nor reduce subjectivity by some method. The relationship with the participants and their narratives becomes an integral part of the data.

For example, Casey is open about her pre-understandings about politically active high school teachers.[27] She acknowledges her philosophical framework. She recognizes her emotions, especially as she engages these thoughtful and moving narratives. Casey embraces the influence this research has on her. Therefore, the reader is forced to acknowledge her stance and react accordingly; becoming aware of Casey's place in the dialogue, readers thus recognize their own social locations. They actively engage the interpretations and resist being neutral about the issues discussed. Casey's motive for reflexivity is connected to the maxim— understanding self is a precondition to understanding others.[28] As I read about the teachers in Casey's research, I was obliged to use her lens. I could not adopt another lens without first appreciating and respecting these women teachers as persons. Refusing to objectify these narratives, Casey forces me, the reader, to remain human and sympathetic.

My own research on preaching professors is a dialogue co-authored by my participants and me.[29] These professors are active agents, co-constructing the meaning and interpretation of my research. This collaboration is ultimately a negotiation of the meaning presented. I pose questions, probes, and alternative perceptions while considering and reflecting on the text at hand to offer interpretations within a collaborative relationship. Although commenting on their words and selecting what to talk about and not talk about, I do not have the right to "unsay"

26. Ibid.

27. Casey, *I Answer*.

28. Casey, "New Narrative Research," 24.

29. Sensing, *Pedagogies of Preaching*.

their words.[30] My intent in the reflexivity component of the project was to allow the reader of the dissertation to discern the trustworthiness of my conclusions.

I am convinced that reflexivity is an ethical concern that cannot be ignored or dismissed. By recognizing the position of the researcher, including emotions and perspectives, preconceptions can be bracketed from the analysis and acknowledged in the interpretation. "Since we believe we already know, we need to recognize and keep at bay our beliefs."[31] To summarize, researchers should not pour data into a preset mold but should minimize the distortion of the meanings presented by openly acknowledging their roles as researchers.

The Graduate School of Theology at Abilene Christian University adopted a set of classroom virtues that are included in every syllabus in the curriculum. The virtues were constructed considering both intellectual and relational aspects of a student's life. I offer them as a summary and example of the academic responsibility needed from DMin students.

Classroom Virtues[32]

The GST invites students to participate in a process of theological and spiritual formation. Knowing how to think theologically comes by habit and by imitation, not simply by acquiring isolated facts. The assumption here is that books alone are insufficient for addressing difficulties of life and forming people into the image and likeness of God. Ultimately, we strive to form communities of inquiry, inviting you to inhabit a shared world of learning. Within such an environment, the goal is to cultivate critical skills of reflection, spiritual disciplines, interact authentically with one another, and learn to function as a community of inquiry. A large part of this involves connecting areas of life rather than pitting them against one another. Prayer, study, and other dimensions of life are all integral to the process of formation. Consequently, we invite you to participate in a set of practices; nurtured within this context, you pursue

---

30. Lather, "Research as Praxis," 264.

31. Van Manen, *Researching Lived Experience*, 47.

32. Co-authored by Frederick Aquino and the GST Student Services Committee (Tim Sensing, Mark Love, and John Willis).

"intellectual, moral, spiritual excellence" the result of which is the formation of the whole person.

1. Desire for truth in the context of love—the aptitude to discern whether belief-forming processes, practices, and people yield true beliefs over false ones. People motivated by this desire will be more likely to conduct thorough inquiries, scrutinize evidence carefully, investigate numerous fields of study, consider alternative explanations, while respecting and caring for others.

2. Humility—the capacity to recognize reliable sources of informed judgment while recognizing the limits of our knowledge and the fallibility of our judgments. This is not created in isolation but takes into account feedback and correction from other sources of informed judgment.

3. Honesty—the capacity to tackle difficult questions without seeking simple answers. Ignoring complex and difficult questions only solidifies vices such as intellectual dishonesty, close-mindedness, and rash judgments. These vices preclude the possibility of refining our thinking and of participating in conversations with others.

4. Openness—the desire to engage in an open-ended search for knowledge of God, including receptivity to different ideas, experiences, and people. Listening becomes a discipline that acknowledges the other and respects diversity. The art of being a student and a teacher is an ongoing process that necessitates hospitality, patience, and love.

5. Courage—the ability to articulate one's position while considering other perspectives. The aptitude to express convictions involves risk yet fosters opportunities for meaningful dialog. Responding to objections entails tenacity but should not be confused with close-mindedness.

6. Wisdom—the capacity to offer a synthetic discernment of knowledge on behalf of the community. The aim is not merely the dissemination of information but a pastoral implementation of faith for the building up of the community. It solidifies various pieces of data, practices, and experiences and aptly applies knowledge and faith to particular situations.

7. Stewardship—the commitment to one's accountability to the gifts and responsibilities that one brings to the classroom. Classroom engagement includes proactively participating in the course goals, seeking mastery of course competencies, and collaborating with faculty and fellow students in the developing of a learning environment. Committing oneself to spiritual and intellectual well-being and growth is a faithful response to the opportunities graduate education affords.

8. Hopefulness—the receptivity to the future possibilities of God. The cultivation of thankfulness for our heritages and expectation for our future ministries engenders a guard against cynicism and a spirit of perseverance during times of stress and disorientation.

9. Prayerfulness—the making of space to commune with God. The task of learning and teaching so that we are formed into the image of Christ through the Spirit involves our consistent reliance on God's sanctifying work.

3

The Big Picture

During my DMin program, the graduate school changed directors. The former director utilized a descriptive methodology,
while the new director implemented a quasi-experimental approach.
My cohort group arrived at the research methodologies class ready to
write our proposals according to one tactic and found our ideas being
deconstructed one by one. The experience introduced me to the feud
that often occurs between methodological schools of thought. I quickly
learned about flexibility. I wanted to graduate, so I adapted. Some in my
cohort neither adapted nor graduated.

During my tenure of teaching research methodologies, I have interviewed various DMin directors around the country. A diversity of
approaches still pervades the discipline. Some directors advocate an
exclusive approach to methodology that mirrors their own research and
discipline. Other directors use whatever system they inherited from a
founder or influential predecessor. A third group seeks the Holy Grail,
the perfect method suitable for the DMin. My own way is eclectic but
controlled by the following rule: The problem and purpose statements
are the determining force for making methodological decisions. My
biases lean towards project theses that are qualitative in nature, but a
multi-methods approach is flexible enough to use quantitative tools. The
Holy Grail of research methods does not exist. In the structure below,
let the suggestions provide you with both order and inspiration to adapt
your approach to your particular context.

Chapter 3 of the thesis delineates the methodology of the project,
including the rationale, intervention, and evaluation. You will explain
not only how you conducted your research but also why you chose your
strategy. You will describe both the design and the rationale of how the

research was accomplished. You will answer questions like: "What is the nature of the data?" "How was the data collected, organized, and analyzed?" And, "How will you present the data to your readers?" Once you choose a particular approach, you will need to go beyond the descriptions in this textbook and find resources that describe your methodological rationale and choice of method in more detail.

THE NATURE OF RESEARCH

Research, simply defined, is a family of methods that share common characteristics of disciplined inquiry. Research methods contain data, arguments, and rationales that are capable of withstanding careful scrutiny by members of an associated guild. Research prompts us to understand problems, ask questions, and pursue specialized modes of inquiry.

Within the larger category of "research," there exist various procedures that ask different questions and solve different problems. Richard Jaeger's classic text, *Complementary Methods for Research in Education*, describes seven standard methods for research. He lists them as (1) Historical Methods, (2) Philosophical Inquiry Methods, (3) Ethnographic Methods, (4) Case Study Methods, (5) Survey Methods, (6) Comparative Experimental Methods, and (7) Quasi-Experimental Methods.[1] Lee Shulman's opening chapter states, "What distinguishes disciplines from one another is the manner in which they formulate their questions, how they define the content of their domains and organize that content conceptually, and the principles of discovery and verification that constitute the ground rules for creating and testing knowledge in their fields. These principles are different in the different disciplines."[2]

What Shulman says about research in general is also true of qualitative research. Qualitative methods as research disciplines have their particular philosophical foundations and methodological integrity. Although there are many typologies, Patton's approach is typical. He states,

> Decisions about design, measurement, analysis, and reporting all flow from purpose. Therefore, the first step in a research process is getting clear about purpose. The centrality of purpose in making methods decisions becomes evident from examining alterna-

1. Jaeger, *Complementary Methods*.
2. Shulman, "Disciplines of Inquiry," 5.

tive purposes along a continuum from theory to action: 1) *Basic research*: To contribute to fundamental knowledge and theory 2) *Applied research*: To illuminate a societal concern 3) *Summative evaluation*: To determine program effectiveness 4) *Formative evaluation*: To improve a program 5) *Action research*: To solve a specific problem."[3]

Some authors are protective of their turf. Mixing methods is a taboo. If Patton is right, and purpose is the criteria, then mixed methods are sometimes appropriate. I am intentionally crossing these methodological boundaries. I am advocating a multi-methods approach in qualitative research. Riesmman states, "Students who combine methods will have to cross borders, risk being defined as illegal aliens, transgress the 'hedgerows that define and protect traditional interests and practices.'"[4]

The practical mandate to gather the most relevant data to address the project's purpose "outweighs concerns about methodological purity based on epistemological and philosophical arguments."[5]

It is not my intent to lay the philosophical groundwork in a defense of qualitative research. Patton asserts, "The classic qualitative-quantitative debate has been largely resolved with recognition that a variety of methodological approaches are needed and credible, that mixed methods can be especially valuable, and that the challenge is to appropriately match methods to questions rather than adhering to some narrow methodological orthodoxy."[6] While the biases against non-quantitative

---

3. Patton, *Qualitative Research*, 213. Patton describes this typology as a "continuum." Some DMin projects may resemble summative or formative evaluation. Patton admits that action and formative research are at times indistinguishable (pg. 221). I choose the term *action research* because DMin projects depend upon the engagement of the participants.

4. Riessman, *Narrative Analysis*, 55–56. Another common metaphor for a pragmatic qualitative methodology that crosses the boundaries is *bricoleur*. A "jack of all trades or a kind of professional do-it-yourself person . . . produces a *bricolage*, that is, a pieced-together, close-knit set of practices that provide solutions to a problem in a concrete situation. . . It changes and takes new forms as different tools, methods, and techniques are added to the puzzle." See Denzin and Lincoln, *Handbook of Qualitative Research*, 2.

5. Patton, *How to Use*, 62. Many pastors engaged in DMin work are not comfortable with constructivist, phenomenological, or interpretivist approaches. They will classify themselves as "logical positivists" or "realists." Instead of rejecting qualitative approaches and opting for quantitative methods, I encourage these researchers to explore Miles and Huberman, *Qualitative Data Analysis*. See Patton, *Qualitative Research*, 91–96.

6. Patton, *Qualitative Research*, xxii, 79. For a detailed discussion as to why there exists an increase in legitimacy for qualitative methods, see 584–8.

modes of inquiry persist, the debate is well worn and exhaustively discussed in the literature.[7]

Instead, I follow the lead of Wolcott, who discourages the qualitative researcher from spending time defending a methodology or describing in detail the techniques of particular methods. He encourages giving "your attention to the substance of your research."[8] He later qualifies his intent by telling writers not to assume too much about method. "Readers must be informed about the nature and extent of your database. When, exactly, did you conduct the fieldwork? How extensive was your involvement? . . . To what extent do interviews constitute part of your database, and what constituted an interview? Are you claiming to triangulate your data? Under what circumstances was information cross-checked, and how are data reported that were not so checked?"[9] The reader needs to know how methods were applied in your particular study to follow your research path, to develop confidence in the rigor and trustworthiness of the project, and to possibly replicate or utilize the project in their context. Therefore, Wolcott advocates full and open disclosure about data-gathering techniques.[10]

On the one hand, I understand how language and perceptions determine how we see reality; I am not fully persuaded, however, by the notion that reality is nothing but a social construct. There is a construction of the knowledge about reality but not a construction of reality.[11] On the other hand, congregational life is complex, and no one has insider information that allows him or her to claim the "real" interpretation.

---

7. Kleinman and Copp, *Emotions and Fieldwork*; Lather, "Research as Praxis," 257–77. Ornstein notes how quantitative methods miss the complexity of an event by focusing on isolated behaviors, methods, and processes while ignoring the larger patterns and relationships of human experience. See Ornstein, "Teacher Effectiveness," 2–23.

8. Wolcott, *Writing Up*, 26.

9. Ibid., 27.

10. Ibid.

11. Patton, *Qualitative Research*, 101, quotes Thomas Schwandt, *Qualitative Inquiry: A Dictionary of Terms* (Thousand Oaks, CA: Sage, 1997), 134, qualifying the term *constructivist*. "Although some versions of *constructivism* do not appear to deny reality, many (if not most, I suspect) qualitative inquirers have a common-sense realist *ontology*, that is, they take seriously the existence of things, events, structures, people, meanings, and so forth in the environment as independent in some way from their experience with them. And they regard society, institutions, feelings, intelligence, poverty, disability, and so on as being just as 'real' as the toes on their feet and the sun in the sky." Throughout this book, I use *construct* in this delimited sense even when I am pressing for dialogical and evolutionary interpretations.

The multi-methods approach advocated in this book allows various perspectives to engage in a critical dialogue that leads to several sets of rich data, resulting in the possibility for deeper understandings. And those understandings can be communicated to readers in such a way that makes the information useful to others.[12] "All of our understandings are contextually embedded, interpersonally forged, and necessarily limited. Any notion of 'truth,' then, becomes a matter of 'consensus among informed and sophisticated constructors, not of correspondence with an objective reality.'"[13] My pragmatic approach to "truth" resembles C. S. Peirce's understanding of the evolutionary development of knowledge over time and generations.[14] By capturing and honoring different perceptions of reality, a dialogue ensues that, given time and input, results in clearer understandings of truth. However, the process is evolving and closure is elusive.

As noted above, I do not intend to enter the debate about the rationale of one approach over another.[15] I simply advocate a form of action research that employs a multi-methods approach within community

---

12. See Patton, *Qualitative Research*, 96–102.

13. Ibid., 96.

14. The nature of the universe and all human thought moves towards thirdness (purpose). Peirce describes that progression using the terms *Tychism*, where all essence begins as chance or mere actions; *Synechism*, when actions associate with one another to create patterns and order; and *Agapism*, the logical conclusion of the evolutionary process derived by the eschatological community (*the final conclusion that the community of inquirers will reach given enough time and resources*). (*Grounds of Validity of the Laws of Logic*, EP 1.72, *Evolutionary* Love, EP 1.357ff). EP refers to Peirce, Houser, and Kloesel, *Essential Peirce*.

15. Patton, *Qualitative Research*, 134, lists six questions that help researchers determine their theoretical frame. He insists that there are no right answers to these questions. "*What do we believe about the nature of reality?* (ontological debates concerning the possibility of a singular, verifiable reality and truth vs. the inevitability of socially constructed multiple realities); *How do we know what we know?* (epistemological debates about the possibility and desirability of objectivity, subjectivity, causality, validity, generalizability); *How should we study the world?* (methodological debates about what kinds of data and design to emphasize for what purposes and with what consequences); *What is worth knowing?* (philosophical debates about what matters and why); *What questions should we ask?* (disciplinary and interdisciplinary debates about the importance of various burning questions, inquiry traditions, and areas of inquiry); *How do we personally engage in inquiry?* (praxis debates about interjecting personal experiences and values into the inquiry, including issues of voice and political action)." You will need to realize that no matter how you answer, there will be strengths and weaknesses, possibilities and limitations.

located in a specific setting and is intended to bring transformation.[16] While my approach has a constructivist underpinning rooted in phenomenological and philosophical pragmatism, it is beyond the scope of this work to lay that foundation.[17] My approach is an orientation to inquiry rather than a particular method. Greenwood and Levin state,

16. My approach is similar to William Myers's third category "The Pro-Active Research Method." Myers, *Research in Ministry*, 29–31. Technically, Patton, *Qualitative Research*, 213–25, might classify my approach as "Evaluation Research: Summative and Formative," since the evaluation of the intervention is primary, but I prefer the category of action research due to the employment of an intervention and the high involvement of a participant group in the process. See Stringer, *Action Research*, for a complete description of participatory action research that seeks change within and for a community.

17. *Pragmatism*, a term coined by Charles S. Peirce, differs from the popular definition associated with "utilitarian." Many scholars cite the origin of pragmatism to the Metaphysical Club (1872–1875). Modeled after other Saturday Clubs that gathered around Cambridge, this club included William James, Chauncy Wright, John Fiske, Nicholas St. John Green, Oliver Wendell Holmes Jr., and Charles Peirce. Alexander Bain's definition of belief ("that upon which a man is prepared to act") fashioned their preliminary understandings of pragmatism. See Alexander Bain (1818–1903), Scottish philosopher and psychologist; *The Emotions and the Will*, 505. Under the category of the will, the essential articles in the theory are these: 1) Belief belongs to "the active part of our being." Preparedness to act is not merely the test or criterion but the essence of belief. 2) The opposite of belief is not disbelief but doubt or uncertainty. 3) Belief is primary; doubt is "an after product, and of the primitive tendency." Peirce cites Nicholas St. John Green as the one who pressed Alexander Bain's definition of belief among the rest of the club (*Pragmatism*, EP 2.399). West, *American Evasion*, 50, summarizes Peirce's philosophy stating, "For Peirce, pragmatism is not a philosophical *Weltanschauung* or a new metaphysics of truth and reality. Rather it is a method of rendering ideas clear and distinct and ascertaining the meaning of words and concepts." West, 42, cites C. I. Lewis saying, "Pragmatism could be characterized as the doctrine that all problems are at bottom problems of conduct, that all judgments are, implicitly, judgments of value, and that, as there can be ultimately no valid distinction of theoretical and practical, so there can be no final separation of questions of truth of any kind from questions of the justifiable ends of actions." Or as John Dewey, "Pragmatism of Peirce," 301–2, one of Peirce's most famous intellectual heirs succinctly says, "He [Peirce] framed the theory that a conception, that is, the rational purport of a word or other expression, lies exclusively in its bearing upon the conduct of life." William James regarded the ideas in Peirce's two famous essays that first appeared in *Popular Science Monthly*; namely, *The Fixation of Belief* (Nov 1877) and *How to Make Our Ideas Clear* (Jan 1878) as the origin of pragmatism. Peirce's famous Pragmatic Maxim, "Consider what effects, which might conceivably have practical bearings, we conceive the object of our conception to have. Then our conception of these effects is the whole of our conception of the object" (*How to Make Our Ideas Clear*, EP 1.132).

Patton, *Qualitative Research*, 71–72, describes pragmatism: "My pragmatic stance aims to supersede one-sided paradigm allegiance by increasing the concrete and practical methodological options available to researchers and evaluators. Such pragmatism

Action Research ["AR"] is social research carried out by a team that encompasses a professional action researcher and the members of an organization, community, or network ("stakeholders") who are seeking to improve the participants' situation. AR promotes broad participation in research process and supports action leading to a more just, sustainable, or satisfying situation for the stakeholders.

Together, the professional researcher and the stakeholders define the problems to be examined, cogenerate relevant knowledge about them, learn and execute social research techniques, take actions, and interpret the results of actions based on what they have learned. AR rests on the belief and experience that all people—professional action researchers included—accumulate, organize, and use complex knowledge continuously in everyday life. This belief is visible in any AR project because the first step professional action researchers and members of a community, organization, or network take is to define a problem that they seek to resolve.[18]

Stringer says it well:

Formally, then, action research, in its most effective forms, is phenomenological (focusing on people's actual lived experience/reality), interpretive (focusing on their interpretation of acts and activities), and hermeneutic (incorporating the meaning people make of events in their lives). It provides the means by which stakeholders, those centrally affected by the issue investigated, explore their experience, gain greater clarity and understanding of events and activities, and use those extended understandings to construct effective solutions to the problem(s) on which the study was focused.[19]

So, in the spirit of reflexivity, I name my location and proceed. My approach is an eclectic borrowing from the field of qualitative research in order to address a particular research agenda, namely, the DMin project thesis. My approach is heuristic in nature (see chapter 6). My personal

---

means judging the quality of a study by its intended purposes, available resources, procedures followed, and results obtained, all within a particular context and for a specific audience.... Being pragmatic allows one to eschew methodological orthodoxy in favor of *methodological appropriateness* as the primary criterion for judging methodological quality, recognizing that different methods are appropriate for different situations. Situational responsiveness means designing a study that is appropriate for a specific inquiry situation or interest."

18. Greenwood and Levine, *Introduction to Action Research*, 3-4.

19. Stringer, *Action Research*, 20.

experience and insight shapes my research. My identity, social location, experiences, skills, and insights are the primary tool in my inquiry. And since I am working with others, my research is participatory action research as described below.

The Nature of Qualitative Research

Merriam describes five characteristics that all qualitative research has in common, namely, "the goal of eliciting understanding and meaning, the researcher as primary instrument of data collection and analysis, the use of fieldwork, an inductive orientation to analysis, and findings that are richly descriptive."[20] Furthermore, qualitative research systematically seeks answers to questions by examining various social settings and the individuals who inhabit these settings. Qualitative research is grounded in the social world of experience and seeks to make sense of lived experience. Qualitative researchers, then, are most interested in how humans arrange themselves and their settings and how inhabitants of these settings make sense of their surroundings through symbols, rituals, social structures, social roles, and so forth.[21] Denzin and Lincoln, describing qualitative research, state,

> Qualitative research is multi-method in focus, involving an interpretative, naturalistic approach to its subject mater. This means that qualitative researchers study things in their natural settings, attempting to make sense of, or interpret, phenomena in terms of the meanings people bring to them. . . . Qualitative research involves the studied use and collection of a variety of empirical materials—case study; personal experience; introspection; life story; interviews; artifacts; cultural texts and productions; observational historical, interactional, and visual texts—that describe routine and problematic moments and meanings in individuals' lives. Accordingly, researchers deploy a wide range of interconnected interpretive practices hoping always to get a better understanding of the subject matter at hand.[22]

20. Merriam, *Qualitative Research*, 11.

21. Berg, *Qualitative Research Methods*, 7. Mason, *Qualitative Researching*, 3, describes this social understanding of qualitative research as an "interpretivist" stance rooted in a phenomenological understanding of the world. See also Patton, *Qualitative Evaluation Methods*, 6.

22. Denzin and Lincoln, *Handbook of Qualitative Research*, 3-4. Currently there are three editions of the *Handbook of Qualitative Research*. All three editions are substantially different each containing various authors and chapters..

Qualitative research produces culturally specific and contextually rich data critical for the design, evaluation, and ongoing health of institutions like churches.

As stated before, within the DMin field that utilizes qualitative research, various interpretations of what is a superior project vary widely. On one end of the spectrum lies a simple ethnographic study that describes a particular ministry setting. On the other end, some programs advocate a quasi-experimental approach. Much of the debate is rooted in the nature of the tensions surrounding the disciplinary boundaries within and across the humanities and social sciences. A particular institution's approach to the method used in a DMin program is often related to the training received by an individual faculty member. I believe the approach described here allows the adaptability necessary for a broad range of seminaries.

Within the human systems and relational constructs of research, I propose that DMin projects are a type of participatory action research that introduces an intervention in order to provide ministerial leadership for the transformation of the organization.[23] Patton offers the following list of principles for participatory and collaborative inquiry:

1. The inquiry process involves participants in learning inquiry logic and skills, for example the nature of evidence, establishing priorities, focusing questions, interpreting data, data-based decision making, and connecting processes to outcomes.

2. Participants in the process own the inquiry. They are involved authentically in making major focus and design decisions. They draw and apply conclusions. Participation is real, not token.

3. Participants work together as a group and the inquiry facilitator supports group cohesion and collective inquiry.

23. By definition, DMin research is not "purely" a participatory form of action research. Participatory action research (PAR) by definition would require the community under study to be the primary actor in defining the project's problem, data collection, methods of analysis, and how and where to use the findings. Yet, DMin projects are not completely a principle investigator paradigm either. The DMin project will involve a partnership with the project's participants who will co-author the study with the DMin pastor-student. A "type" of participatory action research addressed by DMin projects is a modified model that mediates between the more distinct classifications. Modified models are described by Szala-Meneok and Lohfeld, "Charms and Challenges." Similarly, DMin research could, but often does not, possess the same political activism intents most often ascribed to PAR.

4. All aspects of the inquiry, from research focus to data analysis, are undertaken in ways that are understandable and meaningful to participants.

5. The researcher or evaluator acts as a facilitator, collaborator, and learning resource; participants are coequal.

6. The inquiry facilitator recognizes and values participants' perspectives and expertise and works to help participants recognize and value their own and each other's expertise.

7. Status and power differences between the inquiry facilitator and participants are minimized, as much as possible, practical, and authentic, without patronizing or game playing.[24]

That description sounds like pastoral leadership that leads through incarnational and cruciform practices. Understanding the DMin project from the above perspective discourages approaches that favor authoritarian ways. Furthermore, the DMin student will engage the field, rather than the library, as the locus of inquiry. Historical and descriptive approaches, while viable, are not preferred. Patton concludes, "Regardless of the terminology—participatory, collaborative, cooperative, or empowerment—these approaches share a commitment to involving the people in the setting being studied as co-inquirers, at least to some important extent, though the degree and nature of involvement vary widely. My purpose here has been to point out that these participatory approaches often employ qualitative methods because those methods are understandable, teachable, and usable by people without extensive research training."[25]

Returning to the name—action research—Bell describes it in the following way: "The essentially practical, problem-solving nature of action research makes this approach attractive to practitioner-researchers who have identified a problem during the course of their work and see the merit of investigating it and, if possible, of improving practice."[26] Patton states, "Action research aims at solving specific problems within a program, organization, or community. Action research explicitly and

24. Patton, *Qualitative Research*, 185. See also, Reason, "Three Approaches." Reason compares and contrasts three approaches to research as participation: co-operative inquiry, participatory action research, and action inquiry.

25. Ibid.

26. Bell, *Doing Your Research Project*, 9.

purposefully becomes part of the change process by engaging the people in the program or organization in studying their own problems in order to solve those problems. As a result, the distinction between research and action becomes quite blurred and the research methods tend to be less systematic, more informal, and quite specific to the problem, people, and organization for which the research is undertaken."[27]

The DMin projects are ministry interventions designed to address particular problems for specific contexts. DMin researchers do not have the same issues that confront other fieldwork investigators relating to "reactive responses," "entry to the field," "familiarization," and "departure from the field." Since the minister-researcher is primarily perceived as minister, the reactive effects of an "outside" researcher are minimized. While the congregation and the participants are informed that the minister is working on the DMin project and is conducting research, most congregants let that information settle in the back of their minds. To them, the DMin researcher is pastor first.[28]

Although some argue that "pure" research requires not crossing any of the boundaries between methodological domains, DMin projects vary widely, addressing manifold issues and situations, thus requiring a flexible stance. The lines between methodological domains are thin and blurry anyway. Mowat and Swinton state, "It is our opinion that the most effective way that practical theologians can use qualitative research methods is by developing an eclectic and multi-method approach which seeks to take the best of what is available within the accepted modes of qualitative research, but is not necessarily bound by any one model."[29] At the heart of a multi-methods approach is the

27. Patton, *Qualitative Research*, 221.

28. For more information about the reactive effects of the researcher's presence see, Shaffir and Stebbins, *Experiencing Fieldwork*, 13–16. This collection of essays is organized around the issues of "entry," "learning the ropes," "maintaining relationships," and "departure." Although DMin research is fieldwork, ethnography is primarily "exploratory" while DMin research is "action."

29. Swinton and Mowat, *Practical Theology*, 50. For further support of an eclectic approach see Denzin and Lincoln, *Handbook of Qualitative Research*, 5 and Flick, *An Introduction*, 229. Theoretically, triangulation and the use of multi-methods in research has sometimes come under attack when the goal is to ascertain an empirical "true" account of the setting or activity. Even with multiple lenses, the interpretation is still limited and bounded by the context. The "whole picture" is impossible to ascertain. Triangulation allows the researcher to substantiate (or not, as the case may be) the picture that is being seen and interpreted but it is not the pot of gold at the end of the

assumption that "different procedures are employed to ask different questions and to solve different problems. . . . Research . . . requires judgment and selectivity grounded in broad understanding, certainly broader than can be provided by any single explanatory perspective. Ways of seeing are ways of knowing and of not knowing. And knowing well is knowing in more than a single way."[30]

Various problems are addressed by DMin action research projects. What if the congregational leadership lacks understanding of the congregation's context, ecology, or story? The project could implement an ethnographic analysis of the congregation in order to provide a descriptive narrative account of the church. What if the congregation desires to develop a ministry program or activity, implement a curriculum, develop people for more effective leadership, or evaluate a current practice? The project could implement a strategy to develop or evaluate the desired activity. Since the possible research problems available for study are countless, then the implementations, interventions, or strategies are likewise countless. What does count is that coherence exists between the project's problem, purpose, theology, action/intervention, and evaluation. The multi-method approach is an important aspect of triangulation and the issues of validity (both described below).

THE RECIPE

Patton states, "There is no recipe or formula in making methods decisions."[31] True, but chefs often turn recipe writing into an art form. Good chefs begin in the kitchen, experiment, test, and record what works. There may not be an ideal recipe for making apple pie. Your grandmother may have done it differently than mine. Yet, out of their vast experience and expertise, each bakes an apple pie that is the best in town. The "truth" is in the tasting. And my taste may differ from yours. Patton continues, "Any given design inevitably reflects some imperfect interplay of resources, capabilities, purposes, possibilities, creativity, and personal judgments by the people involved."[32] Whether in writing or from memory, good chefs still follow a recipe. Design is essential.

rainbow. Subsequently, the theory of triangulation and multi-methods is not a quick and easy substitute for the positivists' search for "validity."

30. Shulman, "Disciplines of Inquiry," 7, 23.

31. Patton, *Qualitative Research*, 12.

32. Ibid.

Qualitative methods are preferred for DMin projects. You may use quantitative methods if your project requires it; however, DMin programs are not aimed at quantitative research competencies. Nevertheless, neither qualitative nor quantitative methodologies are specifically taught as separate courses in most DMin programs. A PhD program has more resources to be able to teach a separate course for any possible method used by a student, whether it be case study, survey instruments, narrative, focus group, etc., etc., etc. The DMin program does not assume your expertise in a particular research methodology, nor does the program train you to be an expert researcher using a "pure" approach. You will need to learn (or find a consultant on your own) to employ any particular approach as a "pure" method of inquiry. For example, technically, there is a difference in using the case method as a basis for your inquiry and using the case method as a tool for evaluation. Your project intervention will guide your choice of methodologies and evaluation strategies.

The central purpose of the methodological chapter in your thesis is to describe to readers how the research was accomplished. Methodological decisions need to be explained and footnoted. Vague statements, such as "standard content analysis techniques will be utilized," communicate little to your reader. Even a simple phrase like "standard choices" has various alternative definitions and philosophical biases. A discussion and justification of the strategies chosen and the correlating theoretical framework must be offered.[33] The primary purpose of this textbook is to provide you with resources and rationale to support your methodology. Throughout the process, you are finding and assessing serendipitous outcomes, both negative and positive, whether expected or unexpected. Know how you are going to do this early, in the proposal, not as a tacked-on afterthought.

Descriptions of your methodology should be clear. If you are using a case study methodology, then be clear in your thesis about the theory of case studies. If you are using questionnaires, be clear in your thesis about the theory of questionnaires you are using. There are philosophical assumptions working behind the scenes of all research methods and tools. Epistemological and ontological underpinnings influence the decisions

---

33. Many of your professors (not all) used a descriptive or historical methodology for their PhD dissertations. They will be less familiar with the DMin methods utilized for your projects. Subsequently, they too need the fuller description as to the rationale and the protocols for your methodology and evaluation techniques.

that the investigator makes while conducting research.[34] Sometimes the multi-methods approach leads to a careless eclectic use of tools that induces the researcher to employ methods that are incommensurate. Even within the same category (e.g., interviewing), the researcher may borrow an idea from a text rooted in phenomenology and blend it with a protocol from a resource that advocates a more positivist and experimental foundation. Such blending may have the appearance of sophistication; however, a careful reader will see the glitch and question the findings. The whole study becomes suspect and is judged untrustworthy. That is why the methodology of the project thesis must be explained and justified. Transparency about the methodological choices and analytical decisions and practices will improve the acceptance of the final product.

The methodology will include three primary areas, namely, the rationale, the intervention, and the evaluation. The rationale is described above. The intervention primarily talks about the action that is taken to address the problem and fulfill the purpose of the project. It will include a description of the participants (Who? Why? How many?) and the setting. The evaluation section will include the issues of data collection, analysis, and interpretation.

THE INTERVENTION

The DMin project as described above is a type of action research where the researcher becomes a co-participant with the community in the process of gathering and interpreting data to enable new and transformative modes of action. DMin projects are not designed just to understand phenomena but to provide the minister an opportunity to impart pastoral leadership that implements change. DMin students engage in the project thesis, hoping to effect change through the specific plans of action they have in mind, like training teachers, improving their preaching, initiating a new social justice program, or addressing issues of inclusivity. The process began by analyzing the context. From analysis emerged a problem and purpose for the project. The next step involves formulating an action, an intervention, that will fulfill the purpose of the project. The idea for the intervention might come from the pastor-student's imagination as the congregational situation is contemplated in the library, office,

34. Throughout Mason's work, *Qualitative Researching*, she explicitly addresses epistemological and ontological issues.

or prayer room. However, the most effective interventions will be imagined, shaped, and implemented in and by community.

Figure 3: An Action Research Cycle

In the DMin context, process is cyclic in nature. The pastor-student already lives and works within the context. Various ministries and practices are occurring on an ongoing basis. Within the context, the pastor-student identifies a particular problem that needs addressing. An action, an intervention, is taken to address the problem. Data is collected and analyzed to discern whether the intervention accomplished its purpose. Conclusions are drawn about the feasibility and sustainability of the intervention in the future life of the context. After the project is over, the pastor will continue working in the context and will introduce new actions. The DMin project thesis is simply one focused look at a process that is ongoing in the life of congregations and other para-church organizations. By examining the cycle through the lens of an intentional project thesis, expectantly, the pastor will develop habits of thinking and acting that will enhance the development of a novice into an expert. Afterwards, the pastor continues the path of lifelong learning.

The purpose statement explicitly lays out how the intervention will address the problem of the study. A common trap at this stage of the process is to do too much. Remember the axiom—*do less, more thoroughly.* Projects that are too big lead to students who do not graduate. More importantly, the process becomes overwhelming and frustrating. For example, you have identified the problem that diverse voices within the congregation have little influence in the decisions of the church. Further examination reveals that the current church board has no intentional mechanisms for soliciting or hearing the concerns or opinions of the membership. Part of the dynamic involves a lack of diversity on the church board itself. The scope of the project is narrowed when you choose only one of these issues to address in your project. Advisors are keenly aware of the temptation to do too much and should quickly intervene.

Another common trap that quietly ensnares students and advisors alike involves not doing first things first. Ministry is never an isolated activity unconnected from the larger life of the community. Interventions are always one step in a series of processes that serve the congregation. Sequentially, some steps are prior to others. More importantly, some steps are more theologically significant than others. Often, I hear students say, "I'm going to train teachers." But they do not have a training curriculum. They say, "The church is going to start a prison ministry." But they do not have any trained personnel. Although they have a worthwhile intervention in mind, a prior step may involve a lengthy preparation that must be completed in advance. In the example above, although you could choose any of the issues described in the intervention to include diverse voices, for the purposes of your project, opt for the one at the beginning of the process. Your purpose could be to lead the congregation in a selection process that will expand the membership of the board. However, before that happens, you will need a new selection procedure. The old process led to the present board demographic. The intervention would involve putting together a team, Task Force A, authorized to write a new board member selection process. Or, Task Force B could be assembled with the assignment of drawing a congregational road map for the inclusion of diverse voices in the decision-making process.

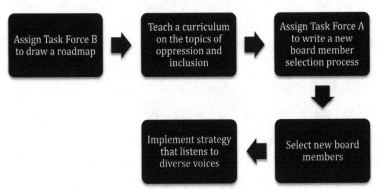

Figure 4: Steps in a Process

Both Task Force A and B have narrowly defined duties. Both are feasible and manageable. Both are necessary and significant. However, Task Force B would be doing a project that logically and theologically comes prior to the needed but more routine duty assigned to Task Force A. Again, do what comes first, first. Finish implementing the road map for the inclusion of diverse voices in leadership decisions after you are a doctor. When the road map is completed, evaluated, and analyzed in a thesis, you will not only walk across a stage listening to *Pomp and Circumstance*, you will also have a plan of action that will guide you for several years.

Interventions utilize projects of all shapes and sizes: retreats, classes, planning sessions, training exercises, homework, case studies, among others. The format of the sessions or activities of the intervention must be spelled out in detail. If a training program has seven sessions, then describe the schedule, lesson plans, room setup, childcare arrangements, invited participants, and other activities. In the final thesis, lesson plans should probably be included in an appendix.

The methodology section will include a consideration of the subjects involved in the study, data collection, setting, and analysis techniques. If a cook is using a recipe, the recipe must be written in a style that any cook could duplicate the dish. If other people wanted to replicate your project, they should be able to follow your path. They should be able to precisely follow your methodological protocols and successfully reproduce the intervention.

Some items in your recipe are:

- The purpose and objectives of the project's intervention
- The tasks to be done
- The steps to be taken for each task
- The people involved (see "sampling" in chapter 4)—Including secondary groups (e.g., childcare)
- The places where activities will occur
- The timelines and durations of activities
- The ethical issues related to informed consent and confidentiality
- The resources required—Handouts, projectors, posters, videos, guest speakers, etc.

- The types of data that will be collected

- The tools for gathering information needed—Recording equipment, observers, field note protocols, etc.

- Protocols for using tools (precise recipes); notes about training others who might use your protocols (e.g., participant observers).

- The analysis/evaluation procedures and methods required (e.g., coding of data)

The following examples do not provide the entire recipe described here but merely the ingredients of the intervention itself.

Example 1: Allen Burris, "Sermon Preparation for Hearers: A Collaborative Approach to Preaching in the Mitchell Church of Christ," convened a study group that would meet on Wednesday nights for seven weeks, attend the Sunday morning service, and commit to a daily engagement in spiritual practices.[35] After discussing sampling issues (the selection of the team), Burris describes his intervention as follows:

> Each Sunday during the intervention, the participants in this project received the preaching topic and biblical text for the Sunday sermon one week before it was preached. The "experience sheet" for each week is found in the appendices of this thesis. The text was printed for them on a regular sheet of paper. I printed the text in the New International Version. This version is used by a large majority of the congregants, and it is the version from which I normally preach.
>
> On the same sheet of paper, in addition to the text, a reflective question governed the reading of the text each day. A suggested meditative activity and a suggested prayer followed this. On Monday, Tuesday, and Wednesday the same text was presented, but the reflective question, meditative activity, and suggested prayer changed each day. The participants were instructed to read the text daily and to follow the directions for using the meditative activities and prayers.
>
> The exercise on Monday was designed to help the participants understand how the selected biblical text fit in its broader context. Monday's exercise also was designed to help the participants become familiar with the text by encouraging the use of imagination. The participants were asked, in essence, to enter the story described by the text to see and to hear what was taking place.

35. Burris, "Sermon Preparation," 38.

Monday's prayer was a request for a greater awareness of the text in thought and imagination.

The exercise on Tuesday focused on the activity of Jesus. The participants were asked to use their imagination specifically to see Jesus. Tuesday's prayer was "Lord, help me to see you."

The exercise on Wednesday moved the focus to the participants. They were asked to consider how God was speaking to them through the passage. Further, they were asked to contemplate how the passage could make a difference in their lives. Wednesday's prayer was a request for God to reveal what he wanted the participants to hear and to learn from the passage. Additionally, the participants prayed to be prepared to discuss their three-day experience with the preaching text in the group meeting that evening.

On Wednesday evening, during the normally scheduled Bible class time for the congregation, the participants sat with me at a round table. Together we discussed the text and their three-day experience with it. I took notes as I conversed with the participants.

On Thursday, Friday, and Saturday the participants were encouraged to continue to read the text and to reflect upon the Wednesday evening discussion. They were encouraged to allow their thoughts and experiences to direct their prayers. On Sunday they listened to the sermon preached in the worship setting. Following the sermon, they, along with the rest of the congregation, received a preaching response questionnaire.

[After describing his own tasks, Burris continues.] The purpose of the study [Wednesday night] was for the participants to express their reflections regarding the text. The following questions were used to begin the group conversations: Did you notice the broader context? What in this text strikes you as remarkable? Does anything arrest your attention? Have you seen a similar idea elsewhere in the Bible? What aspects of the text does our congregation need to hear? I then invited the group to discuss their experience with the text.

Following the Wednesday evening study, I completed the sermon and prepared to deliver it on Sunday. My final preparation involved reflection on comments made during the Bible study. I also reviewed the notes taken during the Wednesday evening study, looking for themes and patterns in thoughts expressed by the participants.[36]

36. Ibid., 38–42.

Example 2: Jonathan Camp, "Bridging the Generation Gap at the Church of Christ at White Station," (you may recall Camp's thesis from chapter 1) states, "The purpose of this project was to equip members of an intergenerational planning group to provide recommendations for bridging the generation gap at White Station."[37] He describes the intervention as follows: "My equipping strategy included content transmission and focused discussion to guide the composition of the document. . . . This project involved eight one-hour planning sessions intended to provide 1) a theological foundation for generational bridge building and 2) recommendations for bridging the generation gap at White Station to be submitted to the leadership team and the elder administration committee."[38] The first five sessions concentrated on content transmission and the final three sessions involved exercises designed to produce the recommendations document.

Example 3: Steven Martin, "Envisioning Self-emptying Practices for the Union Hill Church of Christ,"[39] writes,

> The intent of this project was to facilitate the development of a road map that would promote the formation of the Union Hill Church of Christ into the likeness of Christ through self-emptying practices. . . . It was an expectation that a team of opinion leaders within Union Hill, directed by the Holy Spirit, would envision such a road map as they participated in self-emptying practices and communal discernment. . . . The project utilized eight sessions in which a selected team of Union Hill opinion leaders reflected upon self-emptying principles, participated in self-emptying practices, and formulated a road map to navigate the congregation as a whole toward self-emptying. Furthermore, two of the eight sessions engaged the congregation as a whole with observational assignments for the team. . . . In the spirit of appreciative inquiry, which entails a collaborative and generative process of organizational change, this project sought to build upon what the church is already doing right, through a highly participative form of discussion based on positive appreciative questions. Such an approach honored the embedded narrative of self-emptying within Union Hill.[40]

37. Camp, "Bridging the Generation Gap," 38.
38. Ibid.
39. Martin, "Envisioning Self-emptying Practices," 27.
40. Ibid., 27–28.

Martin then describes the eight sessions in detail, including sampling details, session descriptions, road map construction, and tools for evaluation. Appendices include handouts used to describe each session and the associated protocols.

EVALUATION

How do you know if the intervention was successful? Did the intervention accomplish the purpose of the project and appropriately respond to the problem of the project? If not, how should the intervention be modified? Once the intervention has been implemented, you will need to assess the outcomes or changes to see how the intervention accomplished its task.

Evaluation is the systematic collection, analysis, and interpretation of information about the activities, characteristics, and outcomes of actual programs in order to make judgments about specific aspects of the program, improve the program's effectiveness, and make decisions about the program's future.[41] "When this examination of effectiveness is conducted systematically and empirically through careful data collection and thoughtful analysis, one is engaged in evaluation *research*."[42]

In other words, evaluation involves choosing a meaningful way to assess the effects of your project compared to the goals you set out to reach. Evaluation allows you to get inside the mind of the folks and determine the effectiveness of the intervention. Evaluation of the intervention provides information and feedback to ascertain what works or does not work. Such an assessment of goals will inform you about strengths and growth areas of your intervention. Therefore, the next time you do the intervention, you will anticipate a more effective outcome because you have enhanced your methodology from the previous implementation.

Evaluation needs to be clearly focused on the research problem, the core of the project; otherwise, it can be counterproductive, directing attention to the wrong areas of activity, and distorting the research process. All aspects of the thesis must display a unified thought. From the problem and purpose statement, to the theological and theoretical foundations for addressing the issue, and culminating with the method and evaluation, a cohesive whole must be conceptualized and concretized.

41. Patton, *How to Use*, 145.
42. Patton, *Qualitative Research*, 10.

One way to test the cohesive nature of a thesis is to read it backwards. Do thesis results emerge from the assessments employed? Do these evaluation tools triangulate the research (as discussed below)? Does the methodology derive from the theories and theologies described? Are the theories and theologies appropriate to ground the purpose of the project? Does the purpose address the identified problem? Does the observed problem for the thesis represent the context of the project? Any aspect of the thesis should cohere with every other section.

Patton emphasizes another widely missed issue related to evaluation:

> It is important to know the extent to which a program is effective after it is fully implemented; but to answer that question it is first necessary to know how and the extent to which the program was actually implemented. . . . Unless one knows that a program is operating according to design, there may be little reason to expect it to provide the desired outcomes. Furthermore, until the program is implemented and a 'treatment' is believed to be in operation, there may be little reason to even bother evaluating outcomes. . . . Implementation evaluations tell decision makers what is going on in the program and how the program has developed.[43]

Tools to collect data from the setting are chosen based on the particular demands of your project. The question of what complex of tools could/should be used is answered by the kind of data you need for evaluation. When you gather data, look for what people experienced: their reactions, behavior changes, and/or organizational impact, etc.

When reporting about your data, give an accurate accounting of what actually took place in the course of the project. Give details about what went well and what obstacles you faced. If session 3 was cancelled due to weather, let the reader know, and tell how you adjusted your procedures. Include complete descriptions of how you collected and analyzed the data. Chapter 3 of the thesis should not only explain what you did, but should also justify what you did. If there are particular weaknesses and limitations to your approach, describe them in more detail than the generalizations you made in chapter 1. Now you will have an actual case to describe the limitation.

DMin projects generally employ qualitative methods for evaluation. Protocols for the evaluation tools need to be carefully described

---

43. Patton, *How to Use*, 27.

and footnoted.[44] Quantitative methods should only be used if an outside expert or consultant is employed or if the student has specialized training. Since you are not trained in the research methodologies being employed in your project, you will need to be clear how you are addressing validity and reliability issues by means of *triangulation*.

Triangulation

The key to interpretation is not in the tools, or the reporting of the information guided by a set of techniques, but rather in how one makes sense of the experiences of everyday life. Any single approach will have limitations. Subsequently, triangulation (multiple data-collection technologies designed to measure a single concept or construct) provides a complex view of the intervention enabling a "thicker" interpretation.[45] It is a way to cross-check your data that provides breadth and depth to your analysis and increases the trustworthiness of your research. It is a means of refining, broadening, and strengthening conceptual linkages and perceptions. Triangulation is "cross-checking the existence of certain phenomena and the veracity of individual accounts by gathering data from a number of informants and a number of sources and subsequently comparing and contrasting one account with another in order to produce as full and balanced a study as possible."[46]

The term *triangulation* derives from an analogy with navigation and surveying.[47] A person can fix her location or gain her bearings by knowing two other landmarks or signposts. For example, triangulation networks showed people how a point on a map could be located from an unknown point rather than from previously fixed points. And according to the detectives on television, a cell phone can be located by triangulating it between two towers.

> [Triangulation] means comparing observational data with interview data; it means comparing what people say in public with what they say in private; it means checking the consistency of

44. Berg, *Qualitative Research Methods*, 6.

45. Ibid., 60

46. Bell, *Doing Your Research Project*, 102. Sometimes "breadth" and "depth" are talked about only when using studies that are extended over a long period of time—longitudinal studies. Although beneficial, longitudinal studies are not practical for DMin students who routinely start and finish their interventions within one year.

47. Hammersley and Atkinson, *Ethnography*, 231.

what people say over time; and it means comparing the perspectives of people with different points of view. It means validating information obtained through interviews by checking program documents and other written evidence that can corroborate what interview respondents report. Sometimes these divergent types of data provide a consistent picture. At other times the different data sources point in different directions. What people say they are doing and what they are doing are often in tension. It is best not to expect everything to turn out the same. The point is to study and understand when and why there are differences. Finding that observational data produce different results than interview data does not mean that either or both kinds of data are invalid. More likely, it means that different kinds of data have captured different things, so the analyst attempts to understand the reasons for the difference.[48]

Denzin has identified four basic types of triangulation that augment our ability to see varying perspectives on complex issues and events:

1. Data triangulation—the use of a variety of data sources in a study. For example, comparing and contrasting data from observation, documents of official records, and interviews will give you a richer description than you could otherwise know.

2. Investigator triangulation—the use of several different evaluators or social scientists who are investigating the same problem. Researchers who are studying the same location or phenomenon could come together and compare notes and initial interpretations. They need to compare and contrast their accounts, recording contradictions, recognizing the gaps in the data, and emphasizing the common themes they share. DMin projects could employ multiple researchers, but usually this approach lies beyond the scope and resources of most projects. The primary purpose of the program focuses on the local minister as researcher.

3. Theory triangulation—the use of multiple perspectives to interpret a single set of data. If the study focused on the outreach program of the local missions committee, examining the findings through the lenses of different atonement theories will reveal more than restricting the study to one particular doctrinal approach.

48. Patton, *How to Use*, 161–3. See the description of "slippage" in chapter 7.

4. Methodological triangulation—the use of multiple methods to study a single problem or program, such as interviews, observations, questionnaires, and documents.[49] For example, correlating the findings that result from a family systems approach with the data generated through a statistical analysis of a survey and the conclusions of an independent expert will sharpen the focus of your interpretation more so than any of the methods used alone. Methodological triangulation provides the best rationale when using quantitative techniques.[50]

Which of the four types is best? It depends on what you are doing. The following text assumes that data triangulation enhances validity and reliability of the student's research and is accessible to DMin students. Students sometimes ask why my approach is not methodological triangulation. If you choose to use methods that are more complex in the gathering of the data, then you have a case for methodological triangulation; however, the methods as described in the next chapter are simply data collecting techniques.

Be specific when describing what data collection tool is being used for a particular angle of interpretation. Just saying that "field notes, a participant observer, and an independent expert are being utilized in this project" is not sufficient. All three of those angles might involve field notes and observations. Instead, be clear and descriptive. For example, "The insider angle represents the twelve participants working with me in my project. On the final day of the project, Session 9, the participants will take part in a group interview. [Elaborate on the description of the rational and protocol of the group interview]. Throughout the nine sessions, I will be taking field notes. [Elaborate on the description of the rational and protocol for the field notes]. Finally, I will ask Dr. Mike to function as an independent expert. [Elaborate on the rational and role of the independent expert. Provide the protocol the expert will utilize]."[51]

49. Patton, *How to Use*, 60.

50. Denzin, *The Research Act*. Denzin modifies his understanding of triangulation in the 3rd edition (Englewood Cliffs: Prentice Hall, 1989). The modification recognizes the caution of equating triangulation with objective views of validity. A further clarification of using triangulation for the purposes of validation is explored in chapter 8.

51. See Patton, *Qualitative Research*, 172–3, for the theoretical support of using an independent expert at the center of the evaluation process.

The three angles I suggest are outsider, insider, and researcher (yourself). The data collected from these sources covers the entire spectrum of the project. Seeking an independent expert or utilizing the judgment of the larger community that the intervention will serve easily imparts the outsider perspective. Moschella's advice suggesting respondent validation parallels my insider angle. The researcher asks the research participants to check if the interpretations of the data are "accurate and appropriate."[52] The participants in the project are often the most valuable sources of evaluation for your project. Finally, your expertise as the minister, researcher, and active participant will be the filter of all the data. Therefore, it is imperative you record your observations, interpretations, and insights in a formal way and display them as a data set.

Figure 5: Data Triangulation from Distinct Perspectives

Using a Venn diagram to illustrate the triangle emphasizes the perceptions the angles have in common and the perceptions distinct to each angle (described as patterns or themes in chapter 7). What does the diagram not illustrate are the perceptions not captured by the research (described as silences in chapter 7).

Ways of seeing are also ways of not seeing. No one can look through a window into a house and see every aspect of the room. A view from the north window may give you an excellent vantage point to see the south wall, but you may miss altogether the mirror hanging next to the north window and have only limited views of the east and west walls. No single field of vision is all-inclusive of every aspect of a vista. The landscape of a research problem is similarly too large, complex, and dynamic for one snapshot to capture. Subsequently, when a researcher can increase the

52. Moschella, *Ethnography*, 185.

number of angles of vision upon a particular problem, discernment and knowledge also increase.

For qualitative research, three angles of vision are considered the saturation point to support the criteria of trustworthiness. Nevertheless, caution needs to be exercised. Do not claim too much or overstate your case. Three angles of interpretation will not produce the whole picture. Triangulation provides more conversation partners to inform your judgment but does not include every conversation partner. For instance, in your study of a particular congregational system, later evaluators (even from the next generation of members) will have insights and understandings that will substantiate, modify, or reject your interpretations.

The three angles of vision is just one metaphor to illustrate the researcher's gaze upon a problem, the intervention, participants, etc. is normally described under the category of observation. Another metaphor—that of conversation—assists the researcher to also respect that qualitative research involves human participants and social networks. It is not only what one observes that is crucial for interpretation, but also what one hears. The participants have voice. What people say allows them to co-author the interpretation with the researcher. Such hospitality on the part of the researcher will also give great weight to the findings of the project, while at the same time enhancing validity and reliability.

Camp's project to equip group members in order for them to write recommendations for bridging the generation gap at White Station utilized triangulation in its evaluation. Camp used participant observation to gather data about his own perspective and interpretation. After each session, he recorded field notes about the characteristics of the participants, their styles of interaction with one other, the content and manner of their conversations, as well as more subtle factors, such as silences, body language, and tone of voice. He also recorded reflections about his own reflexive awareness.[53] To analyze his field notes, he used a coding system adapted from Barney Glasser and William Strauss, *The Discovery of Grounded Theory* (Chicago: Aldine, 1967). This was the researcher's angle. The second angle of evaluation involved two focus groups divided along generational lines in order to allow respondents to give feedback more freely according to the communication patterns and perspectives

---

53. Camp, "Bridging the Generation Gap," 47.

unique to their generation.[54] The decision to have homogenous focus groups accorded with the literature.[55] A trained note-taker who also possessed interpretive skills observed the focus groups. The focus groups provided the insiders' perspectives. Finally, an independent expert was sent the recommendations document. He responded as the outsider angle of interpretation.

John Siburt's project, designed to discern and articulate virtues, demonstrates the use of an independent expert, a professor of theology at a local seminary, in addition to the insider and researcher's angles. Siburt utilized a group interview, described in chapter 4, as the insider's angle. He videotaped all sessions as a resource to supplement his own observations and field notes (the researcher's angle). And he asked a seminary professor from another institution to read the content of the sessions, read the articulation of Christian virtues that emerged from the sessions, and provide insight and critique concerning the theological strengths and weaknesses of the process and outcomes.[56] The expert attended the last two sessions. During the last session, he interviewed the participants in a quasi-focus group setting. He did not utilize predetermined questions or an agreed-upon protocol. He relied upon his qualifications and experiences that distinguished him as an expert. Many of these qualities remained implicit in the thesis. Finally, he supplied Siburt with an oral evaluation that provided a key third (and complimentary) alternative to the other two angles of interpretation.[57]

Using the examples from the previous section describing interventions, the following chart identifies their angles of evaluation.[58]

54. Ibid., 54.

55. Patton, *Qualitative Evaluation*, 173.

56. Siburt, "Crossing the Threshold," 46.

57. Ibid., 65–70. Also note the previous description in chapter 4 of how an independent expert used a case study to evaluate whether the participants could utilize principles learned during the intervention.

58. Chapter 4, "Tools of the Trade," provides more options, variety, and flexibility than this chart.

Intervention	Insider's Angle	Outsider's Angle	Researcher's Angle
Burris's Collaborative Approach to Preaching	Survey—*Preacher Response Questionnaire* given to the congregation and to the intervention participants	Independent expert—professor of homiletics at a seminary from a neighboring state	Field notes as a participant observer
Camp's Bridging the Generation Gap	Two focus groups utilizing a moderator and a participant observer	Independent expert—sociology professor at a university in a different state	Field notes as a participant observer
Martin's Self-Emptying Road Map	Open-ended questionnaire administered after the last session of the intervention	Independent expert—a Catholic priest and professor of religious studies at a nearby university	Field notes as a participant observer
Siburt's Articulation of Virtues	Group interview	Seminary professor at a nearby seminary who read the documents and interviewed participants	Field notes as a participant observer, supplemented by videotaping all sessions

Evaluation of the intervention is a key component in the project thesis. In the busyness of the pastorate, evaluation of programs, interventions, or other ministry activities rarely gets attention. By the time a curriculum is implemented, the educational director is planning for the next quarter. When the small group ministry kicks off its new vision, the associate minister begins another assignment. As soon as the capital campaign reaches its goal, the next phase of development is launched. The cycle continues throughout the lifespan of healthy churches. However, evaluation and reflection are often put on the back burner. The project thesis requires the student-pastor to slow down and attend to closing the loop. The intent of requiring focused attention to the evaluation side of the equation is to set in motion a pattern of behavior, a way of thinking, that the graduate will rely upon in years to come.

4

Tools of the Trade

DATA—MY FAVORITE CHARACTER ON *Star Trek: The Next Generation*. What an appropriate name for an android with a positronic brain. If Captain Picard needed anything, Data provided it. Data could fix a warp drive. Data could analyze a planetary system. Data could assess conflicting theories about physics. Data could solve all problems the scriptwriters conceptualized. Data was the perfect quantitative researcher since he did not have an emotion chip. Data was open, objective, and neutral. However, if you watched the show, Data wanted to be more human. His own problem required him to be a qualitative researcher. He studied human behavior and society with the skill of an ethnographer. Data's thirst for understanding could not be solved with numbers and equations. Therefore, with tentative humility, Data listened.

What does data provide you? To be able to say anything in your thesis or to conclude something from your project, you need data. Data collection procedures and techniques are included in the section of your thesis that describes the methodology's evaluation. Data includes items you count, like attendance. Data includes items that are difficult to gather and measure, like feelings. Most of the data in qualitative studies will involve words and observations gathered in field notes, transcripts, and questionnaires. Once the research problem is determined and the intervention is implemented, you will need to decide what data will be required to evaluate the effectiveness of your action.

Patton summarizes what any qualitative textbook will tell you about tools. Researchers of all philosophical shapes and ontological sizes use three overarching data collection methods. These are as follows:

> (1) In-depth, open-ended interviews; (2) direct observation; and (3) written documents. Interviews yield direct quotations

79

from people about their experiences, opinions, feelings, and knowledge. The data from observations consist of detailed descriptions of people's activities, behaviors, actions, and the full range of interpersonal interactions and organizational processes that are part of observable human experience. Document analysis includes studying excerpts, quotations, or entire passages from organizational, clinical, or program records; memoranda and correspondence; official publications and reports; personal diaries; and open-ended written responses to questionnaires and surveys.[1]

All the tools described in this chapter collect data that is context sensitive and specific.

I sometimes buy a new tool and use it without reading the directions. Sometimes I can intuitively figure it out. How hard is it to use a nail gun anyway? No, that is not true. There is nothing intuitive about it. I watched my dad use a screwdriver many times before I picked one up. Through experience, I learned a few tricks. Holding a light fixture in one hand, a screw in the other, and the screwdriver in my mouth did not produce the results that I wanted. I climbed the ladder higher to hold the light fixture with the top of my head. You do not want to hear what came next. Likewise, since I did not have the guidance of a skilled artisan, I had to read the instructions to the nail gun to learn how to load the nails. It may seem intuitive to know how to ask a question or to watch a parishioner bowing in prayer, but there is a first time. And there is a correct way. And let's face it, instructions are boring and for "nerds." Nevertheless, the instructions and protocols below are intended to help you learn the basics. Do not hesitate to follow the path of my footnotes for more detailed instructions. More importantly, remember that using qualitative research tools is a skill that is acquired over time. I suspect your first interview will resemble your first sermon, your first grilled salmon, your first attempt at changing a diaper, and my first attempt at hanging a light fixture. Yet, through practice, perseverance, and experience comes expertise. It is my hope that the details given below will help you avoid seeing whether or not your congregation has developed the fruit of the Spirit of long-suffering.

Using qualitative tools with people is not like buying a screwdriver from Sears. When I use my screwdriver instead of my chisel, the tip is

---

1. Patton, *Qualitative Research*, 4.

chipped. The next day, I use my screwdriver instead of my crowbar and I twist the edge. It no longer fits the slot. I buy my tools at Sears. They have a lifetime guarantee. I have never been questioned as to why my screwdriver has developed so many battle scars. However, you will want to be more careful in your research. Respect for people requires you to choose the appropriate tools for your particular project. Since you are designing your techniques, writing your protocols, wording your questions, and applying your methods, it is even more important for you to understand the nature and purpose of the tools in your toolbox. Yes, I can use a hammer to drive a screw—but only once.

DMin students are often not trained in seminary to use qualitative research tools. Times are changing and the study of congregations is a growing field, but for many of you, the tools described here will be your first venture into the field. The following schema of this long and winding chapter is organized according to how I have seen tools used and applied by my students. Some of the tools do not fit neatly into Patton's categories listed above; yet, all of them have produced data that enabled students to see and analyze their projects in appropriate ways. Your employment of any tool should include an understanding of the theoretical constructs that shape its use. Likewise, hands-on experience with a tool, protocol, or instrument prior to its implementation in your project will increase its usefulness and credibility. You will then be able to appreciate its strengths and weaknesses.

TOOLS EVERYBODY NEEDS

As I said, I am not much of a home repair specialist. But I try. It sometimes saves me money. That means, sometimes it does not. Like the day I tried to remove the faucet with a pipe wrench. I carefully examined the matching replacement faucet I bought at Lowe's. It had threads. After twisting the copper pipe into a spiral, I discovered the faucet was welded. I did not own a torch. Every plumber needs to own a torch. Through years of trial and error, I have slowly purchased and learned to use various tools. There are some tools that everyone needs. A screwdriver, for example, is used for attaching a hinge to a door, connecting a wire to a switch, and assembling a bicycle. Everyone needs a screwdriver. Carpenters, plumbers, electricians, auto mechanics, and many other professionals use screwdrivers everyday. That same principle applies to qualitative research tools too.[2]

2. Some topics like field notes, choosing a sample, and asking a question fall into

Sampling

Before we begin thinking about sampling, one caution needs sounding. The Hawthorne Effect is a theory that questions research dependability due to cases when subjects know they are being studied.[3] On the one hand, congregants want their ministers to do well. When they know the minister is doing the project for a grade, they want their minister to make an A. On the other hand, most participants are chosen because they believe in the project, want the project to succeed, and subsequently, forget about the research side of the equation. They become engrossed in the workings of the project, accept, and soon ignore note-takers and other design features. During the interpretation phase of your thesis, ask, "Does my data from this sampling exhibit the Hawthorne Effect?"

Once the intervention is determined, many decisions about sampling are also decided. Who are you going to interview? Who will attend your focus groups? Who will be given the questionnaire? Normally, your data collection tools will be given to all the participants in your intervention. Once the decision is made about who is participating in the project, then the decision about who will be interviewed or fill out a questionnaire is already determined. Sometimes, however, you will include different populations. The design of the project may dictate who will participate. If the design of the study specifies choosing a sample group from the larger congregation or organization, then the following principles will assist the decision-making process.[4]

Random samples are normally used during quantitative research projects when a large number of participants are needed. Random sampling is derived from statistical probability theory. Qualitative studies are designed to investigate an issue in great depth. Quantitative studies are designed to investigate an issue with great breadth. The tension between depth and breadth is resolved by determining the purpose of the study. If examining a larger population enhances the design of the project, then selecting a random sample is necessary to protect the validity of the data. How is the random group selected? Various methods are employed, but

multiple categories and so will be mentioned more than once. Field notes will be specifically discussed in chapter 6.

3. Parsons, "What Happened," 922–32; Gillespie, *Manufacturing Knowledge*; and Draper, "Hawthorne Effect."

4. Babbie, *Practice of Social Research*, 175–213, gives a comprehensive discussion of sampling in social science research.

the most common utilizes a table of random numbers that is located in the back of many statistics books. Because most DMin students are not trained in statistical analysis, it is wise to hire a consultant or seek assistance from a trained volunteer from the church or organization.

Theoretical sampling allows you to choose the population to study based on the theoretical constructs of your project. According to Corbin and Strauss, theoretical sampling is "a method of data collection based on concepts/themes derived from data. The purpose of theoretical sampling is to collect data from places, people, and events that will maximize opportunities to develop concepts in terms of their properties and dimensions, uncover variations, and identity relationships between concepts."[5] Theoretical sampling does not begin with a predetermined population or gather all the data before analysis. On the contrary, samples are taken step-by-step until a category reaches a "saturation" point. The analysis of the data collected guides the researcher to the next phase of the project. A researcher using theoretical sampling often does not know who will be asked questions, what questions will be asked, or where the journey will arrive.[6]

Purposive samples select people who have awareness of the situation and meet the criteria and attributes that are essential to your research. They are more common in qualitative research and will be more useful for DMin projects. Patton argues that the usefulness of purposeful sampling lies in selecting "information-rich" cases that can provide depth to your data.[7] The selection process is guided by choosing appropriate principles from the following list.

1. Folks that are politically savvy, have a vested interest, or are key stake holders

2. A typical population that is generally knowledgeable about the subject at hand

3. A group that fits a certain demographic (But do not assume that because someone fits the target group that it means they either care or have something to say about the subject.)

---

5. Corbin and Strauss, *Basics of Qualitative Research*, 143. See also Mason, *Qualitative Researching*, 92–94.

6. Corbin and Strauss, *Basics of Qualitative Research*, 146.

7. Patton, *Qualitative Research*, 230–46.

4. Participants chosen by someone else (often a key informant like a church board or ministerial staff)

5. Extreme or deviant cases that exemplify the outliers of your particular study

6. *Snowball* or *chain sampling* where people you interview first give you leads and connections about who to ask next

7. The confirming or disconfirming case

8. The outsider or the newcomer, who may sometimes be quite perceptive and offer a different way of looking at a familiar problem

9. People who represent the emerging case

10. People who represent the typical case

11. People who have a particular reputation

12. Folks who represent a certain opinion

Lincoln and Guba suggest *maximum variation sampling* as the most useful method for selecting people to participate in your project.[8] By selecting people who represent a broad range of perspectives, you increase the inclusivity of your project. Therefore, choose people who vary in age, gender, marital status, employment, ethnicity, length of membership, etc. Your wide net will gather many differing opinions. Small samples from a heterogeneous group might seem like a problem because no one will be alike, but when any common pattern emerges from great variation, then value of the information increases. If divergent people share core experiences, then the discovery is of greater significance in answering your question. Stringer agrees, "Researchers, therefore, need to ensure that all stakeholders—people whose lives are affected—participate in defining and exploring the problem or service under investigation. Although it is not possible for all people to be thus engaged, it is imperative that all stakeholder groups feel that someone is speaking for their interests and is in a position to inform them of what is going on."[9]

Two cautions: Because you are using an approach that has a smaller sample size, you will need to exercise care not to overgeneralize.

---

8. Lincoln and Guba, *Naturalistic Inquiry*, 202. Patton, *Qualitative Research*, 234–5. Especially note exhibit 5.6, 243–4, where Patton lists 16 types of purposeful sampling strategies and the associated purposes for selecting a particular type.

9. Stringer, *Action Research*, 44.

Furthermore, be careful about "talkative" people who may not represent the larger population. Once in my ministry I chose a key informant who seemed to be wise, informed, and above all else gracious. His opinions appeared to represent the whole group. He was in a position of power, and most folks within the congregation deferred to him. It was not until four years later that I realized that his opinions were not respected, most people who opposed him had already exited the church, and the rest avoided controversy by letting him dictate. I realized that I had not listened to the church. I had only heard a filtered version of "the way things were." I erred by not getting a fuller picture of the whole by including voices that were more diverse.[10]

Both cautions lead to the question, "How many people are you going to interview?"[11] Maybe everyone in your context is feasible. However, if a large population is chosen, then a statistical analysis will be needed to interpret the large amount of data that will be generated. Most DMin researchers will need to hire a statistician to both crunch the numbers and guide the interpretation. Qualitative tools also can produce too much data to be analyzed easily. Patton notes that a one-hour interview will yield 10–15 single-spaced pages of text and may take several hours to process.[12] I once conducted six narrative interviews that asked preaching professors to tell me the stories of their lives. It yielded 90 pages of transcripts.[13] You will need to consider any extra costs in transcribing that might be incurred. A local college that teaches transcription may have students who want to practice their skills at a lower rate. Whatever the decisions about sample size, justify and footnote the theoretical rationale for your choices.

A rule that guides this decision about sample size is, "Quality is more important than quantity." There are actually no rules about how many people will be included in a study. Each situation and project will prompt different decisions.

10. Patton, *Qualitative Research*, 321–2, agrees saying, "The danger in cultivating and using key informants is that the researcher comes to rely on them too much and loses sight of the fact their perspectives are necessarily limited, selective, and biased. Data from informants represent perceptions, not truths. Information obtained from key informants should be clearly specified as such in the field notes so that the researcher's observations and those of the informants do not become confounded."

11. Vyhmeister, *Quality Research Papers*, 130.

12. Patton, *Qualitative Research*, 440.

13. Sensing, *Pedagogies of Preaching*.

In the end, sampling size adequacy, like all aspects of research, is subject to peer review, consensual validation, and judgment. What is crucial is that the sampling procedures and decisions be fully described, explained, and justified so that information users and peer reviewers have the appropriate context for judging the sample. The researcher or evaluator is absolutely obligated to discuss how the sample affected the findings, the strengths and weaknesses of the sampling procedures, and any other design decisions that are relevant for interpreting and understanding the reported results. Exercising care not to overgeneralize from purposeful samples, while maximizing the full the advantages of in-depth, purposeful sampling will do much to alleviate concerns about small sample size. . . . The validity, meaningfulness, and insights generated from qualitative inquiry have more to do with the information richness of the cases selected and the observational/analytical capabilities of the researcher than with sample size.[14]

Questions

The art of asking a question seems so simple. Even a two year old practices and refines the art daily. Yet, the art of asking a question is difficult to master. If you want your art to appear someplace other than your refrigerator door, then do not assume expertise. Face-to-face interviews, focus groups, and questionnaires employ the same basic techniques for asking a question—techniques that involve wisdom and skill to employ. Wording, sequencing, and selecting questions require the skilled mind of an artisan who may take weeks and months before putting brush to canvas, chisel to stone, or words on a page.

Most often, open-ended and informal questions are used in qualitative interviews and questionnaires. The questions often employed are:[15]

1. Grand Tour Questions: ask an opening question to set the stage for the interview. Global questions enable participants to describe the situation in their own terms. Grand tour questions are open-ended questions that establish rapport. A typical grand tour ques-

14. Patton, *Qualitative Research*, 244–46.

15. The list of possible question types is consolidated from Patton, *Qualitative Research*, 348–51; Merriam, *Qualitative Research*, 76; Springer, *Action Research*, 71; and for further investigation see Spradley, *Ethnographic Interview*. He also explores in depth the categories of descriptive, structural, and contrast questions.

tion allows participants to talk about how activities usually occur (e.g., "How does your task force usually work?" "Describe a typical Sunday here at First Church?") A specific grand tour question may follow and focus on specific activities (e.g., "Can you tell me about last Sunday?). Grand Tour questions are asked first.

2. Guided Tour Questions: ask the participants to take you on a tour (e.g., around the office, tour of a situation, an explanation of a task).

3. Descriptive Questions: ask for more information about an action, a phenomenon, or a behavior. "I noticed that the congregation does not gather for a fellowship meal until a prayer is offered in the foyer. Are there other occasions within the life of the church where prayer functions similarly?" Notice the question is not asking about why. Why questions place the participant in the role of expert and often change the dynamics of the interview. Ethnographic research emphasizes the "what" and "how" questions that lead to concrete examples. Deciphering meaning about the action or the behavior will come later.

4. Task Questions: ask the participants to engage in an activity that will clarify the subject. Draw a map or a picture (e.g., "How do you see yourself in this committee?").

5. Hypothetical Questions: ask what the respondent might do or what it might be like in a particular situation. Hypothetical questions usually begin with "What if" or "Suppose." "Suppose it is my first time to visit your services, what would it be like?"

6. Quotation Questions: challenge the respondent to contemplate an opposing view or consider abstract issues. "Some people would say that the folks who left this church during the crisis were the ones with weak faith and faulty convictions. What would you say to them?"

7. Ideal Position Questions: ask the respondent to describe an ideal situation allows the respondent to dream or imagine possible alternatives. "What do you envision the ideal board meeting to be like?"

8. Knowledge Questions: ask for specific information possessed by the interviewee. Even if the information is not "true," it is what the interviewee believes to be factual.

9. Interpretive Questions: advance tentative interpretations of what the respondent has been saying and asks for a reaction. "Would you say that traditional styles of worship practiced here contribute to spiritual formation more than you anticipated?" "Who," "What," "When," "Where," and "How" questions that extend interpretation to deeper levels.

10. Behavior Questions: ask about what people have or have not done. The questions aim at eliciting descriptions of experiences from people. "If I had been with you on that day, what would I have seen you doing?"

11. Opinion Questions: move beyond actions and behaviors and explore why from the interviewee's perspective. Opinion questions tell us about people's goals, intentions, desires, and values. "What do you believe?" What do you think?"

12. Feeling Questions: seek to understand how this person feels and is emotionally affected by an issue, action, or subject. You are asking the participants how they experienced the subject being addressed. It is easy to confuse opinion questions with feeling questions. Listen carefully to the response to make sure you are receiving the answer you intended with the question.

13. Sensory Questions: ask about what is seen, touched, smelled, heard, or tasted. The unusual odor that comes through the air vents might prove useful when investigating the hospitality practices of a local congregation. Asking questions about the barbecue at a South Carolina picnic saved me from wrongfully accusing someone of bring spoiled meat (it had a mustard base).

14. Background or Demographic Questions: ask about age, occupation, education, or any number of standard background questions that describe identity characteristics.

Any of the questions above could be asked in the present, past, or future tense. For example, you can ask folks what they are doing now, what they have done in the past, and what they plan to do in the future.[16]

16. Patton, *Qualitative Research*, 351.

Write questions that will elicit the information you are seeking. Patton identifies "good" questions as "open-ended, neutral, singular, and clear."[17] Open-ended questions let the interviewee pursue any direction and use any words to express what they want to say. It is easy to "lead the witness" by indicating what you think is the best answer. A singular question contains only one clear idea. The fact that a question is open does not mean that multiple items should be included.[18]

When possible, use the language and idiom of the congregation to shape the questions.[19] This is possible even when you borrow questions from another instrument. For example, you will want to choose the language for communion that represents your local congregation (i.e., "Lord's Supper," "Communion," or "Eucharist"). When writing questions, avoid emotionally charged and leading questions that reveal your bias but may not be shared by the participant. For example, when you ask, "What emotional problems have you experienced since the pastor's departure?" you are assuming that people have had an emotional problem due to the event. That is not true for everyone. Avoid ambiguous or misleading words and phrases like, "What is your mission when experiencing fellowship activities?" Avoid inflammatory comments like, "How do you feel when *those people* visit your assembly?" Additionally, avoid questions with two objects that could lead to more than one acceptable answer. Thumma lists several possibilities that fit into this common pitfall—

- This error is occasionally seen where one is asked either to agree or disagree with a statement. Questions of this type include, "Do you favor longer Sunday school time and more in-depth teaching for the children?" and "The Bible is essential to my faith; I read it daily." Ask yourself for each question, "Could I both agree and disagree with parts of this statement?" If so, rewrite it.

- Likewise, be careful not to write comparative statements for which no adequate comparison is given, such as "The singles ministry is better now (agree or disagree?)." A respondent might ask, "than when? Last year, when I first joined, or when the new singles minister took over?"[20]

17. Ibid., 353.

18. Ibid., 353–62, provides a guide about writing questions that are open-ended, neutral, singular, and clear.

19. Thumma, "Methods," 225.

20. Ibid.

Field-testing the questionnaire or the interview guide will help you avoid many of these pitfalls. Piloting questions ensures that they are well worded. After pretesting, some questions might be eliminated or rewritten. You may learn what questions you failed to ask but should have included in the first place. At times, even the order will be changed. There are three options for piloting the questionnaire. You can use two or three thoughtful people who take the questionnaire and offer feedback. You can ask an independent expert to assess the questionnaire. Or you could field test the questionnaire in another setting. The field test should be followed by a statistical analysis that assesses the questionnaire at a deeper interpretive level. The more often a questionnaire is used and tested, the more the validity and reliability aspects of the instrument can be trusted. Many DMin students do not have the time for field-testing a questionnaire. If that situation applies to your setting, then choose options one or two. Alternatively, you could use an instrument already constructed and tested, or do not use a questionnaire but some other method to garner the information required. Do not assume that questionnaires are easy and will automatically gather the data you need. A strong instrument only comes through intentional and thoughtful construction and implementation.

SPECIFIC TECHNIQUES
FOR DATA COLLECTION & EVALUATION

In the previous chapter, the concept of data triangulation was introduced. Evaluation of the project's intervention will occur from three different fields of vision. The participants' angle of vision, an outsider's angle of vision, and the researcher's angle of vision provide an intensive gaze upon the effectiveness of the project. Various social science techniques and the associated skills to employ them are available to the researcher to evaluate the project's success. Key questions to ask to ascertain the best methods to employ for this particular study are, "What procedure best gathers information that I need for this particular angle of vision?" "Is the tool suitable for the purpose of the project and will the tool yield usable data?" "Will it measure what needs to be measured in order to ascertain whether the intervention addressed the problem of the inquiry?" Once appropriate tools are selected, data collection can begin.

Data collection is a critical issue for the project. If not done well, the whole process will be jeopardized. Preparing for data collection requires certain skills. The evaluation tools described below require preparation and training on the part of the investigator to ensure the project's integrity. Data collection begins with setting the boundaries for the study; it continues by collecting information through observations, interviews, documents, and visual materials, etc., and concludes by establishing the protocol for recording the information.[21] After describing the setting, the subjects (actors), the events (intervention), and the process, the methodology needs to indicate the types of data to be collected and provide a rationale for the data collection.[22]

Data collection and analysis techniques should be appropriate to, and, in fact, driven by the research questions. Casey desired to be inclusive in the gathering of data. By allowing techniques to be as open ended as possible, Casey controlled her own interference.[23] Her inclusive stance required respect for the participants as persons rather than subjects. She maintained the interpersonal character of her research throughout the project. Although Casey asked open-ended questions unaware of the journey before her, she chose her subjects to correlate with her research questions concerning political discourse about social change.

Riessman also suggests that the researcher use open-ended questions and techniques so that the listener is able to "construct answers" and generate data without unnecessary prodding.[24] The lack of a researcher-structured agenda creates a relaxed, conversational atmosphere necessary for eliciting narratives.

Quantz describes the process of data collection as follows:

> This "emic" approach requires the interviewer to eliminate as much as possible the urge to apply external structure to the interview. Instead of a formal interview schedule which has all the questions planned ahead of time, the interpretive interview must be a process which is flexible enough to follow the lead of the interviewee while not losing sight of the object. The typical interview might begin with what Spradley and McCurdy (1972) call the "grand tour" question. Such questions are designed to be directive enough to require concrete and precise responses, yet open enough to allow the interviewee to go in any direction. . . . Such questions allow the interviewees . . . to recall anything they think might be

21. Creswell, *Research Design*, 148–50.

22. Ibid., 149.

23. Casey, *I Answer*.

24. Riessman, *Narrative Analysis*, 54.

important or amusing. On the basis of their usually very lengthy response to this initial question, the interviewer should have a wealth of material to begin more specific questioning. In this way, a typical interview has been structured by the interviewee, but is clarified by the follow-up questioning of the interviewer.[25]

Most narrative researchers only gather one narrative from each participant. This approach taps in on the belief that people speak and tell their stories in patterned ways. People have consistent perspectives, use common metaphors, and maintain the same identity throughout time, and we presume that folks tell their stories generally the same way on different days. Various episodes may be recounted on different days, but the patterns of identity remain. Lather, while affirming the notion that single narratives may tend to become paradigmatic and consequently dogmatic, encourages the researcher to gather sequential interviews to facilitate collaboration and deepen the probing process.[26] Although it may be assumed that people follow the same basic patterns when retelling their stories, Lather's desire to demonstrate coherence in the research encourages researchers to consider subsequent interviews of the participants. Asking, "Does the transcript appropriately record and interpret your narrative?" could accomplish this objective. The question of what lens a participant is using while telling her story can be determined by comparing her story to a larger collective subjective to which she belongs.

Throughout the research process, you should take a neutral stance. It is sometimes difficult not to interject your feelings and opinions when people say and do things that cause you to disagree. Both verbal and nonverbal clues need to be presented as an interested but nonreactive response. Your job is to gather and record a participant's perspective and experience. You can add your initial feelings and interpretations in a side column or a different page, but the data that is recorded for future analysis cannot be tainted.

How much data is enough? As noted in chapter 1, qualitative researchers have few strict guidelines governing when to stop the data collection process. Most DMin projects will delineate in the methodology section the number of people to be interviewed or focus groups to be conducted, etc. Likewise, researchers may stop gathering data when

---

25. Quantz, "Interpretive Method," 189.
26. Lather, "Research as Praxis," 257–77.

patterns repeat and no new information is being added to the existing categories. This is often called the "saturation" point.

Observations

What people say they believe and do is often contradicted by their behavior. How and where people spend their money, time, and energy is often a poor witness to their public identity. Given the frequency of this aspect of humanity, observation is a powerful way to check the consistency of what people subjectively report about themselves during interviews, questionnaires, and focus groups. Additionally, observation gathers information about people's physical, social, cultural, political, and economic contexts, among others. By observing the interactions of the participants in the study, the researcher can understand more about their relationships, ideas, norms, habits, and practices.[27]

Participant observation is the primary tool used in ethnography, the study of living human beings in their social and cultural contexts. In ethnography, the researcher would be observing people as they engage in their routine activities of worship, meetings, service, fellowship, and education. Participant observation allows the researcher to encounter members of the project team who are engaging in the project's activities.[28] But in a DMin project, you will be observing folk as they engage the activities and interventions outlined in the methodology section of your project. As qualitative researchers, you are assuming that there will be multiple perspectives within any given community and the activities of that community. You want to know what those perspectives are and understand the interplay among them. Primarily, participant-observers will be using all their senses in order to ask questions, gather data, and take notes according to a prescribed protocol.

27. Common ethnographic terms you will encounter often when reading the literature about observation are: *Etic*—to observe and analyze beliefs and actions from an outsider's perspective. *Emic*—to observe and analyze beliefs and actions from an insider's perspective.

28. As a technical term in ethnography, participant observers are immersed into the daily activities of the culture being studied. Living daily with people, learning to speak their language, understanding their rituals and symbols, enables the researcher to minimize her own presence upon people's responses. I am adapting the term to refer to anyone who is assigned to witness and record a specific activity within the DMin project. The minister and the participants in the project are currently living within the culture of the congregation.

Figure 6: Degrees of Involvement

Ethnography normally asks the observers who participate in the social life of the context observed to maintain cognitive distance in order to do scientific work. However, most DMin researchers are "insiders," people who are invested in the life of the congregation. Merriam describes the role you will take as a DMin researcher as that of the "*collaborative partner. . . .* The defining characteristic of this stance is that the investigator and the participants are equal partners in the research process."[29] The participants you have asked to join you in your project are also "insiders." It is difficult for an "insider" to see the familiar. It may be as "plain as the nose on your face," but if it is always in front of you, you may miss it week after week. As James 1:23–24 says, it is "like people who look at their faces in a mirror and, after looking, go away and immediately forget what they look like." You may need to train yourself and your participants to see the context with new eyes. For example, if you are examining a problem related to how visitors are received on a Sunday morning, your task force may want to visit neighboring churches and experience being an "outsider." Then, back at home, the group can imagine their own experience on any given Sunday. That knowledge will influence what you observe and how you interpret what you see.[30] Finally, with participant observer eyes, a particular set of events can be scrutinized for the purposes of the project.

Problems that "insiders" have include being biased against or biased for a particular person, project, or activity. In either case, such bias will hinder your role as a researcher. As a DMin researcher, you are an advocate for the intervention. You are prone to be biased for a positive outcome. Too much attachment is a liability. However, swinging the pen-

29. Merriam, *Qualitative Research*, 101.
30. Thumma, "Methods," 199.

dulum to an "outsider's" perspective often creates too much detachment. In a DMin project, pulling away may even create unwarranted problems. Detachment often leads participant observers to miss key words and moments in the study. Finding the boundary or border position between "insider" and "outsider" is difficult even for trained ethnographers. The pastor-researcher will find the task virtually impossible. Reflexivity when it comes to the difficult task of maintaining a liminal state between the two realms will enhance your credibility. Taking field notes is the most effective technique for letting the researcher pull back from being too fully engrossed in the participation of the project. Taking notes is not a routine activity for participants and helps create a degree of detachment.

Always remember, the researcher is historically rooted. Take me for example. I have an ethnicity, economic position, political views, gender biases, etc. . . . My parents raised me. It cannot be otherwise. Their background and perspectives have an affect on my way of viewing the world. I attended public schools. I attended Purdue, Harding, Duke, and UNCG. I married young, have two children, and continue to enjoy the wife of my youth as I advance in years. I worship in the same denomination of my parents. My perspective on any given congregational experience will be partial and biased. Again, it cannot be otherwise.

The idea of a non-participant observer is not possible.[31] The presence of a note-taker, even in the corner of the room, affects how the system reacts and how people behave. The researcher might try to hide behind a two-way mirror, but most folks do not engage in life in such contrived locations. While researchers strive for accuracy in their observations and validity in their analysis, they also must reflect on how their role as researcher influences the setting.

The Star Trek Syndrome infects researchers, making them feel inoculated from outside contamination. The researcher believes a vaccine exists that ensures that "real" research possessing "neutrality and objectivity" is possible. In the world of TV, the Star Trek Syndrome is connected to the prime directive of non-interference. As the adventurers traveled through space, they were directed to maintain their distance from alien cultures. Nowhere was this more evident than when the crew of the starship Enterprise made first contact with beings from another world. The plot of many episodes revolves around the conflict of ignoring or disobeying the prime directive. The captain often made exceptions

31. Gobo, *Doing Ethnography*, 6–7.

because he deemed that particular situations demanded that the crew act on the behalf of higher ideals of justice or mercy. Why did the prime directive create such conflict of interests? Because the prime directive is an unachievable ideal, a utopian Vulcan value placed upon humanity. Similarly, why is the ideal of a non-interfering participant highly prized? Because some researchers maintain the values of a positivist worldview that sees scientific inquiry as an endeavor to run experiments that will be unpolluted by the hands of the scientist. But human societies do not live their lives in sterile laboratories. The mere fact you have entered the room, breathed the air, and asked a question has altered and "tainted" the evidence. Again, it cannot be otherwise.

The question of what is to be observed in a specific setting is not always an easy one. Particular projects will require differing sets of information. The protocol should spell out the exact details of what is to be observed. Spradley offers nine major dimensions of every social situation:

1. Space: the physical place or places

2. Actor: the people involved

3. Activity: a set of related acts people do

4. Object: the physical things that are present

5. Act: single actions that people do

6. Event: a set of related activities that people carry out

7. Time: the sequencing that takes place over time

8. Goal: the things people are trying to accomplish

9. Feeling: the emotions felt and expressed[32]

By selecting the nine dimensions one at a time, you can describe most features of any social situation. The interrelationship of the dimensions takes your observation to the next level. An easy way to see the interrelationships is to formulate descriptive questions designed to focus your attention. For example, "What are the major events in this social situation?" "Who are the actors in this social situation?" "Which actors

---

32. Spradley, *Participant Observation*, 78. Spradley constructs a 9x9 matrix that delineates all the possible descriptive questions you could ask about these interrelationships. See Patton, *Qualitative Research*, 331, exhibit 6.6, for summary guidelines for a field observation.

participate in which events?" And "In what ways do events change relationships among actors?"[33]

One generic example from the public health field offers the following possible list:

What to observe during participant observation[34]

Category	Includes	Researcher should note
Appearance	Clothing, age, gender, physical appearance	Anything that might indicate membership in groups or in sub-populations of interest to the study, such as profession, social status, socioeconomic class, religion, or ethnicity
Verbal behavior and interactions	Who speaks to whom and for how long; who initiates interaction; languages or dialects spoken; tone of voice	Gender, age, ethnicity, and profession of speakers; dynamics of interaction
Physical behavior and gestures	What people do, who does what, who interacts with whom, who is not interacting	How people use their bodies and voices to communicate different emotions; what individuals' behaviors indicate about their feelings toward one another, their social rank, or their profession
Personal space	How close people stand to one another	What individuals' preferences concerning personal space suggest about their relationships
Human traffic	People who enter, leave, and spend time at the observation site	Where people enter and exit; how long they stay; who they are (ethnicity, age, gender); whether they are alone or accompanied; number of people
People who stand out	Identification of people who receive a lot of attention from others	The characteristics of these individuals; what differentiates them from others; whether people consult them or they approach other people; whether they seem to be strangers or well known by others present

Before you arrive at a situation, anticipate what you will be observing and recording. It is easy to be overwhelmed at all the possibilities an

33. Spradley, *Participant Observation,* 80–83.

34. Mack, et al, *Qualitative Research Methods,* 20.

event or setting has to offer. A little planning, spelled out in the protocol, will ease any disorientation that occurs. Moschella describes this as a way to "train your gaze."[35] It is impossible to capture the whole event, so you will need to be selective. Additionally, Moschella encourages the observer to use all his senses. Sights, sounds, smell, and textures can give the observer a sense of the room. The moldy odor in the fellowship hall, the dusty and cluttered foyer, or the fresh cut flowers on the tables all can contribute to the meaning that you are seeking to discover and interpret. Some items may seem unimportant at the time. "Because you cannot judge the significance of each aspect in advance, starting out with a wide angle and recording as much detail as possible serves the process well."[36] Soon, you will "narrow your gaze" onto the particulars of your study.

It is not just the structured times that need careful observation. Sometimes great insights can emerge during hallway conversation, waiting in line for coffee, or afterwards in the parking lot. People may express opinions during the unstructured times that they would not during a program even if asked directly. Moreover, observe significant items that did not happen. If you expected the group to make a decision, but there was no motion or vote, then note it. If during the coffee break people sat around the room with little conversation, note it. Not everything that did not happen is worth noting. If the police did not show up to intervene in a domestic dispute, you do not have to record that in your notes (unless, of course, there really was a domestic dispute and the police ignored the 911 call). However, the purpose of your being there, the protocol in your methodology, and the purpose of the gathering are indicators that narrow your gaze on what was presumed to happen.

During observations, you will often have opportunities to engage people in conversations or informal interviews. Be prepared. Know ahead of time the possible topics and questions that you will ask. Ask them to describe the situation, explain in their own words what you are observing, or recount stories that relate to the activity. The "casual" or "impromptu" conversation provides you the opportunity to verify your observations and to delve deeper into the meaning of events.

Your protocol will include observations of people, actions, context, and physical materials. For example, if your project focuses on hospitality to strangers, you may choose to observe three activities where visitors

35. Moschella, *Ethnography*, 116.
36. Ibid.

and newcomers interact with members. Second, you can narrow what you are seeing at those locations by selecting key concepts (e.g., greetings, distributed literature, or other routines). Furthermore, your observation can focus on the conversations visitors are having with greeters or other church members. Finally, you could follow selected individuals or objects related to hospitality. Follow the path of a visitor (without lurking or stalking) throughout his time with the church, or observe how a welcome basket is distributed, utilized, or discarded. By narrowing the observation using the lenses of activities, concepts, conversations, and objects, you reduce the pressure on yourself to observe everything and everybody.

The protocol offered in *Studying Congregations* is a checklist of options. Not all the items will pertain to your particular study, but the following list can assist you in covering your essential categories.

Observation Protocol[37]

1. Demographics: (1) What is the social composition of those you are observing—their age, sex, race, ethnicity, apparent family composition, and social class? (2) How do ordinary members compare demographically to the clergy? To others within the congregation's local community? (3) Are there significant minority groups within a larger membership majority? Are there well-defined subgroups, sitting apart from the whole, such as parents with babies, teens, or older adults? (4) What is the dress of the participants? Are the members formally or informally attired? How does their dress compare to the leaders' dress? Are there special costumes for the clergy? Are the laity expected to wear a prescribed "uniform" or particular articles of clothing? (5) What can be deduced about their social, moral, and economic commitments based on their attire; the type of vehicles they drive; bumper stickers; and the bike, gun, or ski racks?

2. Physical Settings: (1) What do the church grounds look like? Is the landscaping similar to or different from the surrounding community? Is the church visible to passersby? Is a sign evident and readable from the road? What is the parking area like? Is it paved, well

---

37. Thumma, "Methods," 200–201. An observation tool used by the Association for Case Teaching (ACT) is included in Appendix 5 (used with permission).

kept, lighted, patrolled, and marked with special handicapped and visitor parking spaces? (2) Describe the exterior of the building(s). What is the church architecture like? How does it compare to neighboring buildings? Does the building connote anything about what takes place inside? Is the primary entryway clearly marked and evident to visitors? What does the entryway and greeting foyer imply about the welcoming attitude of the church? (3) Describe the interior of the building(s), the physical space. Is it plain or ornate, well-lit or dark, small or large, traditional or contemporary? Is the building "user-friendly," with ushers, informational signs, handicapped access, and visitors' stations? (4) What is the arrangement of seating and standing space? Describe the seating: theater-style seats, bequeathed pews, folding chairs? How is the sacred space arranged, decorated, and set off from the other parts of the sanctuary? (5) What props or equipment are used or displayed? Describe the altar, chairs, tables, railed areas, pulpit, musical instruments, choir lofts, audio and video devices, and sound system. What explicitly religious icons, symbols, or artifacts are evident, such as Bibles, candles, statuaries, scrolls, wall hangings, stained-glass windows, murals, baptistery, shrines, hymnals, or prayer books?

3. The Event: (1) What happens in the course of the worship event? What is the format, length in time, number and order of distinct segments, such as informal gathering time, announcements, testimonials, prayers, sermons, ritual celebrations, music, and singing? Describe what takes place during these activities and the roles of both the leaders and the congregation. Is there considerable bodily movement? Are these activities formal or informal, highly ritualized or seemingly spontaneous? (2) Who participates in each segment of the service: many people or a few; only ordained leaders or also lay people; only one demographic group of the membership or a diversity? Does the congregation participate in unison, in groups, or individually? What are the interactions like? Are they formal or informal, explained or dependent on insider knowledge? (3) How is the event orchestrated: by the senior clergy person, by a worship leader, by a written source like a bulletin or prayer book, by unspoken traditions and habits? What programs or worship guides are announced or published? (4) What other events take place at the church throughout the week? Who presides over these? Who

attends and participates? What do these say about the concerns of the congregation?

4. Interactional Patterns: (1) Who interacts with whom? Prior to the service, where do people gather? Is there a subtle segregation by sex, class, race, or cliques in these gatherings? Are all equally incorporated into the interactional patterns? Who is left out? Are the membership interactions stiff and formal or casual and informal? (2) Are the congregational members highly focused and engaged in what is taking place, or are they minimally involved and easily distracted? Do they follow along in the sacred texts and hymnals and participate in the ritual motions? Are they actively recording sermon and announcement notes or doodling on the bulletin? Are any members asleep, flirting, or disciplining children? During the service, do disruptive interactions take place? How are these kept to a minimum? Are there pockets of rebellious or unruly participants, and how are they treated? (3) From the interactions within the service, can you tell anything about the governing structures or power hierarchy of the church? Who seems to be in charge? Who seems to be respected and honored? Who are those without power? Does congregational authority seem highly concentrated or diffused? (4) What is the nature of interactions following the event? Do the members have access to the leaders, formally or informally? Is the tone or mood of the members light, serious, fired up, sleepy, relaxed, or hurried as they leave? Are there other events following the service to encourage lingering or increased participation, such as meetings, lunches, trips, and recreational activities?

5. Verbal and Written Content: (1) Listen carefully to what is being said by the members in the pews, halls, classrooms, and parking lots. Record jokes and gossip, complaints and grumbling that are shared with you. Do not eavesdrop, however. You have no right to information you overheard if the speaker did not know you were a researcher or that you were listening. Are there common greetings, "buzzwords," or concerns voiced. Is there a difference between what is said officially and what is heard informally? (2) Read carefully everything passed out or available on racks, tables, or in the pews. What groups or causes are sponsored or supported by the church? What does this literature report about the concerns

of the church? (3) Notice the words of the hymns. Do members seem to be paying attention to these words? Record the prayers but also listen for the emotional content. What is being said and why? Are these hymns and prayers addressed to a deity or to each other? Do they evoke a distant or close, warm or cold, formal or familiar relationship with the sacred or within the community? (4) Carefully pay attention to the words of the preacher and other lay leaders. What is the style, tone, and language of speaking? (5) Has this message changed recently with a new pastor, a new contextual situation, or a new ministry direction? Is there a call by the leaders or others to change direction? What future hopes and visions are members offered?

6. Meaning: (1) Rather than focusing specifically on what is said, pay attention to the meaning conveyed in the message, especially concerning who the people are as a social, moral, and spiritual community. How is members' involvement with the world described? Are members instructed to care primarily for their own, for local needs, or for global issues? Are ethical codes and behavioral norms rigid and absolute or flexible and relative? What is the character and content of the theology being espoused? (2) What is the overall message: one of challenge, comfort, criticism, exposition, invigoration? What is the character of the service? How does is seem to relate to the lives of the membership? What does salvation mean to these people? What implications can you draw about the faith of the members and its role and importance in their everyday lives?

Knowing what to observe and recording those observations are complementary activities. Refer to the discussion on field notes in chapter 6 for appropriate ways to record your observations.

Interviews

Tavis Smiley sets the standard in television interviewing. In a recent YouTube posting, he addresses the dilemma of how to get the most out of your subjects. His intent is to elicit openness and honesty from his guests. He begins by noting the difference between an interview and a conversation. An interviewer often prepares 8–10 questions, lists them on a card, and runs down the list of questions regardless of the answers. "You ask, they answer." A conversation is not scripted. As the interviewer, you ask the first question. That question is based on your homework. You have to know the subject material and the background information. Your second question depends on what they say. It will trigger something that prompts you to ask another question. However, your second question is not just a flow of consciousness but again will be informed by your homework and by the intent you have for the interview. Smiley next advises interviewers to be generous listeners. If you listen, they will tell you where to go next with your questions. After you get the first question out, listen to what they are telling you. You are not leading the conversation but you are following the conversation. They will end up telling you more than they intended to say.[38]

Interviews allow people to describe their situations and put words to their interior lives, personal feelings, opinions, and experiences that otherwise are not available to the researcher by observation. A researcher might arrive at certain conclusions through observation that will be confirmed, modified, or even corrected through interviews. Interviews not only provide a record of interviewees' particular views and perspectives, but also recognize the legitimacy of their views. While even interview data is only a representation of the interviewee's opinions, experiences, and understandings, it does allow you to gain insight into thoughts that are not expressed through a person's actions or that are too sensitive for people to discuss in a group setting.[39]

38. Smiley, "How to Get More." See Swinton and Mowat, *Practical Theology*, 64–65, who differentiate between a conversation and an interview noting that interviews are intentional and interviewers are in a power position. Because of the power dynamics, the interviewer must be cautious and protective of the gift that the interviewee has granted.

39. A specialized interview is Key Informant Interviewing that involves an individual in whom you invest a disproportionate amount of time because that person appears to be particularly well informed, articulate, approachable, or available.

It's not just what you say...

Tone refers to the volume and sound quality of a person's voice. It can reveal biases such as excitement, approval or disapproval, scorn, surprise, and disbelief. Remember that cultural context affects how tone of voice will be interpreted—what is moderate in one context may seem inappropriately loud in another. For example, depending on where you are, increasing the volume of your voice might indicate that you have become irritated or angered by a particular response, or it could be perceived as a fluctuation of the voice typical of everyday conversation. The age, gender, social status, educational background, and economic class of both you and the participant might also factor into which tone you should adopt. Generally, you should aim to use a friendly tone that will not betray your personal opinions or emotional state.

Body language is the culturally specific interpretation of what it means to move or position the body in a particular way. Facial expressions are perhaps the most obvious example, but gestures, posture, and constant movement can also be powerful indicators of a person's mood, opinion, and evaluative stance. Interviewers should be conscious of their body language at all times and be careful not to imply, for example, boredom, aggression, or exasperation. Instead, body language that indicates patience, a pleasant mood, an open attitude, and sincere interest will serve to encourage participants to express themselves without reserve.

The main purpose of the interview is to obtain a special kind of information. The researcher wants to find out what is "in and on someone else's mind."[40] Patton states, "We interview people to find out from them those things we cannot directly observe. . . . We cannot observe feelings, thoughts, and intentions. We cannot observe behaviors that took place at some previous point in time. We cannot observe situations that preclude the presence of an observer. We cannot observe how people have organized the world and meanings they attach to what goes on in the world. We have to ask people questions about those things. The purpose of interviewing, then, is to allow us to enter into the other person's perspective."[41]

When determining what type of interview format (or questionnaire) to use, you first consider your problem and purpose statements. What information do you need that would help you evaluate whether or not the intervention was effective in answering the problem and fulfilling the purpose of the project? The kinds of questions you want to ask and the sort of answers you expect to be offered must cohere, or you will

40. Patton, *Qualitative Evaluation*, 278.
41. Ibid., 196.

gather piles of data that will tempt you to manipulate it in order to be useful.

When it comes to interview protocol, you must be explicit about protocol in the methodology section of your thesis. Describe your procedures in detail. How does this methodology function? Why this methodology? How does this methodology function in relation to reliability and validity?[42] Decisions about many practical issues are solvable early in the process. "The length and number of the interviews, the place or places where you will conduct them, obtaining informed consent, the process for selecting particular persons to interview (and the rationale for these choices), plans for recording or transcribing interviews, and managing the time and expenses that interviews require."[43] A standard protocol would include the following components:

- Instructions to the interviewer (opening statements)

- The key research questions to be asked

- Probes to follow key questions

- A welcome for the person being interviewed, giving them thanks for their participation (At the end of your session together, thank the interviewee again for their participation and let them know about any follow-up contact that will occur.)

- Transition messages for the interviewer

- Space in which the researcher records reflective notes (Taking notes during the interviews helps capture nonverbal and initial reactions.)

- Identification of yourself, your role, your purpose (Don't assume they know.)

- Ways of acquiring permission to talk with people and record information

- Ways of checking that the time is convenient for an extended discussion, as well as ways of negotiating alternative times and places for interviews

42. See Berg, *Qualitative Research Methods*, 57ff. for extensive rationale, protocol, and analysis of interviewing.

43. Moschella, *Ethnography*, 66. To understand the issues relating to transcriptions, see Bischoping, "Quote, Unquote."

- A plan in case the interview is interrupted

- A reminder to the interviewee of the volunteer nature of the interview (They are not obligated to respond to any question.)

- Protocols for recordings

- Communication to the interviewee about how the issues of anonymity and confidentiality will be handled

- Procedures for authentication[44]

Cite the sources. Interview methods have a variety of approaches and underpinning philosophies. The literature is not uniform at all. Cite the particular approach and who offers it as an appropriate protocol for the methodology under discussion.

When determining what type of interview format to use, you must consider the kinds of questions you want to ask and the sort of answers you expect to be offered. *Structured interviews* that include fixed response options increase the number of participants available for interviewing. Telephone interviews are an example of a structured interview. Structured interviews must be field-tested for reliability and validity and will probably involve statistical analysis.

Unstructured interviews must develop, adapt, and generate questions and follow-up probes appropriate to the given situation and the central purpose of the investigation. Sometimes during the course of a field observation, an unstructured interview may augment what is observed to gain additional information about various phenomena. Unstructured interviews allow the interviewee to take you on a journey. You may not know where you are going, but be open to the serendipity of discovery. It is because you do not control the direction of the interview that you may find the richest discoveries. If you knew enough to ask a question, then you probably already have ideas about the answers.

44. Authentication: Will you allow the participant to authenticate what they say or not? For example, will the interviewee be able to check the transcript for accuracy or make appropriate deletions, additions, or changes? Authentication is sometimes called "member checking" (see "credibility" in chapter 8 for a more complete description). There are different theories as to the necessity for authentication. For example, researchers assume that people on different days may have diverse moods or emotions causing them to respond with atypical and even contradictory answers. However, Casey, "Class Notes," records that people speak in patterned ways. Even if they tell a different story or use different language if asked the same question on a different day, the patterns and themes from their lives will still emerge.

But in an open interview format, you may learn about the questions you should be asking.

Your role as an interviewer in an unstructured interview is to facilitate conversation. You may introduce topics but not control the conversation by addressing issues or specific questions directly. In the midst of the conversation, you probe for deeper answers and or meaning, identify new topics, and probe new topics. Finally, you watch for non-verbal clues. If needed, you can schedule a follow-up interview for clarification on a topic.

Somewhere in between the structured and the free-flowing interview style are the *semi-structured interviews*. Specified themes, issues, and questions with predetermined sequence are described in the protocol, but you are free to pursue matters as situations dictate. However, the probing is narrowed by a preset protocol that correlates with the project's problem and purpose statements. An interview guide lists the questions or topics that the interviewer desires to explore. It ensures that the basic information is obtained from each person. There are no predetermined responses, and the interviewer is free to probe and explore for more depth. An interview guide ensures good use of time, makes the process more systematic and comprehensive, and keeps the interviewer focused on the purpose of the interview.[45] The intellectual task is to try to assess when to probe an answer for more depth or to move to another question. While you will have notes about the topics that need to be covered to generate the data you need for your study, you will also need to make connections between relevant issues not anticipated and the purpose of the study.

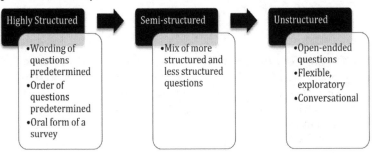

Figure 7: Interview Structure Continuum[46]

45. Patton, *Qualitative Research*, 344–5.

46. Adapted from Merriam, *Qualitative Research*, 73. See also, Fontana and Frey, "Interviewing."

Interview Protocols: Interview guides that provide you direction in your project do not need extensive explanations. You already know the background and the rationale for the guide. A simple listing of the questions and space to record your notes will be the extent of the guide. However, if you will be using other people to lead a group interview or conduct several face-to-face interviews, you will need to provide training as well as an extensive interview guide. Whitney and Trosten-Boom suggest a comprehensive guide has the following six parts:[47]

1. An introduction that sets the stage for the interview and includes an overview of the inquiry process, significance of the interview, and details about confidentiality and how the data will be utilized in the future.

2. Stage-setting questions that build rapport.

3. Topic questions that explore in depth the subject at hand.

4. Concluding questions that wrap up the interview. For example: "Anything you want to add?" "What should I have asked you that I did not think to ask?"

5. Summary sheets that allow you to collect the interview data. They serve two purposes. First, they function as a repository for the best stories, quotes, and ideas. Second, they provide space for reflection, where initial interpretations are recorded.

6. Quick action sheets to collect items that require immediate action or attention. For example, changes that need to be made in the interview protocol, future questions to ask, or items needing attention before the next session.

Various forms of questions are elaborated as:

> *Backward questions* generally come first. They invite us to remember high-point experiences—times when we have experienced the Affirmative Topic to be most alive and most present. . . . *Inward questions* generally follow backward questions. They refer back to the high-point experiences, asking us to make meaning of those peak experiences, and to extrapolate learnings about their root causes of success. . . . *Forward questions* generally come last. At their best, they solicit our hopes, dreams, and inspirations. They encourage us to imagine futures in which the Affirmative Topic

47. Whitney and Trosten-Bloom, *Power of Appreciative Inquiry*, 156–7.

is the best it can possibly be. . . . *Transition questions* are often embedded within the forward questions. They are retrospective reflections from the imagined future state—an opportunity for the interviewee to consider first steps and transitions from the current reality to the imagined future."[48]

Training others to use your protocol involves giving them the background and purpose of the study, practice interviewing, guidelines regarding note-taking, practice redirecting negative feedback, information about the interview schedule (who, when, and where), and ethical considerations.[49]

An example of the protocol given in an interview guide is found in the Profiles of Ministry (PoM) assessment constructed by the Association of Theological Schools (ATS). Although the questions are open ended, there is a precise structure. For example, after some of the questions are specific instructions to the interviewer about what to ask next. Typically, those instructions read like, "If the respondent answers 'yes,' ask them to explain. If they answer 'no,' move to the next question." "If the respondent answered 'yes,' ask them . . . . Otherwise, move to the next question." The POM instructions for the interview are as follows:[50]

> Before turning on the recorder, read the following text aloud to the person to be interviewed:
> "This interview is one part of the Profiles of Ministry program. It consists of a series of questions dealing with your view of yourself and your approach to ministry. Please consider each question as an invitation to express yourself as honestly as you can, not as a demand for one particular kind of answer that may seem more 'right' than another."
> "Sometimes a word or two will be all you want to say in response to a question. Sometimes you will need several sentences to answer. It is up to you to judge how much needs to be said. Several questions direct me to ask follow-up questions or for a fuller explanation. Your responses to these may be as brief as you wish."
> "Throughout the interview you may hear several questions that seem to relate to the same issue. This is to help get a clearer picture of where you stand, not to see whether you are consistent.

48. Ibid., 152–3.

49. Ibid., 160.

50. Brekke and Williams, *Profiles of Ministry*, 5.

You will also notice changes of subject matter between one question and another."

"I will read the questions as they are written and I can repeat any question you wish to hear again. I am asked not to define any words or interpret meanings. You should fell free to go back and add to previous answers any time you want."

"Whatever you say during this interview will be confidential. It will be used only in coding your answers. Please do not discuss these questions with anyone who has not taken the interview."

"Unless you have a question, I will turn on the recorder and we will begin. Please speak loudly enough for your taped answer to be clearly understood."

Sometimes it is difficult to schedule an interview with some people. They will do a lengthy face-to-face interview in an informal setting when they claim they are too busy to answer a questionnaire or sit down for an official interview. Or, their reticence may be due to their introversion, quiet disposition, or lack of confidence. Sometimes informal interviews facilitate getting information from someone reluctant to share in a formal way but who will talk to an interested listener. In such cases, downplay your perceptions, interests, agendas, and biases. Do not lead, but use neutral questions and minimize governing the framework of meaning or the constructing of reality.

When using open-ended questions in an interview, the interviewer is free to pursue new topics or explore in more detail a vague subject. Prompts or probing questions are used if the respondent's answers are brief or unclear. If at points during the interview, it seems that the respondent is waiting for a reaction from you, or when the person seems to be holding back key information, then a prompt or a probing question is appropriate. The following list of prompts or probing questions will prove essential for the skilled interviewer.

1. Silence: The long pause encourages the participant by indicating you are ready to hear more.

2. Extension: "Tell me more about. . ."

3. Encouragement: "Go on, yes . . ." Or a simple "un-huh" or "I see" will prompt the person to keep speaking. Such signals indicate you are interested and are still carefully listening.

4. Clarification: Asking the participant to help you understand some aspect of their answer that puzzles you. "What did you mean when

you said . . ." "I don't understand . . ." Don't assume that you know what they are talking about just because you know the words they are using. You are there to learn. You are interviewing these people because they have something to teach you.

5. Elaboration: Asking the classical questions of who, what, when, where, why, and how. "How did this happen?" "Why do you think. . . ?" "What happen then?" "How did you handle . . . ?"

6. Repetition: Allows you to check a response by mirroring back a previous statement. "You were saying earlier that. . ." "If I understood you correctly, you said . . ." "So you were 19 when . . ."

7. Example: "Can you give me an example of . . ." You are asking the participant to engage in a story based upon information that has emerged in the interview. For example, "Can you describe the time when . . ." or "Would you tell the story about the time when you. . ."

Knowing how to conduct an interview and recording people's responses are complementary activities. Refer to the section on field notes about appropriate ways to record what people say.

Hints For Interviewing[51]

1. Schedule your interview well ahead of the meeting date. Confirm the time with the interviewee the day before you are to meet. Do not schedule an interview for longer than two hours. Arrive on time.

2. Allow the person being interviewed to select a place that would be most comfortable for him or her. Encourage the person to choose a location with as few distractions as possible; restaurants are seldom good for formal interviews.

3. If you use a tape recorder, check your tape, batteries, and sound levels before you start.

4. Be prepared with a list of issues you want to cover and an opening question. Otherwise, allow the direction of the conversation to be determined as you go along. Even if you use a tape recorder, make notes during the interview about what you have covered and those issues to which you wish to return.

---

51. Ammerman et al., *Studying Congregations*, 204.

5. Begin your meeting with informal and casual small talk. Wait for a lull, a question, or another verbal bridge into the formal interviewing. Describe the reason for the study, define your participation, and detail your use and protection of any recorded material. Then begin with your predetermined opening question.

6. Use photos and other concrete objects on occasion, if necessary, as stimulants to conversation.

7. Focus on events or specific experiences that have led this person to his or her beliefs or opinions. Rather than pushing the interviewee by using *why* or *what do you mean* questions, ask *for examples* or *for instances*, especially when trying to flesh out ideological issues or abstract ideas.

8. Listen, listen, listen. Do not give advice or argue, and interrupt only to clarify. Encourage the person with nods and smiles. Pay attention, be warm and personable, and do not overplay the researcher role.

9. Beware of asking questions that could only be answered by damaging either the interviewee's or other congregational member's esteem or social standing. Do not encourage gossip, but record it if it arises. Do not push sensitive issues if you perceive discomfort by the interviewee. Remember, this person is part of your congregation.

10. Use interviews to check out the information provided by others, but do not break confidences by relating what took place in other interviews. Let the person know what you already know, and ask him or her to tell you more, to fill in details only he or she can provide, or to correct misinformation.

11. Pay attention to what happens and what you see in the surroundings during the interview. For instance, note how the person responds to family members, whether he or she prays before meals, the prominence of religious symbols or literature in the home, and so forth. Likewise, record the interviewee's response to the interview process: Was the person outgoing or reserved, forthright or reticent with opinions? These characteristics may tell you much of the person's place and role in the life of the congregation.

12. If you are less familiar with those you will be interviewing, it is good to record a set of brief demographic facts (age, race, gender, occupation, approximate socioeconomic level, years of member-

ship, and depth of involvement in church life) about each person you talk to. Often this information, once tallied, will help you check to see if those you interviewed adequately represent the congregation as a whole.

13. You will want to test your questions on a spouse, friend, or other study members prior to conducting the interviews. Your questions may need to be refined further as you begin the interview process.

Questionnaires

A questionnaire is a paper and pencil instrument for doing an interview. Many of the suggestions and principles for interviewing discussed above apply to questionnaires. If you are using a standard questionnaire, you do have the freedom to re-word or rearrange the questions. However, if you want to compare results with other groups that have utilized the instrument, your comparison will be suspect. Be careful changing questions and sequence because you could change the intended meaning. For example, when question 2 is asked after question 1, certain implications may emerge that do not come to a person's mind if the question sequence is reversed. Likewise, a question might not be asked if it is subsequent to a similar question, but it might be essential if asked first. Scott Thumma gives the following example, "You might for example get different answers depending on which of the following two statements you put first: 'Caring for the earth is essential to being a good Christian' and 'Recycling should be a social priority for our church.'"[52]

There are various question types commonly used in questionnaires. The open-ended questions will be used most often in DMin projects. Sometimes these questions can be narrow in focus requiring only one or two sentences or even just one word. For example, "In the past two years, what event has inspired you to grow spiritually?" At other times, a broad question may prompt some responders to write several paragraphs. For example, "What role does preaching have in the life of the church, your family, and your personal walk with God?"

Other question types may resemble a survey (described below):

---

52. Ibid., 226.

1. Fixed choice: Asks the question in a set fashion and provides a choice of predetermined answers. The simplest of these is the *yes/no* question. Multiple-choice questions fit in this category.

2. List: Select items from a list.

3. Category: Often demographic questions (e.g., age 20–29).

4. Ranking: Place items in rank order.

5. Scale: The primary purpose of scaling is to provide a technique for efficient data reduction. Interpreting scales will often require statistical analysis. Babbie describes the Bogardus Social Distance Scale, Thurstone Scales, Likert Scaling, Semantic Differential,[53] and Guttman Scaling.[54]

To increase the number of questionnaires returned, choose your time and place wisely, and personally collect the finished questionnaires. Be specific in your methodology section about the details of distribution and return to ensure a systematic set of procedures. During my DMin project, the questionnaires were distributed during the worship assembly. People return the questionnaires by putting them in boxes that were placed at the exits.

John Siburt's project demonstrates the use of a questionnaire. To put the project in perspective, he states, "The problem addressed by this project was the lack of an intentional process of catechetical instruction through which the elders of the Richardson East Church of Christ articulate relevant virtues for the members of the Richardson East Church. . . . The purpose of this project was to formulate a process through which the Richardson East elders discerned and articulated relevant Christian virtues within the communal life of the Richardson East Church of Christ."[55] From the insider's perspective, he gave the participants a questionnaire asking the elders the following questions based upon Watson's five areas of a training program:[56]

> *Reactions*: Describe your experience as a participant in these sessions? Did you have a positive experience? If so, what made this

---

53. See my "Preacher Response Questionnaire" in Appendix 3. E.g., Clear—Hazy.

54. For a detailed description of scale construction, see Babbie, *Practice of Social Research*, 165–71.

55. Siburt, "Crossing the Threshold," 20.

56. Friedman and Yarbrough, *Training Strategies*, 223.

a meaningful experience for you? What was the most fulfilling aspect of this process for you? How do you feel John performed in this process? How do you feel the elders performed in this process? What was the most positive or helpful aspect of the process? How could the process have been more helpful? *Learnings*: What new knowledge or insights did you gain as a participant in this process? In what ways did the process enhance your education or formation as a Christian leader? *Job Behavior*: How will the knowledge gained from this process inform your behavior as an elder? Has the process led you to behave differently in the role of elder? Has the process affirmed any of your current behaviors as an elder? Has the process redefined the role of elder for you in any way? *Organizational Impact*: How has this process served or contributed to the values and mission of the Richardson East Church? How might this process impact the Richardson East Church? *Additional Outcomes*: Please describe any additional outcomes associated with this process.[57]

While it might be argued that the questionnaire did not directly use the word "catechesis" or refer to the document that was produced to articulate Christian virtues, the term "process" functioned to communicate the purpose of the project. Additionally, some of the particulars of the questionnaire sidetracked it from accomplishing its primary function. For example, the question about "John's" role as facilitator was not necessary since the project was not designed to enhance or evaluate the practices of group dynamics or the leader's performance.

Surveys

A survey is a lengthy questionnaire that employs fixed choice responses. The purpose of a survey is to describe characteristics or understandings of a large group of people. When the desired sample size is so large that it is not feasible to interview or use a questionnaire, then the survey is the best option. If you choose to mail surveys, it will be more economical than face-to-face surveys, but the cooperation and return rate will decrease. Also, a mailed survey will need to be self-explanatory. Telephone and face-to-face surveys will increase both time and costs. However, face-to-face interviews increase participation, your ability to clarify, and the probability of gathering additional information. If the survey is used as one angle of the triangulation, then the questionnaire is interpreted

57. Siburt, "Crossing the Threshold," 100–101.

using qualitative standards even if the hiring of a statistician is necessary to process the information.[58]

Bell summarizes the use of surveys as follows:

> In surveys, all respondents will be asked the same questions in, as far as possible, the same circumstances. Question wording is not as easy as it seems, and careful piloting is necessary to ensure that all questions mean the same to all respondents. Information can be gathered by means of self-completion questionnaires (as in the case of the census) or by means of questionnaires, schedules or checklists administered by the interviewer. Whichever method of information gathering is selected, the aim is to obtain answers to the same questions from a large number of individuals to enable the researcher not only to describe but also to compare, to relate one characteristic to another and to demonstrate that certain features exist in certain categories. Surveys can provide answers to the questions What? Where? When? And How?, but it is not so easy to find out Why? Causal relationships can rarely if ever be proved by survey method. The main emphasis is on fact-finding, and if a survey is well structured and piloted, it can be a relatively cheap and quick way to obtaining information.[59]

Allen Burris, in his "Sermon Preparation for Hearers: A Collaborative Approach to Preaching in the Mitchell Church of Christ," intentionally used a survey that required statistical analysis as one angle of evaluation.[60] He states the problem in the following way: "Preaching is not as effective as it could be because those who hear the Sunday morning sermon are unprepared to hear its message."[61] As a response to the problem he states, "The purpose of this project was to help a selected group of participants collaborate with the preacher in preparing the Sunday morning sermon to enhance their hearing it."[62] The intervention took place as a six-day process involving a devotional guide with meditative activities. The group met on Wednesday evenings in a round table discussion of their experiences. Following the Wednesday session, Burris completed writing the sermon for the following Sunday.

---

58. Babbie offers a more complete description of surveys for social science research. Babbie, *Practice of Social Research*, 237–73.

59. Bell, *Doing Your Research Project*, 14.

60. Burris, "Sermon Preparation for Hearers."

61. Ibid., 11.

62. Ibid., 12.

Burris used a preaching response questionnaire in order to survey the congregation's reception of the sermon. The *Preaching Response Questionnaire* was designed to garner feedback measuring audience participation and logical organization of the sermon.[63] This tool was developed for the specific purpose of soliciting listener reaction to the deductive and inductive method of preaching.[64] The survey results (from the control group) were compared to the results from the group contributors who participated in Burris's intervention. After analysis by a trained statistician, who utilized a two-sample test of proportions or z-test, Burris stated, "Nineteen of the twenty-six questions, statements, or word pairs revealed a significant difference between the congregation and the project study group. These nineteen questions or word pairs were significant in the strongest response possible, for example, 'strongly agree' or 'strongly disagree,' rather than 'agree' or 'disagree.'"[65] Burris's analysis of the nineteen questions was triangulated with the data from his field notes and the data from an independent expert who interviewed the project study group.

63. Tim Sensing, "Testing of the Validity." See Appendix 3.

64 This instrument was found to be a valid instrument. Cronbach's Reliability Coefficient [alpha] was calculated to be 0.9458 indicating the internal consistency of the response tool. The positive correlation between the 26 items was observed to be high. The multivariate t-test (Hotelling T2) was used to test the hypothesis of no difference between the mean vectors of the 26 variables (questions 1–26) for the two sermonic models. The observed $F_{(26,274)}$-test statistic value 1.80598 with the p value of less than 0.011. This means, the hypothesis of no difference may be rejected. This tool did distinguish between the two models in a significant way. A Roy-Bargman Step-down F-test could be conducted in order to determine the significance of the questions asked in this particular order. Preliminary observations indicate that while both the Pearson Chi-square value and the univariate F-tests give evidence of significance for questions 1–3 when asked independently of each other, question 3 is not significant when questions 1 and 2 are asked before it. Questions 5, 8, 16, and 21 also indicate a high level of significance when asked in this sequence. This observation is due to the high correlation structure of the variables (questions 1–26). However, this level of statistical analysis is beyond the scope of this research project. The null hypothesis states there is no significance difference between listener participation and the inductive movement of the sermon (HO: $\mu 1 = \mu 2$). The alternate hypothesis states there is a correlation between listener participation and the inductive movement of the sermon (HA: $\mu 1 \neq \mu 2$). Although it may seem preferable to pursue a directional alternative hypothesis assuming a positive correlation between inductive methods and listener participation, preliminary studies indicate a negative correlation. Since the null hypothesis has been rejected in this study, this tool can be used as an effective measure of the listener's participation in a sermon.

65. Burris, "Sermon Preparation for Hearers," 56.

Ammerman offers the following caution about using surveys:

> Finally, a word about surveys. Many questionnaire items have been developed for discovering various aspects of people's beliefs about God. . . . Seeing how your congregation responds to such a set of questions can often be very revealing. One should always, however, take actual observations more seriously than, or at least alongside, responses to a survey. How people actually use and talk about the Bible is far more important than which preset response they choose on a questionnaire. In addition, the questions asked on the survey may not really reflect either the particular questions most pertinent to this congregation's operative theology or the way they would put things. The range of responses many not be their range at all. Finding out that 60 percent of respondents chose a given answer to a question about faith may only tell you that answer was the least unpalatable of the alternatives. If you use a survey to find out about your congregation's theologies, choose the questions with care. Avoid items that contain language or presuppositions that seem foreign to you. Keep the language as close to what is familiar as possible. And use the results more as a conversation starter than as a final verdict on what the congregation believes.[66]

GENERAL SUGGESTIONS FOR WRITING SURVEYS[67]

1. The questionnaire format should be eye-catching and uncluttered, with plenty of white spaces. The zoom feature on many word processing programs works well to evaluate the aesthetics of a questionnaire.

2. Use a clear, readable font but vary the size of the font or use bold and *italics* type (sparingly) to guide the eye through the questions.

3. Briefly introduce the survey form with a short statement about who is sponsoring the survey, why it is being done, whether the information will be confidential or not, what will be done with the final results, and any special instructions about how to fill out the form. Include this statement even if a cover letter will be attached to the form.

---

66. Ammerman et al., *Studying Congregations*, 101.
67. Ibid., 213.

The purpose of this questionnaire is to help our church think about its present life and plan for the future. Please take a few minutes to respond to these questions. In most cases, you can just mark (X) the response that fits you best (though perhaps not perfectly) or fill in a brief answer. Where you are asked for your belief or opinion, we really want to know what you think. There are no "right" answers. When you really cannot answer, just skip on to the next item. We guarantee that your individual answers will be anonymous and held in the strictest confidence. When you have completed the survey, deposit it in the special boxes by the exits as you leave. We hope you enjoy filling out the questionnaire. After the results are tallied and the self-study is completed, a special church meeting will be held to discuss the future of our congregation. Thank you for your assistance in helping us better understand ourselves as a congregation.

4. Use topic headings and perhaps a short descriptive sentence to introduce a new section of the survey.

   - *First, a few questions about your participation in the congregation.*

   - *Beliefs and Values*

   - *Please respond to each statement with a check (√), indicating whether you strongly agree, agree, are neutral or unsure, disagree, or strongly disagree.*

   - *Finally, some background information about yourself.*

   - *Thank you for time and thoughtfulness. If you have any further comments about the church or the self-study please write them below in the space provided.*

5. Use the same format to define the space where answers should be written for all your questions. Generally, it is best to ask the respondent to make an X, rather than a check mark, in the space defined by a box or brackets [ ] or by parentheses ( ). For certain questions, a blank line can be used to define where respondents are to answer. Never just leave an open space, unless you are asking an extended, open-ended question. At times it is also acceptable to ask the people to circle a response, for example, to indicate which is the most important of the several items they identified. Remind people to mark only one answer.

6. When using several sections of questions with different foci, maintain a common format. For instance, if you use parentheses to indicate where an X should be made, use them throughout, and always put them on the same side of the question. If you offer a range of response choices, for example, from agree to disagree, keep them in the same order throughout the survey.

Group Interviews

Group interviews are sometimes called focus groups.[68] Through group interaction, data and insights are generated that are related to a particular theme imposed by a researcher and enriched by the group's interactive discussion. The synergy of the group will often provide richer data than if each person in the group had been interviewed separately. One person's response may prompt or modify another person's memory of an event and its details. Because not everyone will have the same views and experience, participants influence one another. Differences in age, gender, education, access to resources, and other factors will prompt a variety of responses that may not emerge in a homogeneous group setting or from the individual interview.

The group responds to a series of questions that allows the researcher to quickly gather data from several points of view. Yet, it may hinder individual expression. People may choose not to reveal intimate details to the group or in a group setting that they would otherwise tell in a private and confidential setting. Possibly some people will slant their version in a group setting in order to maintain their pretenses or protect their secrets.

The methodology section should clearly describe the group structure, including such items as the agenda, questions, moderator involvement, and note-taker. Purposeful sampling techniques are used to give you data related to the project's rationale. Focus group theory advocates selecting participants along homogeneous and theoretical meaningful dimensions and criteria. If you need diversity, heterogeneity, then add more focus groups. Although not likely within DMin projects, research shows focus groups work best when the participants are strangers. As Lee observes, "Acquaintances are more likely to share tacit, taken-for-

---

68. However, a "pure" focus group methodology is self-contained. See Morgan, *Successful Focus Groups*; Morgan, *Focus Groups*; and Krueger, *Analyzing and Reporting*.

granted assumptions; discussion among focus group members with stronger acquaintanceship ties can be relatively difficult to interpret, understand, and evaluate."[69] Persons not well acquainted with each other, however, are more likely to speak without the unexpressed knowledge that is common among friends, and their conversation will be easier for the researcher to interpret.

The optimum group size depends on group interest in the topic, but 8–12 is often cited as average. Additionally, the literature often delimits the number of groups to a theoretical saturation of three. The number of topics covered depends on how specific and in depth the participants discuss the individual topics. While fewer topics are possible in a group setting versus individual interviews, participants will not be able to explore any topic to the extent they could when being interviewed separately.

The moderator should be familiar with the protocol and the list of questions. The more rehearsed the moderator, the more comfortable the setting, thus encouraging the participants to be more relaxed. The facilitator's role will include mediating difficult topics and tensions that may emerge, while being careful of dominant players and the forming of sub-groups. Similarly, the facilitator will need to know how to tone down the talkative person and draw out the silent one. Focus groups are notorious for getting off topic. Knowing how much leeway a group needs while maintaining focus is often a tight-wire act difficult to balance. Mack offers the following suggestions to moderators for handling common issues in focus group discussions:[70]

1. *Talkative.* If a participant holds the floor for too long, you may need to intervene. You could start by thanking the person for his or her contribution and inviting others to comment on what the person said or to provide alternative views. You might also try encouraging a talkative person to make only one point at a time. You could, for example, step in as the person is introducing a new topic and encourage the group to discuss the first point. You might also use body language to discourage someone from taking for an excessive amount of time, such as decreasing your eye contact

---

69. Lee, *Using Qualitative Methods*, 70.

70. Mack, et al., *Qualitative Research Methods*, 62.

with the talkative participant and increasing eye contact with other participants.

2. *Prone to interrupt.* One strategy is to remind the group that one of the ground rules of the focus group is to refrain from interrupting other people. You might also thank the individual and suggest returning to his or her point after the first speaker's contribution has been completed.

3. *Aggressive.* You might first remind participants of the ground rule that no one is permitted to insult or personally attack anyone else. You could also try to decrease the level of aggression by calmly asking the individual in question to explain the reasoning behind the stated negative opinion and then involving the rest of the group in the discussion.

4. *Shy.* Some participants will be hesitant to join an ongoing debate or discussion. You could offer them a safer opportunity to speak by pausing the discussion and asking whether anyone else has something to contribute. You could also pose questions directly to individuals who have been especially quiet, thank them afterward for sharing their experience, and encourage them with body language, such as smiling.

5. *Angry.* If a participant becomes angry, try to soften the level of emotion by acknowledging the issues at hand are indeed sensitive or controversial. If you consider it preferable to address the person's anger, steer the conversation toward the idea that it is the issue that is upsetting rather than another participant.

6. *Crying.* If a participant begins to cry, it is up to the moderator to gauge whether it is better to address the issue directly or not call attention to the person. If you decide to discuss it, you might ask the person to identify the source of his or her distress. When the source is an issue related to the content of the discussion, ask the group if other people feel emotional as well. If the issue has to do with group dynamics, react accordingly, reminding people of the ground rule of mutual respect, and so on. In some situations, the note-taker might take the crying participant aside to resolve the situation.

7. *Tired.* If more than one participant begins to appear tired or irritable, it may be time to take a break. Encourage people to get up and move around, use the restroom, and have refreshments (if provided).

The moderator's guide or instructions should also contain ground rules for focus group dynamics. Ground rules allow you to set the tone of kindness, respect, and confidentiality. These ground rules are best read before the session begins. You may want to distribute them on a separate sheet of paper. Mack offers an example of ground rules:[71]

1. Ask participants not to discuss details of the content of the discussion once they leave the focus group site.

2. Ask the participants to respect other group members by not divulging what any participant says during the discussion or the identity of any individual present once they leave the focus group site. Remind them that in the informed consent agreement, you have pledged not to disclose anything concerning their participation in the study with anyone other than the research team.

3. Ask the participants speak one at a time. A moderator may prefer to have participants speak in turn according to seating, in the order in which participants indicate having something to say, or according to no particular arrangement. Speaking one at a time lets everyone hear and react to each contribution; it also makes the note-taker's job easier.

4. Ask participants to treat one another with respect. This means not doing anything that could cause another member of the group to feel uncomfortable, such as singling out an individual for criticism, name-calling, or making pejorative comments about any given contribution. All participants need to feel free to express their opinions without fear of being attacked by the group.

Focus groups work best when two people partner together. The person leading the group is often called the moderator or facilitator. The second person is the note-taker. The note-taker should be prepared to step up to the moderator's role if circumstances require it (e.g., sickness). Immediately after the session, the note-taker should convert his notes into a fuller description of the event. In this case, the research team has

71. Ibid., 61.

the advantage of two perspectives. Shortly after a debriefing session, the facilitator should add her comments to the fuller description. Although at first their comments may be distinguished by using their initials, the final reporting of the responses will be a synthesized account. Mack offers the following purposes for debriefing sessions:[72]

1. To log any additional information about the focus group while it is still fresh in the memory. For example, even when audiotapes are used to record the session, there will be nonverbal communication, such as gestures, facial expressions, eye contact, tension, that will not be picked up on tape.

2. To discuss issues or comments that need clarification. Field notes explaining confusing parts of the focus group will be valuable for helping other researchers to interpret the transcripts later on.

3. To discuss particular questions that did not work well and why.

4. To note any information that contradicts or confirms data collected in previous sessions.

5. To discuss new topics that arose during the focus group.

6. To identify missing information. Comparing what information was being sought with what was actually learned can help moderators plan how to solicit this information more effectively in subsequent focus groups.

7. To identify information that needs to be researched outside the focus group setting. This may have to do, for example, with cultural norms, fact checking, or specifics about the study.

8. To discuss trouble spots that came up during the focus group, with regard to participants, group dynamics, and questions. It may be necessary to develop new strategies for dealing with a particular issue for subsequent focus groups.

9. To provide the moderator and note-taker a forum for giving each other constructive feedback.

Artifacts

DMin projects often ask the participants to produce a product as the outcome of the intervention. Several sessions are conducted to orient the group before they begin their task. The remaining sessions of the

72. Ibid., 75.

intervention involve participants creatively assembling a document that fulfills the project's purpose. Example products include curriculum, action plans, mission or vision statements, covenants, contracts, agreements, blueprints, leadership transition procedures, guidelines or policy statements, process documents, and much more. There are myriads of products that are produced by committees, task forces, and organizations every year. Martin's road map for guiding his congregation towards self-emptying practices is described below. Final products discussed in other chapters include Ogren's criteria for planting a missional church, and Siburt's catechetical material on Christian virtues.

The work that emerges is subject to evaluation. It can be shipped to an independent expert for examination. The participants can also discern the value of their work. You know what you intended to happen, thus, your angle of interpretation is also vital. The method of evaluation is dependent upon the nature of the product. A majority of the artifacts produced will be documents. Once the final form of the document is determined, it becomes a data set subject to analysis similar to field notes, transcripts, and interview and questionnaire results.

Throughout interventions, researchers often assign the participants activities to engage in, either during a project session or during the following week. For example, the participants may be asked to record their observations of a church service, keep a diary of their personal experiences, engage in a project designed to enhance their interaction with the project session, etc. For example, Jeff Christian asked a group of participants to meet weekly in order to attend to the problem of disconnection between the Sunday morning sermon and daily virtue formation in sermon listeners. "The Wednesday evening group addressed this need by training listeners to approach the Sunday morning sermon as a location for character development."[73] The purpose statement that resulted from this problem involved facilitating "a group that prepared listeners to reflect on the way sermons cultivate virtue."[74] He gathered the homework, coded it in a manner that enhanced later interpretation, and stored it as a data set. The homework became an artifact that he analyzed like he would any other document. Below is an abbreviated account of the journal homework assignment.

73. Christian, "Preaching," 9.
74. Ibid., 10.

Group member journals served as one-third of my evaluation. I asked the group to write for six weeks . . . with the prompt, "Give me reflections on your Christian walk." I did not coach group members to write about sermons or this project in order to gauge whether they would make the connection between sermons and daily Christianity. As my independent expert and I read the journals each week, however, we looked for entries discussing sermons. On one hand, if a journal did not mention sermons, the silence may suggest that preaching does not play a critical role in the listener's walk with God, at least not in an explicit way the listener thinks about on a regular basis. On the other hand, if the journal spent time reflecting on sermons as a part of the listener's spirituality, my independent expert and I took that information as a way to describe the ways preaching helps shape listener's character. . . . I asked group members to begin an electronic journal and email the journal entries to me once a week, each Tuesday evening prior to our Wednesday evening sessions. I printed out a packet for myself and a packet for my independent expert. My copy of the journal was unedited; I gave my independent expert a blanched copy at her request, removing names and identification markers in order to encourage group members to be as open as they wanted to be in their reflections. We both used the protocol described in the evaluation section of this chapter to code and interpret data gathered in the journals.[75]

Steven Martin, "Envisioning Self-emptying Practices for the Union Hill Church of Christ," conducted eight one-hour sessions in order to design a road map to guide the church's future self-emptying practices.[76] After several sessions, Martin assigned homework. The homework provided a starting place for the next week's discussion and the raw materials for the writing of the road map. The team became co-researchers with Martin as they engaged in observation, open-ended interviews, and experiential activities. The data the team brought back each week required the team to interpret and synthesize it into a logical narratival document—the road map. Additionally, Martin's field notes and a final group interview of the team reflected on the efficacy of the final product in fulfilling the project's purpose, namely, "to evoke a deeper likeness of Christ's humility within the life of Union Hill by developing a road map

75. Ibid., 48.

76. Martin, "Envisioning Self-emptying Practices," 29.

to reorient us to the mind of Christ."[77] However, Martin discovered it was difficult to separate the final product from the process of writing. He describes the assignments as follows:

1. Session 1 included instructions about their homework that requested their participation and observation of responses during a timeline exercise on the following Sunday evening. The exercise asked all church members who attended on Sunday evening to mark high-lighted moments in Union Hill's history. Before the congregational timeline assignment, I taped approximately twenty feet of three-foot-wide butcher paper marked with four lines on the wall. The top line served as an annual timeline scale beginning with 1985, the initial merger of two congregations into Union Hill's mother church, and continued through the present. On the remaining three lines, congregants identified church events, community events, and con-temporary cultural events. I provided the project team with the fol-lowing instructions: 1) listen and observe the process and note what you hear and see; and 2) ask one or two others outside the team, "What did you write on the timeline? And why?"

2. Session 2: The meeting concluded with the homework assignment to view the Mother Teresa video shown to the whole congregation on the following Sunday evening. I asked the team to sit dispersed among the congregation and ask one to two people, "What did you think of the video?"

3. Session 3: The concluding homework assignment directed team members to divide into dyads and participate together during the week in a self-emptying activity. Before the close of the session, each dyad selected a self-emptying activity for this exercise from a list previously generated by the team.

4. Session 4: The session concluded with the homework assignment to come to the next meeting prepared to present three ways Union Hill may embody self-emptying practices to one another and to outsiders.

5. Session 5: I asked that the team think of three ways self-emptying practices may be promoted within the Union Hill congregation for the following session.

77. Ibid., 7.

6. Session 6: I concluded the session by assigning the team the task of envisioning these various suggestions for self-emptying in a sequential road map for Union Hill.

7. Session 7 and 8 focused on constructing and editing a road map.[78]

Scales and Testing Instruments

Standardized tests and other measurement techniques are similar to surveys (e.g., MMPI; Myers Briggs; Prepare/Enrich; Profiles of Ministry, various congregational study or profile tools—the list is endless). Participants often consider these instruments intrusive (or at least inconvenient and annoying). The measurement considerations necessary for understanding these tools fall into the quantitative area. You can use a quantitative tool in a qualitative study as one angle of your evaluation if the tool measures what you need to evaluate. I have personal experience with Taylor/Johnson and various speech feedback tools and describe my research on their uses below. I include these caveats to illustrate the necessary considerations that you will need to process before employing any assessment tool in your project.

THE TAYLOR-JOHNSON TEMPERAMENT ANALYSIS (T-JTA), 1984 VERSION.[79]

According to its stated purpose, the T-JTA instrument is "used to measure a number of important and comparatively independent common personality variables or attitudes and behavioral tendencies which influence personal, social, marital, parental, family, scholastic, and vocational adjustment. It is designed to aid the counselor in ascertaining and evaluating the significance and role of these traits in the overall problem or circumstance." T-JTA is also to be used in a "Criss-Cross" fashion, providing a measure of interpersonal perception. Especially applicable

---

78. Ibid., 29–32. The list (edited and paraphrased from chapter 3) does not provide all the details of the sessions Martin conducted. Complete details of the sessions and assignments were given in an appendix.

79. The following summary is taken from my own review of the material, technical manuals, and the Buros Institute, *Tenth Mental Measurements Yearbook*, 357. The history of the Taylor-Johnson Temperament Analysis (T-JTA) goes back to 1941, when Roswell Johnson published the Johnson Temperament Analysis. In the 1960s, the JTA was extensively revised by Robert Taylor and Lucile Morrison and published as the T-JTA. Norms were updated in 1984.

in premarital, marital, and family counseling, Criss-Cross analysis is done when two respondents have been plotted for purposes of comparison. Not only will the individuals take the test, they will take the test again, responding how they feel the other person would respond. The visual graphs used in interpretation of scores can be easily compared. The couple's profile can provide a picture of the personality similarities and differences that may either produce compatibility and counterbalance or conflict and misunderstanding.

T-JTA consists of 180 items equally divided among the nine bipolar traits measured by the test. These tests can be scored by the counselor or scored by a computer. A Regular-Sten profile is available for those who prefer to use standard scores. Norm tables are included for Criss-Cross use, Sten norm tables, and percentile norm tables. These tables are individualized for the general population (male and female) and college students (male and female). There are editions in several languages, as well as editions for lower-level readers. There is no time limit for the administration of the T-JTA, but it usually requires 30–45 minutes.

The T-JTA scales are not useful with people who exhibit extreme maladjustments. The scales are designed to aid in the early identification or screening of problem areas prior to the development of acute problems.

The general population sample on which the present norms are based consisted of 2,316 males and 1,626 females. The age range for this sample was 17 to 73 years inclusive. The college student population sample consisted of 1,644 males and 2,282 females. The age range for this sample was 17 to 25 years inclusive. The Secondary Population (ages 13–18) N was 10,071 (5,045 males and 5,026 females).

The manual provides appropriate cautions concerning interpretation of the T-JTA. It provides systematic instructions for scoring, conversion of raw scores, and plotting of results. The manual provides a practice packet with forms for self-tests and Criss-Cross tests.

The greatest setback to the T-JTA is the need for extensive training. Although one may learn to administer and score the T-JTA in two hours, it may take years of steady use to have confidence interpreting the results. Much of what is communicated to the couple will be dependent upon the individual counselor's ability to translate the results. Several books have been written to help counselors use T-JTA more effectively. For example, T-JTA may identify an individual as one who tends towards depression and scores lower than the population norms by a significant amount. How the counselor interprets and communicates this information is crucial. This makes T-JTA more counselor dependent than the empirical data would indicate.

The research and statistical data for the T-JTA is extensive. According to the data, T-JTA is extremely reliable and valid.[80] Yet, a more detailed look at the validity of the instrument is subject to question. Although face validity is high, the use of comparing other assessments as a whole package with T-JTA as the method of establishing validity is suspect. What is needed instead is a series of studies specifically designed to objectively evaluate the validity of the different T-JTA scales. Ideally, this should involve correlations of each of the scales separately with relevant criteria, including non-self-report criteria. The manual claims empirical research yet does not provide the data nor does it give references.

FEEDBACK TOOLS

Acquiring feedback has a long and diverse history covering the fields of speech, psychology, education, political science, and management. The purpose of providing feedback in public speaking courses typically has three parts: (1) to inform the speaker about the audience's reactions to the speech, (2) to make suggestions for improvements on future speeches, and (3) to motivate the speaker to speak again or to enjoy speaking. Feedback becomes a primary source for a speaker to understand the self.

In the religious field, most studies relate to the effect a sermon will have on the audience.[81] There are also studies that reflect the effect the feedback has on the preacher.[82] Some studies also relate to the content

80. For example, the lowest correlation coefficient for test-retest reliability for any item was 0.71. Other analysis completed on the data includes split-half correlations, Hoyt's analysis of variance, Spearman-Browns Corrected Correlations, Guttman's Estimated Minimum, ANOVA, and Standard Errors. Construct validity studies were done by comparing T-JTA with 16PF and the Minnesota Multiphasic Personality Inventory.

81. Pargament and Silverman, "Exploring Some Correlates"; Pargament and DeRosa, "What was that Sermon About?"; Price, Terry and Johnston, "Measurement of the Effect"; Engel, *How Can I Get*; Newman and Wright, "Effects of Sermons"; Avery and Gobbel, "Word of God"; Ragsdale and Durham, "Audience Response"; Guthrie, "Quantitative Empirical Studies."

82. Bodey, "Graduated Sermon Critique Forms"; Rife, "Understanding and Utilization"; Gillis, "Role of Feedback"; Jackson, "Feedback in Preaching"; and McDaniel

organization and style.[83] These studies offered a variety of response forms that could be utilized to measure the various responses an audience has to a sermon. Nelson made this conclusion: "Homiletical evaluative forms usually include an evaluation of the sermon's content, the preacher's style and delivery and a host of technical variables important to evaluating the effectiveness of the preacher and his sermon."[84]

Video technology has been used in various teacher-training situations. Beckelhymer notes that cameras were first introduced into homiletic classes in 1968. From antidotal evidence from ten years of experience, he concludes that the camera itself creates anxiety. However, this effect is minimized due to the decrease in self-consciousness and self-doubt that he has observed by using this tool. He notes that both self-image and self-efficacy grow, therefore, he entitles his article, "I Look Like I Belong Up There."[85]

Wilson reviews the use of video technology in teacher training and specifically describes its use in a current program for pre-service physical education teachers. He lists eight benefits:[86]

- It shows the lesson as it really is.

- It promotes an objective analysis of the lesson.

- It allows important segments of the lesson to be reviewed over and over.

- It provides visual as well as verbal evidence.

- It allows for self-evaluation.

- It allows results of the lesson to become immediately available.

- It heightens student interest and motivation.

- It develops self-confidence for student teaching.

He states, "The course evaluations for the class have indicated that the students' confidence has increased, they are aware of their strengths

---

and Watson, "Study of Post-Sermon Discussion." General studies that summarize the research on feedback include: Ilgen, Fisher and Taylor, "Consequences of Individual Feedback"; and Ammons, "Effects of Knowledge."

83. Cathcart, "Experimental Study"; Sikkink, "Experimental Study"; and MaGuire, "Scale on Preaching Style."

84. Nelson, "Comparison of Receptivity."

85. Beckelhymer, "I Look"; Porter and King, "Use of Video-tape Equipment."

86. Wilson, "Video Technology Revisited."

and weaknesses, and they are motivated to continue their pursuit of a teaching certificate."[87] Their desire to persist is a positive measure of motivation.

Quigley and Nyquist argue that video can provide effective feedback in speech performance courses by creating opportunities for students to take the role of observer. Students are able to identify specific skills that are either strengths or growth areas in their public presentations. The speaker, instructor, and peers simultaneously with the performance offer feedback. They can easily make comparisons with past presentations. Students are often surprised at how well they performed, from the observer's perspective, even though they remember they felt nervous or awkward during the actual performance.[88]

Quigley and Nyquist discuss how video can be used in three areas: skill evaluation, modeling, and self-modeling. Both performance and content skills (gestures and voice projection, as well as use of logical argument and the presentation of evidence) can be evaluated. By showing the student how particular skills are performed and how they are contextualized within the dynamic action of a particular speech, the student's self-efficacy increases. The student's belief in his or her ability to communicate well grows. Modeling works primarily through vicarious experiences.[89] Seeing others perform threatening activities without adverse effects will generate positive expectations by the observers. They will desire to grow and persist in their efforts.

Bandura's theories of modeling are foundational to Quigley and Nyquist's discussion. The underlying assumption of modeling is that the observation of others and self can result in changed behavior for the observer given certain conditions. The effect is dependent upon the model's prestige, status, and perceived power. The choice of model is crucial, for there is the potential to create a negative reaction. Quigley and Nyquist particularly note how a model could remind the observer of his or her own inadequacies, consequently increasing anxiety. They recommend editing a version of the video for self-modeling conditions. Bandura advocates using self-modeling techniques that encourage behavioral change deriving from observing oneself on videotapes that por-

87. Ibid., 57.
88. Quigley and Nyquist, "Using Video Technology."
89. Bandura, "Self-efficacy."

tray only desired target behaviors.[90] This study confirmed that a positive version of the performance that demonstrates desired target behaviors was found to be more beneficial. Motivated students will engage in the necessary activities to achieve success. Success increases motivation. New goals and challenges are set. Success increases one's belief for future success. Finally, these authors found unrestricted replay of videos of self-modeling behavior as ineffective.[91]

Bradley, however, conducted an earlier study that should caution the teacher from embracing video as a cure-all. Bradley finds no significant help in the use of video in the areas of skill development, comprehension and retention of content, or final grades. However, he states that there is a significant difference in the student's attitudes. "Student's attitudes toward themselves as speakers and their perceptions that they can improve their speaking ability may have long range effects beyond the effects of grades earned on exams or speeches."[92]

Karl and Kopf offer seven suggestions for using video feedback.[93] (1) Instructors should also provide written models of the specified skill performance; (2) video needs to be used in the environment of trust; (3) video is not an enhancement unless used in multiple sessions; (4) all students must be required to be taped; (5) instructors should limit oral feedback before peers; (6) do not let students evaluate themselves; and (7) combine video with other techniques. Karl and Kopf's study offers cautions and limitations that require further investigation into the possible advantages of using video technology in the classroom. Deihl, Breen, and Larson's study suggests the greatest benefit of video technology is when it is used in combination with other instruments.[94]

Teachers evaluating one another are common for peer evaluation and skill development. One example of a peer evaluation tool used in a school is found in Appendix 6.

90. Bandura, "Perceived Self-Efficacy."

91. See Thelen, Fry, Fehrenbach, and Frautschi, "Therapeutic Videotape," for confirmation of this study. Thelen reviews the literature on symbolic modeling using videotape in various fields and concludes favoring its effective use.

92. Bradley, "Experimental Study," 166.

93. Karl and Kopf, "Guidelines."

94. Deihl, Breen, and Larson, "Effects of Teacher Comment."

OTHER SOURCES OF DATA

Humans produce materials throughout life. Anthropologists often term these materials, "artifacts." These artifacts become sources of data that can either substantiate or contradict the way participants in your project have portrayed themselves in interviews. When I first began ministering in a congregation in the southeast, a file in the office desk contained every church bulletin since the congregation's inception. After two full days of digesting the general content, attendance records, giving trends, sermon topics, service projects, graduations, prayer concerns, etc., I was more equipped to listen to the congregational story. I jotted down my understandings and unanswered questions. Those two days of reading allowed me to springboard into the congregational life quickly. On this occasion, I did not have a research agenda. But the value of congregational documents impressed itself upon me. One particular bulletin article caught my eye. It was an explanation as to why the church was removing the table from the front of the sanctuary. The pragmatic explanation was oblivious to any theological rationale, symbolism, or implications. The insight I gained into how physical and materials decisions were processed also enabled me to discover my first pastoral intervention, namely, implementing a theological reflection model for the leadership of the congregation.

Generally, you need to remember your purpose for examining these sources. You may uncover various interesting topics and tangents, but the problem and purpose statement of your project should focus your attention. When examining these sources, keep in mind the following questions: "How do I get access to the documents?" "What level of detail is provided?" "Do I need other sources, accounts, or information to make sense of these sources?" "Why were these sources prepared and preserved?" "In what ways have these sources functioned or been used by others?" "Are these sources authentic and genuine?" "What biases do these sources support?"

Primary sources reflect data that is produced in the actual course of life by the participants in the context. Secondary sources come from outside the context. Just because something comes from a primary source, that does not make it authoritative. For example, what a participant says about the causation of an event is still an opinion. It can be recorded as primary data from the source, but the information cannot be understood as the official account or a scholarly opinion on the subject. The data is still interpreted.

PRIMARY SOURCES

- Oral histories (interview)
- Letters
- Minutes of meetings
- Church bulletins and newsletters
- Films/videos
- Photos
- Journals/diaries
- News
- Memos
- Policy statements, procedure statements, mission statements
- PR materials

SECONDARY SOURCES

Interpretations of events based on primary sources.

- Books
- Journals
- Summaries (e.g., of a survey)
- Interviews with experts

WRITTEN SOURCE DOCUMENTS

Documents that are "found" but were not intentionally developed by the researcher or the project. They are unobtrusive measures of what actually took place in a given setting. You should not assume that these documents represent objective and unbiased views. Like other sources of data, the person(s) who gathered, organized, selected, and recorded the materials had a context and a perspective.

- Newspaper articles
- Minutes
- Church bulletins and newsletters
- Historical documents

- Public records
- Archived materials
- Recorded histories
- Diaries
- Surveys
- Sermon transcripts
- Financial records

NON-WRITTEN SOURCES

Items with interpretive value.

- Photos
- Works of art
- Icons
- Furniture, furniture arrangement
- Maps and seating charts
- Architecture
- Diagrams
- Digital recordings
- Location descriptions, blue prints, and room size

When examining these other sources of data, often people will offer interpretations, descriptions, and explanations of these items in casual conversations. You may also need to explore or interview key informants in order to understand an artifact. Some of these sources may contain too much data. You will need a plan for surveying and selecting the samples you will include in your analysis. Read your problem and purpose statement again. These two statements are the primary lenses for making these determinations.

Nieman explores the study of artifacts in depth. He states,

> Since artifacts and places are similar and interact with each other, we can use the same strategies to understand them better. This begins with recognizing that they fall into a few broad categories, which in turn reveal the special challenges in studying them accurately. Some are self-interpreted. Artifacts or places may have

textual labels that overtly declare a purpose (like signs posted in a church kitchen), or they are so narrow in use that the purpose is relatively clear (like a baptismal font). Of course, anything in this category may still be adapted later to other uses. Other artifacts or places are intentionally ambiguous. For example, an artist may create a work with multiple meanings irreducible to just one. Similarly, strong and highly charged symbolic objects (like water or flame when used in worship) may bear many meanings at once and resist being contained. Another category includes artifacts or places that are reappropriated. Imagine that the original purpose for some product has diminished or become obsolete (such as a mimeograph machine) or perhaps faced some crisis or rejection (such as the location for an American Flag). In such cases, artifacts or places may later be reclaimed with deeper historic, symbolic, or affective values than ever before (which is why churches find it so hard to dispose of anything). Finally, artifacts or places sometimes have an unknown use. Especially in a new situation, the meaning people give to an object or location may seem veiled and mysterious. Some sort of guide or 'culture broker' can open the door to whether this mystery is the result of amnesia, disconnection from the original users, or an effort to mask meanings from outsiders.[95]

Nieman suggests "a series of questions about the material data, which should include at least six interrelated aspects:

1. History—When did the artifact or place originate? What have been its subsequent periods of greater or lesser use?

2. Setting—What is the typical environment for the artifact or place? How is it embedded there as part of an ensemble of other artifacts or places?

3. Users—Who were the original creators of the artifact or place? Who have been the main or authorized users since then?

4. Technology—What were the materials, labor, and design involved in creating the artifact or place? What skills or abilities are needed for its continued use?

5. Function—What were the original purposes for the artifact or place, both intended and actual? How have these shifted or been augmented or diminished since then?

95. Nieman, *Knowing the Context*, 44.

6. Meaning—What significance or narrative is carried by the artifact or place? Is its meaning primarily functional, aesthetic, symbolic or something else besides?"[96]

The document or artifact was created and used for different purposes from those for which you are now appropriating them. Recognizing that issue, Nieman notes that his six questions may introduce typical errors and distortions. These include:

1. Isolating the product from its typical setting, where it becomes an object unto itself;

2. Over-attributing significance to the product, where it is made to say more about the context than it really can;

3. Functionalist interpretations, where the aesthetic or symbolic dimensions are lost;

4. Abstracted significance, where the concrete quality or use is minimized;

5. Intentional fallacies, where the originator's purpose becomes the only valid explanation;

6. Present-time errors, where the investigator's time period dominates the interpretation; and

7. Progress-continuum errors, where biases about the past or present are implicitly justified in how the product is interpreted.[97]

Keep notes about an artifact just as if you were examining other sources of data. Note the date and place you examined the item. Describe its condition and your appraisal of its authenticity. Is it a typical representative of this type of artifact or is it unusual and atypical? Written sources can be analyzed and interpreted according to the methods described in the documentary analysis section of chapter 7.

This chapter has described various tools used commonly in qualitative research for the collection of data. Observations, interviews, questionnaires, focus groups, independent experts, and field notes are the obvious choices for DMin projects. The process of selecting which tools to use is not a matter of preference similar to picking items in a cafeteria line. When students reach this point in the prospectus stage, they

96. Ibid., 45.

97. Ibid., 89, footnote 8. See also, Merriam, *Qualitative Research*, 120–6.

naively gravitate towards the familiar tools that "feel" right. However, tools should be selected because they best fit the intervention and are designed to provide the data necessary to present a complete evaluation of the effectiveness of the project. The best choices emerge when the student imaginatively creates ways to see the intervention differently. The purpose is not to get a passing grade, to jump through a hoop, or to present the results in the best possible light. The purpose is to uncover the data necessary for an open and honest assessment of the project's intervention.

5

Other Toolboxes

THE LAST CHAPTER DESCRIBED general tools found in every qualitative researcher's toolbox. However, sometimes you own more than one toolbox. In my garage, I have three. I have the large five-drawer chest that supports a smaller seven-drawer toolbox that contains a little bit of everything. While the chest is on wheels, it rarely moves. On a nearby table, I have two toolboxes that I can quickly grab and take with me to a work site. One is setup for general carpentry; the other can address plumbing and electrical tasks. All three have some tools in common like screwdrivers, but the latter two have some specialty items that are only used for particular tasks.

Chapter 5 describes three overarching methods that are often described in the literature as self-contained. While a theoretical purist might desire to maintain methodological integrity for these topics, the approach controlling this textbook asserts that an eclectic approach to methods given a set theoretical construct also displays wholeness. Subsequently, the following look at case study, narrative research, and appreciative inquiry not only surveys what is in other toolboxes, it also provides access to other perspectives and options that DMin students have implemented in their projects. While the comprehensive theoretical complex found in these toolboxes will often not be used, the individual insights and tools can be easily tailored in a multi-methods approach to qualitative research.

CASE STUDY

Some in the field may designate the qualitative method in this book as "Case Study" research. A short introduction to the theoretical constructs that undergird the case method will identify why that connection is made and will enhance your ability to incorporate the case method into your project, theological reflection, and practice. The terms *case* and *case studies* can refer to a broad variety of literary and audiovisual material. *Cases* are learning tools that present stories of actual events and dilemmas faced by real people. *Case studies* formally examine cases through an assortment of processes common in field education including ministry reports, verbatims, case histories, and reflections on ethical dilemmas.

The case method is a tool often used by DMin students to enable participants in their projects to access the lived experiences of others. Case studies are particularly useful in congregational and para-church settings because they can help a diverse group of participants become more creative in addressing community issues.[1] They also provide you and your participants the opportunity to experience the complexity of ministerial situations in the safety of a classroom. While it is impossible to foresee every conceivable contingency, tapping into the lived experiences of others may equip your participants with greater resources to achieve the project's objectives. Additionally, the case method is sometimes used as a tool for evaluating the project's effectiveness.

The use of the case method in DMin projects invites focused group discussion by asking the participants to enter the situation, analyze the issues, and propose responsible alternatives backed by sound reasoning. Cases enhance the development of analytical and decision-making skills, help participants apply learning, and synthesize/integrate a variety of subjects for all who participate. Case studies introduce your participants to tasks, dilemmas, and practices of everyday life and enhance their confidence for the next time they engage in similar situations. Broadly speaking, case study research excels at bringing us to an understanding of a complex issue or object and can extend experience or add strength to what is already known through previous research. Case studies emphasize detailed contextual analysis of a limited number of events or conditions and their relationships.

Social scientists, in particular, have made wide use of this qualitative research method to examine contemporary real-life situations and provide the basis for the application of ideas and extension of methods. Yin defines the case study research method as an empirical inquiry that investigates a contemporary phenomenon within its real-life context,

---

1. I am not using the term *case study* as a research method but as an evaluation method. See the Association of Case Teaching, *Case Teaching Institute*.

when the boundaries between phenomenon and context are not evident, and in which multiple sources of evidence are used.[2]

> There are at least five different applications. The most important is to explain the presumed causal links in real-life interventions that are too complex for the survey or experimental strategies. In evaluation language, the explanations would link program implementation with program effects. . . . A second application is to describe an intervention and the real-life context in which it occurred. Third, case studies can illustrate certain topics within an evaluation, again in a descriptive mode. Fourth, the case study strategy may be used to explore those situations in which the intervention being evaluated has no clear, single set of outcomes. Fifth, the case study may be a meta-evaluation—a study of an evaluation study.[3]

Stake qualifies the issue of nomenclature by stating, "Case study is not a methodological choice, but a choice of object to be studied."[4] He narrows the usage further by stating, "The name *case study* is emphasized by some of us because it draws attention to the question of what specifically can be learned from the single case. That epistemological question is the driving question of this chapter: What can be learned from the single case?"[5]

Most case study methods emphasize explaining or describing an event, program, or setting. I advocate an evaluation of an intervention that encourages transformation. DMin projects by definition require participatory action, leadership, and change. When I use the name "case study," the researcher is looking at the single case of the pastoral intervention. Consequently, Lee's perspective on the case study method would eliminate it as a category for DMin projects as I have defined them.[6] He states, "Case study research is best suited to the examination of why and how contemporary, real-life . . . phenomena occur, but under conditions where researchers have minimal control. Case study research addresses many of the questions traditionally answered by laboratory or field ex-

---

2. Yin, *Case Study Research*, 13. See also Stake, "Case Studies."

3. Yin, *Case Study Research*, 15.

4. Stake, "Case Studies," 236.

5. Ibid.

6. Patton, *Qualitative Research*, 298, notes the confusion when using the term *case study*. Is it a method, or is it an approach? The answer lies in defining the object of study.

periments. The major difference, of course, is that case study research does not (and cannot) require control and manipulation of variables."[7]

Myers advocates the case method for DMin projects. He states that "In such research, narrative descriptions (case studies) emerge in which researcher and participants are understood to be pro-active participants in the study."[8] Myers later defines the method as follows:

> A "case study" as a research process borrows tools from other re-search methods in order to focus holistically upon particular practices of ministry with persons, groups, programs, institutions, or systemic mixes of such components. The case study as a completed descriptive narrative (a "story") presents an example of ministry chosen from a natural setting and evaluated using appropriate tools that emphasize observations and interviewing skills as well as interpretations of documents. The case study, therefore, can be understood to interconnect all of the components being studied (the minister, problem context, ministerial action, setting, individuals in that setting, theory, documents, and other data generated by "borrowed" research tools) within a single narrative paper. In this sense, a D.Min. case study offers the story of a careful documentation and a critical reflection upon a specific practice of ministry. Within this manual, the term "case study" therefore refers to (1) the case study process used to evaluate a specific practice of ministry, and (2) the eventual written description (the "story") of how that practice of ministry occurred and what it might mean. There is both a process orientation to the use of the case study approach (how one collects the data), and a product orientation to the use of that same term (the resultant case study).[9]

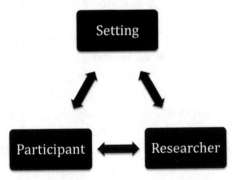

Figure 8: Myers's Case Study Method

7. Lee, *Using Qualitative Methods*, 54.

8. Myers, *Research in Ministry*, xi.

9. Ibid., 5.

The above triangle of Myers's approach is not a triangle of evaluation that I discuss in chapters 3 and 8, but a "snapshot" of an ongoing process that includes the setting, participants, and the researcher. Myers's triangle represents the "story" of the ministry activity. My triangle of evaluation represents the tools employed for gathering and interpreting data around a particular ministry intervention. I am not advocating a "snapshot." I am advocating an intentional proactive intervention into the system, evaluating the effects of the intervention, and drawing conclusions in order to enhance future ministerial practice. In writing the final paper, Myers advocates a "narrative" description that he is reticent to call a thesis. I expect a terminal degree to produce a thesis, an academically recognized document that includes the requisite component parts.

I distinguish the DMin approach from the case study method by differentiating between the objects of investigation. The primary object of the case method is the setting. The primary object of a DMin project thesis is the intervention. To be more precise, the DMin project thesis described in this book is a particular type of case study, namely, the case of a particular intervention at a specific location and timeframe. "Action Research," "Participatory Action Research," or simply "A Multi-Methods Approach," I believe, clarifies the terminology (see chapter 3).

Case Studies in Practice

When implementing his DMin project, Gregg L. Marutzky, "Transforming Leadership Model for the Denver Church of Christ," asked Dr. Jack Reese to function as an independent expert. Reese utilized a case study in his evaluation of the project's intervention. [10] Marutzky identified his problem and purpose as follows: "The leaders of the Denver Church of Christ are struggling to adapt to a healthier model of leadership. . . . The project is designed to orient the leadership of the DCC to a pastoral leadership paradigm that will empower the congregation and restore confidence in the leaders." He continues, describing his intervention in a summary paragraph by saying, "The methodology used in the intervention included a leadership group, five sessions, one expert in case studies, one church consultant, and one outside participant observer. Four of the five sessions introduced the

---

10. Marutzky, "Transforming Leadership Model," 23, 25.

leadership model, while the fifth session allowed participants to practice their new understandings through evaluation of a case study."[11]

Later, Marutzky delineates how the case study was used in more detail.

> The expert, Jack Reese, reviewed the handouts and theological rationale in advance of his presentation and evaluation of the case study. Reese did not participate in the first four sessions, which allowed him to give an objective evaluation of the group's understanding of leadership. Reese evaluated the study according to the protocol used by the Case Studies Institute [The Association for Case Teaching. Dr. Reese served as the co-director in previous years].

The key indicator of the impact of such an intervention lies in the degree of variation from previous actions. For that reason, questions asked in the final session included: What changed as a result of the sessions? How is your thinking different concerning leadership? Are you practicing a different style of leadership with one another? Is there agreement with the teachings from the Corinthian letter? A key issue is the community and the leader/follower relationship. Will the leaders and the congregation open wide their hearts to one another? Was the cross experienced during the intervention?"[12]

The following is an abbreviated report portraying Reese's use of the case study.

> Jack Reese's presentation of the case "Decision to a Split?" to the leadership of the DCC provided a third evaluative angle for the ministry intervention. As a case study expert with experience in teaching and evaluating cases, Reese provided a qualitative analysis for triangulating the entire project. He assessed whether the DCC leadership would be able to articulate, in light of material presented during the four sessions in the two weeks prior to the case study, principles or insights they had learned when applied to a case addressing issues similar to the context of the Corinthian correspondence.
>
> Reese did not want to make this connection overt by telling the group in advance that he intended to draw from them conclusions concerning the leadership model presented previously. He wanted conclusions from the presentations to emerge spon-

11. Ibid., 71.
12. Ibid., 79.

taneously in the discussion. He purposed to give the participants considerable opportunity to respond on the basis of the teaching materials over 1 and 2 Corinthians, but without prompting them to share what they remembered. . . . Reese gave the group several minutes to read the case. He noted, "One of the staff members had left the room to place a food order for lunch. He returned as most were finishing." Reese did not comment in his report on this action other than recording the incident, but it may indicate the lack of priority some in the group viewed the activity. Reese wrote, "Several of the participants took notes. Some began writing Scriptures down, presumably to be prepared to advise John Davis, the outside consultant in the case." . . .

Reese noted, "When I asked the leaders to name the key characters, the first character mentioned was the elders as a group. I expected Bill Jones, Todd Stanley, or John Davis to be named." Reese reported his pleasure that the Denver leaders saw the elders in the case as a group representing a significant character. However, he noted, "The participants did not at first distinguish the five conservative elders from the two remaining progressive ones. So when they talked about Bill Jones, one of the conservative elders, many of the comments were the same." After Reese's prompting, the DCC leaders discussed the significance of the polarization in the elders' group between the conservatives and the progressives.

At first Reese tried to get them to describe the roles and responsibilities of each character, but he changed his approach. He recorded, "Many of the best comments were not about roles or responsibilities but about the larger, more complex issues surrounding each character." Therefore, Reese decided to discuss each character before returning to the talk about the characters' feelings and their values. [Reese's report describes several more discussion questions and a role-playing exercise.]

Reese reported that by the end of the role play, "the issues were clear and the participants quite engaged." . . . Reese led the group in a debriefing session. After hearing from the group regarding the effectiveness of the role play, he addressed the significance of the case for the ministry intervention. This stage of the discussion was a crucial juncture for the project thesis. The question important to Reese was, whether the participants would be able to address the concerns of the case based on the theology presented. . . . He reported no interest in the group making direct reference to the biblical study sessions or even mention of 1 and 2 Corinthians. It was important to Reese, however, that their comments reflect a theology of the cross, the significant doctrine in the four presentations. He noted the move from the overall stakes to the question of which specific Scriptures the leaders would recommend to John Davis. Reese reported that this part of the discussion was focused and quite articulate: "They grasped what was at stake in the case, which was not the elders' authority but how Christians treat one another when they disagree. The first scriptures the mentioned were Romans 12 and Philippians 2. They talked about honoring one another, giving up for one another, seeking the other's best interests, and the implications of the cross in determining how to treat one another. Jesus' example from the Christ hymn of Philippians 2 was quite cogent here; Jesus' emptying himself, being humble, being obedient even to the point of death." . . . Reese noted, "I feel that the participants understood the essence of a healthy theology of the cross." [Reese prompted the group about other scriptures. Eventually the group turned to 1 and 2 Corinthians.] Reese noted, "I was unaware of any place where they quoted Gregg directly or made reference to his presentation the two previous weeks, but I was neither looking for it nor considering it was necessary for the success of the case." Pleased at their responses, he felt that the leadership clearly understood the overall message regarding the transforming leadership model. He noted as well the impossibility of knowing whether they would have said the same things even without the presentations. Reese wrote, "But the responses were well made and reflected a well-thought-through theology of the cross."[13]

Reese's use of a case study as an independent expert clearly demonstrates the value of using cases beyond reporting about the narrative details of a particular context.

The Ins and Outs of the Case Method

In my ministry, I have found the case method an invigorating approach to help congregants to think and learn about various topics vicariously through the lives of others who have traveled down the same pathways. In DMin projects, the case method will be implemented in prescribed ways. Exact protocols will be spelled out in the areas of writing a formal case brief, writing original cases from personal experiences, and presenting cases to others. While you should pay close attention to the instructions and recommendations of your particular program and ad-

13. Ibid.

visors, the following are some key components to the process of analyzing, writing, and presenting cases.[14]

Analyzing a Case

Good cases emerge from current issues and events. Most cases are not timeless and can quickly lose their relevance. I use the following instructions to guide participants as they analyze cases.

1. Analyze the case after reading it through several times. The following six items will guide the analysis: (1) List the characters and note key details about who they are. (2) Develop a chronology of events. A time line places essential facts, events, and developments in a logical order that facilitates keeping the facts straight. (3) Identify the basic issues (especially those things such as acts, values, or attitudes that influence decisions). (4) List all the positions that reasonable persons might take. (5) If applicable, create an organization chart that establishes the relationships of people, institutions, or decisions presented in the case. (6) Include decision(s) and decision-maker(s) in your list. Identify the chief players and stakeholders, useful information in a case that calls for a decision, or where a character faces difficult challenges. Also, list other actors and interest groups who have differing information, power, or objectives.

2. Analysis about a lived experience will offer an answer to these five questions: (1) What was done (act)? (2) When or where it was done (scene)? (3) Who did it (agent)? (4) How did he or she do it (agency)? (5) Why was it done (purpose)?[15]

3. Let the facts of the case and the possibilities you have considered ferment in your mind. Mull over the case, think about it casually, and let things flow through your imagination.

4. Consider any theoretical material or theological resources (e.g., church history or tradition, texts, systematic theology) that would be helpful in clarifying the issues in the case.

14. Throughout this chapter, the sections about analyzing, writing, and presenting a case have been adapted from Reese, *Case Method Approach*.

15. Burke, *Grammar of Motives*. See also Burke, *Rhetoric of Motives*.

5. Decide on your course of action. What decision would you likely make given the conditions and information you have available? Be prepared to defend or substantiate your decision. Remember that no decision is without risk.

6. Participate in any group discussion by sharing your understanding and insights, your ideas and rationale. Listen to what others see in the case; evaluate their positions. Keep an open mind, and be willing to change it with the presentation of new insights or evidence.

Writing a Case

To garner the full impact of the case method for your project, formalizing your analysis will assist you as you prepare to write your thesis. I use the following handout to describe the process of writing a case brief. The case brief will become the data set that describes the experience and records your initial interpretations. The following description delineates how to write a case brief.

1   A case brief is a concise document written in response to a specific case. Case briefs are short and to the point. They focus on a dilemma and describe a decision. Although most dilemmas will have many possible paths, the brief argues for a particular choice.

2. Several skills are used in the paper: (1) The ability to summarize well. (2) The capacity to identify dilemmas and decisions to be made in the case. (3) Sensitivity to the variety of factors that affect the decisions. (4) Application of theology, sociology, ethics, and common sense in a variety of situations.

3   Imagine that you are writing a case brief for the members of the class and will be called on to explain your position. Alternative: Prepare the brief as a consultant's report to a church board.

4. Explore conflicting or contrasting positions on the issue. Put an emphasis on being "objective" (or identify and then bracket your biases). Think with an open mind, and then decide. After you have thought through the alternatives, pick one position to develop. Do not dismiss other perspectives as not applicable, but concentrate on making your position persuasive.

5. Possible outline: (1) Identify the characters. (2) Summarize the case. (3) Identify the problem or issues. (4) Present the facts and

theories that are relevant to the issues. (5) Select and apply a theological construct. (6) State a conclusion. (7) Offer your decision that correlates with your conclusion. That is, describe what you would do in a sentence or two. All briefs must include a decision.

Case studies allow you to examine the lived experiences of others. People tell narratives to make sense of life and experience. Once you have read and analyzed several cases, you begin to feel the impact that this method has for your future teaching and learning. To grow in your use of the case method, you will need to write your own case. When you are reflecting upon the experiences of others through the cases they have written, your ability to incorporate many pastoral practices and integrate ministerial wisdom grows. Now, by writing about your own lived experiences, your professional identity will also continue to develop. After developing the ability to write good cases, your use of the case method in your project will become more effective.

A case is a written description of an authentic event that is fraught with ambiguity. The identities of people, places, and institutions are changed to protect their privacy. The case does not provide all conceivable information, because no one could know everything that happened or what everyone thought. Enough data is provided so that your reader can enter vicariously into the situation. A case is seen through the eyes of one person, the protagonist, who must make a crucial decision about a real-world situation. The case is left open-ended; that is, the reader is not told what decision was made. The reader is expected to study the case and enter into the experience and dilemma of the central character. The basic question becomes: "What would I do?" The focus in the case method is about owning one's decisions and developing an intelligible rationale for one's stance.

Literary theory is a helpful conversation partner when you first begin to write a case. Most people tell their stories in smaller segments often called episodes. Sometimes the episodes are sequenced according to themes, or more commonly, time (chronology). When the story is told, episodes are excluded or included depending upon the purpose and place of the telling. Selection—what episode choices are made for inclusion and exclusion—plays a major role in shaping the content of the narratives. A common narrative sequence as old as Aristotle's *Poetics* involves conflict, complication, climax, and resolution (denouement). The conflict describes the dilemma, an issue or incident that has no apparent way forward. The great white shark eats the unsuspecting swimmer. Next, the plot thickens through complicating circumstances. The white shark is smarter and stronger than any previously encountered. The usual methods for capturing the beast have resulted in more loss of human life and the local tourist economy is devastated. Eventually, the storyline reaches the crucial point of decision and action. From here, there is no going back. Either the great shark hunter succeeds, or all is doomed. And then comes the finale. The shark is destroyed, and all people along the coast are saved.

The case study interrupts the plot sequence by leaving the resolution open. The climax of the story is suspended for reflection purposes. By leaving open "the rest of the story," you provide your peers the opportunity to grapple with a wide range of possible and reasonable pastoral interventions. Stories, and therefore case studies, accommodate the ambiguity and inconsistency found in everyday experience. Furthermore, stories express the multiplicity of meaning and the interconnectedness of phenomena that resist reducing life to simple formulas, facts, and singular interpretations. If a reflection group analyzing the case takes a different route to resolution than you did, then the possibilities to assess your decisions and actions multiply.

I use the following instructions as a guide about writing cases.

1. A good case describes a difficult problem, a dilemma for which there is no single obvious solution. If the solution is obvious, or if the courses of possible action would not produce a difference of opinion, then you do not have the material for a good case. Choose an event or situation that poses a question and requires a decision fraught with sufficient difficulty and ambiguity so that people of intelligence and sensitivity will disagree about what ought to be done. The case can be based on historical events or on personal experiences. Cases that are multi-faceted yet reasonably short are most effective.

2. A case must describe an actual, not a hypothetical, situation. Nothing will draw participants into the discussion of a case more quickly and intensely than assurance that it really happened or is happening. It may be necessary to disguise a case by changing names or places, but avoid exaggerations, embellishments, or alterations that could prompt readers to doubt the accuracy or truthful-

ness of the case itself. Select a case in which the participants will be willing to provide you with the information you need to describe the background, the individuals involved, the situation of the dilemma itself, and the possible courses of action. If you write about a personal experience, you will be the source of information.

3. A case should be about a question or problem with which many people can identify and in which they have genuine interest. Ask yourself, "Will the discussion of the case be beneficial to those I will ask to study and discuss it?" Early in the process of writing a case, you should determine your audience, goals, and themes.

4. A case is written from one person's perspective. Avoid seeing it through the eyes of everyone involved. Do not attribute feelings or motives to anyone in the case unless the person involved verbalizes them. To write a case from one person's perspective may appear too narrow and exclusive, yet it is how we perceive reality, and we must make decisions based on the limited facts and data available to us.

5. A case is a distinct literary form. It is a genre with rules and conventions. It has a certain structure. It is not just a photographic slice of life. A case represents episodes selected from a particular situation by the case writer and is outlined as follows: (1) Focus: The first paragraph sets up the dilemma. The case begins with the suspended climax of the plot. The cliffhanger is posed from the outset. (2) Background: The next few paragraphs give the setting and history of the case so that the dilemma is understood. All participants would agree about this material. Include sufficient information to give the reader an adequate feeling for the case situation without including unnecessary details. Dialogue, letters, or appendices may be helpful tools in this section of the case. The literary device of *flashback* is commonly used. In literature, *internal analepsis* is a flashback to an earlier point in the narrative; *external analepsis* is a flashback to before the narrative started. (3) Development: The next several paragraphs develop the plot. Decide whose eyes the case will be seen through. Use limited third person as opposed to omniscient (the all-seeing) perspective. Select material with the case dilemma in mind by interweaving time structure, plot, character development, and action. Do not portray any characters so negatively that others cannot relate to their experience. (4) Coda:

The last paragraph (or paragraphs) rephrases or highlights the issue or decision. The coda is an *inclusio* with the first paragraph of the case. Like bookends, the first and last paragraphs frame the case by highlighting the dilemma. Ask yourself whether the cut-off point is a good one. Try to avoid ending with a question. Allow the power of suspending the story at a climactic point, a type of cliffhanger, to function to create tension in the reader. Done well, the reader will seek resolution.

6. Pay attention to points of style. (Provide a clear chronology. Check transition points for clarity. Try to be an objective reporter of known facts. Ascribe opinions to those who make them. Quote when possible. Avoid editorializing. Keep adverbs and adjectives to a minimum. Report body language and physical setting to build reader interest and involvement. Present the case in the past tense. Avoid cute names for characters and places when disguising identity so that the tone of the case will evoke serious attention.)

Presenting a Case

Earlier, I described writing a case brief as a formal way to synthesize your analysis of a case. Learning to present a case to a small group or class also develops your understanding of the case and augments your integration of the wisdom garnered from the case into your practice and your project.

There is no substitution for careful planning, and the feedback from an experienced case teacher is priceless. Customarily, an effective teaching plan will cover approximately two hours in order to allow enough time for the group to analyze and reflect upon the case. A typical teaching plan that I have used looks like the following (Total time: 120 minutes):

1. Learning Objectives: Learning objectives are the tentative outcomes you expect to achieve during the case presentation. Spell out 2–4 learning objectives that utilize strong verbs. Possible verbs include: affirm, encourage, demonstrate, synthesize, analyze, appraise, apply, compare and contrast, differentiate, discriminate, prepare, formulate, design, construct, assess, evaluate, and value. Imagine the possible alternatives. From a list of issues within a single case, various pedagogical aims can be achieved. From a single case, applications

are possible from the fields of conflict resolution, leadership, pastoral care, social justice, and missions. A New Testament professor may use the context of a case to engage a class on hermeneutics. A homiletics professor may compare and contrast different scenarios in order to demonstrate the potential of a single text in various contexts. The DMin researcher may set up a scenario that discerns if the participants inculcated the project's intervention. The list is endless and is determined by the particular learning outcomes the teacher has for the students. State these objectives clearly.

2. Distribute the Case: Allow the group enough time to read the case. (10 minutes)

3. Brainstorming Activity 1—Characters: Using a white board or large post-it notes, list all the characters involved in the case. Note 2–3 key identifying characteristics. (15 minutes)

4. Brainstorming Activity 2—Issues: On a different board or post-it notes, list the issues that emerge from the case. When you suggest an issue, note from what part of the case you deem that it emerges. Ask, "For which of our characters is this issue critical?" (15 minutes)

5. Active learning strategies (see below). (one or more activities ranging from 10–30 minutes each)

6. Wrap-Up: Develop a concluding activity that brings closure to the presentation. For example, you might distribute a questionnaire: (1) What have we learned from this case? (2) Choose one character. How would you handle the situation? (3) What wisdom did we garner from the case? The purpose of the questionnaire (or a final writing assignment) allows the participants to concisely describe how they understand the case and what concrete lessons they will apply to their own practice in the future. (15 minutes)

7. Thank everyone for participating.

POSSIBLE ACTIVE LEARNING STRATEGIES INCLUDE:

1. Mini Lecture: A mini-lecture may be delivered before, during, or after the case presentation when appropriate. The lecturer should not preempt the discussion or cut it off by giving the "right answer."

Alternative: A guest speaker, resource person, or podcast could be utilized to give a mini-lecture or presentation. (10 minutes)

2. Small Groups: Small group discussions may provide opportunities for full participation by all those present. The group assignment must be clear, and the teaching plan must allow sufficient time for them to discuss and then to return to the larger gathering. (Pair/ Share is another form of small group discussion that gets everyone involved by simply asking everyone to team up with his or her neighbor.) For example: Divide the class into groups, each representing either one of the characters or a particular issue. Provide the groups with markers and post-it notes so they can record their discussion. Ask them to do the following: (30 minutes) (1) Select one of the issues that emerged in the earlier discussion that you deem vital for your character to consider. (2) Discuss what is most at stake for your character. (3) Discuss some of the alternative decisions or actions available to your character. (4) Identify possible resources available to your character.

3. Role-play is often a good follow-up activity to a small group discussion. Ask the group to discuss possible talking points for the group's assigned character. Pick one person in the group to come in front of the class and play the role of the character. Provide the selected students with large nametags. Reenact or create a scenario for the characters. After the role-play, thank the actors. Debrief with the whole class by asking 1–2 key questions. (20 minutes)

4. Voting or Polling: Asking participants to vote on a key issue before the discussion begins can energize a conversation about the rationale for and implications of various positions. It is often useful to continue with "the minority report" (using the opinion of the minority rather than the majority). When voting or polling is used, the participants may be divided into pro and con groups. The participants' votes place them into two groups that would prepare a "point/counterpoint" discussion about one of the selected issues.

5. "Fish-bowl" is a device that allows the facilitator to select a small group of participants (or allow them to volunteer) who come to the front and discusses pertinent issues/ideas/solutions. The rest of the group listens to the conversation. One modification of this approach is to allow small groups to choose a spokesperson to

present the group's discussion. Another is to leave one chair in the discussion circle empty, so that listening participants can move in and out of the discussion. Additionally, chairs could be labeled in order to represent certain characters.

6. "Jigsaw" is a means of giving individuals with different information or perspectives an opportunity to share with others. For example, if participants are divided into small groups, and each group is given a different topic/issue/character to discuss, they spend a designated period completing their assignment. They are then "regrouped," so that a representative from each small group is included in the new small groups.

For Further Investigation on Case Studies see:

1. Garvin, David A. "Making the Case: Professional Education for the World of Practice," in *Harvard Magazine* 106, no. 1 (Sept–Oct 2003): 56–65, 107. Available from Harvard Magazine, http://www.harvard-magazine.com/on-line/090322.html, accessed 18 November 2009.

2. Lewis, G. Douglass. *Resolving Church Conflicts: A Case Study Approach for Local Congregations.* Harper & Row, 1981.

3. Mahan, Jeffery, Barbara Troxell, and Carol Allen. *Shared Wisdom: A Guide to Case Study Reflection in Ministry.* Nashville: Abingdon, 1993.

4. Sensing, Tim. "Case Studies in Field Education," in *Welcome to Field Education.* Alban, 2011.

5. Swetland, Kenneth L. *The Hidden World of the Pastor: Case Studies on Personal Issues of Real Pastors.* Baker, 1995; and *Facing Messy Stuff in the Church: Case Studies for Pastors and Congregations.* Kregel, 2005.

6. Tomey, Ann Marriner. "Learning with Cases," in *The Journal of Continuing Education in Nursing* 34, no. 1 (Jan/Feb 2003): 34–38.

7. Wassermann, Selma. *Introduction to Case Method Teaching: A Guide to the Galaxy.* New York: Teachers College Press, 1994.

NARRATIVE RESEARCH

My problem statement in my PhD dissertation was: "The problem of this study is to analyze various preaching professors' differing theories and practices of the pedagogy of preaching using a narrative methodology resulting in a phenomenological description of patterns. More specifically, I desire to answer the following question: What patterns and implications can be discerned from different discourse communities concerning the instruction of homiletics?"[16] The problem statement specified a narrative methodology. It did not have to. I could have easily used questionnaires, focus groups, observations, or surveys. The different tools would have produced distinctive data sets leading to diverse conclusions. A secondary study using multiple methods would have provided more texture to my dissertation. I chose not to use multiple methods that would have given more breadth of analysis, but to utilize one approach in depth. My choice was not better, only different. Every study could benefit from a secondary analysis that utilizes a different approach. That is the reason there is no end to the making of books (Eccl 12:12).

The use of narrative research does not fit neatly within the boundaries of any particular methodology. Although it is inherently interdisciplinary, narrative is primarily a vehicle for understanding and explaining lived experiences.[17] Narrative research, rightly understood, is a vital contributor to the collected methods of ethnography, action research, and other qualitative tools. However, the popularity of narrative has led to misapplications thus requiring a more detailed description here.[18]

The purpose of narrative research is to examine how participants impose order on their lived experiences thus making sense of the events,

16. Tim Sensing, *Pedagogies of Preaching*, 2.

17. For a detailed description of the phenomenological approach of researching lived experiences that underlies my use of the term *narrative* see Van Manen, *Researching Lived Experience*. To explore explicit uses of narrative in theological circles see Crites, "Narrative Quality of Experience"; Anderson and Foley, *Mighty Stories*; Niebuhr, *Meaning of Revelation*; Lindbeck, *Nature of Doctrine*; Frei, *Eclipse*; Fackre, *Christian Story*; and Hays, *Moral Vision*.

18. Carl Savage and William Presnell, *Narrative Research in Ministry: A Postmodern Research Approach for Faith Communities*. Louisville, KY: Wayne Oates Institute, 2008. Although this text is being used in various DMin programs, it is a popular rendition of narrative theory and theoretically suspect. For example, it depends on the popular work of L. Sweet et al., *A is for Abductive*, to define abductive reasoning rather than relying on the philosophical pragmatism of C. S. Peirce who coined the word "abductive" and is foundational to current scientific inquiry.

thoughts, and actions in their lives.[19] Human beings do not just live in relationship; they produce relationships to live, thereby producing culture and creating history.[20] Human beings and their identities are neither plastic nor passive. We all have stories existing and being created in a given socio-historical context. Accordingly, our future stories are continuously written and constructed through dialogical human interaction,[21] and a dialogue of multiple voices—heteroglossia.[22] Unless this dynamic interactive and interrelational nature of culture is acknowledged, it becomes hegemonic in nature.[23]

Through narrative, a researcher can explore the ways practical theologians come to know and practice their craft in tacit and unmeasurable ways. Overhearing someone's life story is one way practical theologians are able to incorporate expert and local knowledge about the congregation into their research. Narrative research reflects on this tacit knowledge and translates it into explicit knowledge, allowing it to be integrated with other perspectives.

Narrative itself becomes a research tool to sensitize participants to the dialogical interactive nature of cultural processes. Narratives foster listening to the multiple voices emanating from ever-emerging and developing contexts. Narratives coordinate intersubjective processes. They afford individuals the possibility to construct, co-construct, and reconstruct coherently their identities, and to acknowledge their loyalties, traditions, and inherited roles.[24] When people let you hear their stories, they are sharing a sacred trust, for is through their stories they give meaning and interpret their lives. Narratives facilitate and encourage interpretatively open processes of "becoming" through dialogical and interactive work. Narrative research is a powerful tool that allows for the exposure of both information and interpretation and is an appropriate means by which researchers can examine their beliefs and practices. Postman defines narrative research as follows: "The purpose of a narrative is to give meaning to the world, not to describe it scientifically. The measure of a narrative's 'truth' or 'falsity' is in its consequences: Does it provide people with a sense

19. Riessman, *Narrative Analysis*, 2.

20. Godelier, *Perspectives*.

21. Harré and Gillet, *Discursive Mind*.

22. Bakhtin, *Dialogic Imagination*.

23. Witherell and Noddings, *Stories Lives Tell*; McEwan and Egan, *Narrative in Teaching*.

24. MacIntyre, *After Virtue*.

of personal identity, or sense of community life, a basis for moral conduct or explanations of that which cannot be known?"[25]

Accordingly, researchers can recognize that their narratives have been co-authored and re-authored by the participants in their projects. Other people's experiences allow the researcher to be more experienced. Their narratives inform, shape, and enrich the researcher's narrative and consequently, the researcher's theology. Van Manen advocates the gathering of stories as the essential way to unearth people's pre-reflective understandings of experience. He notes,

> Anecdotes form a concrete counterweight to abstract theoretical thought. . . . Anecdotes express a certain disdain for the alienated and alienating discourse of scholars who have difficulty showing how life and theoretical propositions are connected. . . . Anecdotes may provide an account of certain teachings or doctrines which were never written down. . . . Anecdotes may be encountered as concrete demonstrations of wisdom, sensitive insight, and proverbial truth. . . . Anecdotes of a certain event or incident may acquire the significance of exemplary character."
>
> Subsequently, the "significance of anecdotal narrative in phenomenological research and writing is situated in its power: (1) to compel: a story recruits our willing attention; (2) to lead us to reflect: a story tends to invite us to a reflective search for significance; (3) to involve us personally: one tends to search actively for the story teller's meaning via one's own; (4) to transform: we may be touched, shaken, moved by story; it teaches us; (5) to measure one's interpretive sense: one's response to a story is a measure of one's deepened ability to make interpretive sense."[26]

Doing narrative research from a purposive sample is similar to gathering a life history of a corporate body rather than an individual. You are collecting key stories from individuals, but it is the weaving together of those stories that contribute to the fabric of the community's story. When doing a life history, Ammerman offers the following questions:

- Tell me what this congregation was like back when you first started to attend here.

- How have things changed around here since then?

- What do you think a new member ought to know about the history of this congregation?

25. Postman, *End of Education*, 7.
26. Van Manen, *Researching Lived Experience*, 115–21.

- ⊚ The specific themes you explore might include descriptions of worship services or what the religious education program was like or what sorts of buildings they had and how money was raised. In addition to listening for the general contours of the congregation's history, keep the interview focused in ways that serve your attempts to understand this particular culture. Along the way, keep the people oriented by asking them to relate their stories to other events you know about.

- Was that before or after the big fire?

- Was that while Father Kowalski was here?

- Encourage them to tell stories, not just to relate facts. You are interested in the facts, but it is the stories that will tell you about this congregation's sense of identity.[27]

Casey identifies three strands of narrative research, namely, autobiographical reflection, collective subjective, and plastic identities.[28] The link that holds these new qualitative approaches together is their common interest in the ways that human beings make meaning through language. How do we organize meaning, order experience, and construct reality? These new approaches are based on the speaker's understanding of self and the rediscovery of self. From the narrative of self-perspective, another perspective is given voice that had gone unheard by positivist approaches to research. Other common elements in these post-positivist perspectives are a recognition of one's subjectivity as a researcher and the making visible one's social background, pre-understandings, and relationships.

Researchers rooted in a positivist perspective maintain the myth of objectivity; however, value-neutral research is unrealizable, self-deceptive, and value laden. Correct method does not guarantee true results but only correct guesses. Narrative research is about a different way of knowing. Knowledge is socially constructed, historically embedded, and valuationally based. Olson roots "narrative authority" in Dewey's notion that knowledge is constructed through experience.[29] Practical theologians have personal knowledge of education theory and practice as they interact within their individual contexts. The self is an evolving entity

27. Ammerman et al., *Studying Congregations*, 95.
28. Casey, "New Narrative Research."
29. Olson, "Conceptualizing Narrative Authority."

that changes constantly through social forces and self-reflection. The self is contextualized as far as an individual's identity is tied to community, family, economic and social considerations.

Dialectical theory arises from contextual situations rather than from an abstract theoretical framework.[30] The study of human science must be built upon a different foundation than exists for studying objects. The theory "grows out of the context-embedded data," not from a preconceived notion of the researcher.[31] Research as praxis is a viable alternative to generate social knowledge that is not empirical. In contrast to the more positivist sciences, narrative research does not seek theory first. Rather, theory enlightens prior practice and follows a time of reflection. Theory that follows practice can then assist in developing greater awareness. Therefore, narrative research as praxis, the daily lives of people at church and their self-understanding of what they do, gives rise to theory.

Lather identifies that research from praxis comes forth from contextual situations.[32] Life has the evocative power to generate theory. This encourages the researcher to maintain an open frame of reference and the possibility of new and unexpected discoveries. Primarily, this critical inquiry focuses on the needs of people so that practical and liberating possibilities are made known in their world. By collecting narratives, lived experiences are collected and considered. Interpretation of lived experience points to meaning. The process is both descriptive and interpretive. Such an interpretation is validated when lived experiences are confirmed by lived experiences. Van Manen names this as "the validating circle of inquiry."[33] The concern for reciprocity during research as praxis is addressed early in the process. The researcher and the researched need to be in mutual relationship so there is a shared understanding of meaning and power. The researched need to know how this project benefits them.

Research as praxis generates theory from the data and seeks to minimize hypothesis and researcher-imposed definitions and limitations. Subsequently, greater possibilities for applications in the field and the generation of new knowledge emerge. Lather encourages practices

30. Lather, "Research as Praxis," 267.
31. Ibid.
32. Ibid.
33. Van Manen, *Researching Lived Experience*, 27.

that insure the trustworthiness of the data. In short, self-corrective techniques need to be formalized so that credibility of the data is maintained and personal bias minimized.

Van Manen lists seven aspects of story relevant to this study:

1. Story provides us with possible human experiences.

2. Story enables us to experience life situations, feelings, emotions, and events that we would not normally experience.

3. Story allows us to broaden the horizons of our normal existential landscape by creating possible worlds.

4. Story tends to appeal and involve us in a personal way.

5. Story is an artistic device that lets us turn back to life as lived experience.

6. Story evokes the quality of vividness in detailing unique and particular aspects of a life that could be my life or your life.

7. Stories transcend the particularity of their plots and protagonists, etc., which makes them subject to thematic analysis and criticism.[34]

Furthermore, stories express the multiplicity of meaning and the interconnectedness of phenomena that resist reduction and singular interpretations. Stories accommodate ambiguity and inconsistency found in everyday experience.

Riessman sees narratives ontologically as representations of the deep structures about the nature of life itself.[35] As a representation, narratives fashion identities and relationships. Since all researchers are interpreting their firsthand experiences, the essence of authentic experience cannot be captured by any methodology. Narrative research in teaching is an alternative way of knowing. Individual life stories embody ideologies and theories that are woven with educational practices. What we tell and how we tell it is a revelation of what we believe and what we do. People construct their narratives. They decide what is included and what is excluded in their stories. They plot their stories and add interpretive clues.

34. Ibid., 70.

35. Riessman, *Narrative Analysis*, 16.

People tell narratives in such a way as to make sense of life and experience. Additionally, narratives are shaped by the relationship that exists between the teller and the hearer. Episodic sequence, whether chronological or thematic, is essential for the formation of narrative. Selection, what choices are made for inclusion and exclusion, plays a major role in shaping the content of the narratives. Whether they represent actual events or "truths" is not pivotal to this methodology. Actual events are not being sought. The representation, the construction of reality, is the focus. How people tell their story and what message they desire their story to contain is critical. Actual events cannot be exactly "recovered" anyway. Our memories "selectively reconstruct" the past. Even as events are occurring, we are actively making interpretations and reinterpretations for the purpose of coherence. Riessman emphasizes how language functions as constituting reality. Stories, therefore, do not mirror the world. Stories are constructed, creatively authored, with rhetorical assumptions, and interpretations.[36]

Cortazzi describes one way constructed narratives can be interpreted.

> Every narrative is a version or view of what happened. Most narratives do not simply report events but rather give a teller's perspective on their meaning, relevance, and importance. This perspective can often be seen in structural analysis by dividing the parts of a narrative into at least three major structural categories: an event structure, which reports happenings; a description structure, which gives background information on time, place, people and context necessary to understand the narrative; and an evaluation structure, which shows the point of telling the narrative by presenting the speaker's perspective or judgment on the events, marking off the most important part.[37]

Riessman's theory begins with primary experience and explores the "evaluation structure" of a narrative.[38] The first encounter is prelinguistic (image, color, light, noise, sensations, without analysis). But then the individual attends to the experience. Certain features are made discrete through reflection and memory. Language names observations. Phenomenon is given meaning. Choices are made that determine perception of reality. Next, the experience is told or re-presented in a nar-

---

36. Ibid., 22.
37. Cortazzi, "Narrative Analysis," 384.
38. Riessman, *Narrative Analysis*, 9–15.

rative that already contains an interpretation. The telling moves from an oral stage to a written stage when the experience is transcribed on paper. The experience is now fixed in time and form. The order and style of the telling can now be analyzed. The narrative is now subject to different viewpoints. Decisions are made about why the narrative was told this way. The metanarrative takes shape.

Finally, a reader one day comes to the newsstand and reads the narrative making his or her own interpretations. Different readers in different situations may make different observations. The same reader may interpret the same narrative differently depending upon various factors involved in his or her context. By the final level, there is a transformation of the primary experience. There is now no direct access to the primary experience. Each step involves both an expansion and a reduction due to the choices made in the selection process. The whole has been selectively represented. These selections have been interpreted. The partial narrative of the primary experience imperfectly reflects the whole. The dynamic experience becomes a frozen text. The readers of the text will usually only have access to the published version. Therefore, Riessman concludes that narratives are but interpretations embedded in language and culture (embedded in many elements besides the "truth").

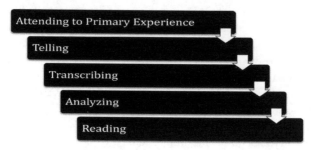

Figure 9: Riessman's Levels of Representations in Research Process

Riessman notes how fully formed narratives have six elements: (1) abstract (summary of the substance); (2) orientation (time, place, situation, participants); (3) complicating action (sequence of events); (4) evaluation (significance and meaning of the action, attitude of the narrator); (5) resolution (what finally happened); and (6) coda (returns the perspective to the present).[39]

39. Ibid., 18.

Further analysis of narratives could utilize Burke's pentad of terms: act, scene, agent, agency, and purpose. Any complete statement about motives will offer some kind of answer to these five questions: What was done (act), when or where it was done (scene), who did it (agent), how he or she did it (agency), and why (purpose).[40]

Casey's theory of narrative centers on her conscious belief that meaning comes from people making sense of their own situations.[41] So much research imposes meaning on others. Casey desires to listen to how others make sense of their experiences. Narratives give the voice a place in time. The perspective of the past is woven into the future to give shape to the present. Propositions are flat and lifeless. Narratives are dynamic. Narratives do something. Sometimes narratives do more than is anticipated.

Casey anchors her theory in two frameworks: The Popular Memory Group and Bakhtin.[42] The former guided her collection of the narratives, while the latter guided her analysis. Narrative, language, and rhetoric are owned and shaped by both individuals and community. Words have meaning only in context, and narratives place words in their context. Therefore, an individual narrative must be interpreted in relationship with the community from which it arises and not in isolation. The community context of language is often not understood. Casey allows each of the three groups she interviews to use their language and metaphors to shape their identity. The languages are distinct yet similar. By locating patterns (Van Manen's "themes") and particulars, understanding and coherence arise. The patterns in the language of a particular community allow the researcher to adopt a method described as "group biography." Relationship is the key concept for narrative theory. By examining relationships and "slippage," concepts of reality (how reality is presented) can be understood at a level that positivist methods cannot. Bullough and Stokes quoting Olney state, "To tell a story is to create a purpose-

40. See, Burke, *Grammar of Motives*, and Burke, *Rhetoric of Motives*.

41. Casey, *I Answer*. Casey used a narrative method to research the lives of African American, Catholic, and Jewish women school teachers who were actively involved in public social transformation. The themes that emerged from her study allowed her to theorize about effective prescriptions for change by diverse individuals who otherwise were silenced by hegemonic discourses.

42. Ibid., 17–28.

ful coherence of meanings, to impose a pattern that, despite inevitable ambiguity, enables consistency of interpretation and action."[43]

Narrative Research in Practice

I have implemented narrative methodologies in three different settings: the classroom, research, and personal development as a teacher of preaching. In the classroom, BIBM 656, *Supervised Practice of Ministry*, I asked students to collect narratives from practitioners whom they consider vocational role models. Upon completion of the data collection phase of the assignment, students were grouped according to vocational aspirations. They coded their interviews, sought for emerging patterns and themes, and reflected upon incongruencies. Their final report depicted metaphors that emerged to describe their practitioners and a summary of a philosophy of work that clarified this particular vocational practice.

Secondly, I applied a narrative methodology to complete a grant in which I studied the preaching lives of African American preachers.[44] I interviewed seventeen African American preachers who studied with either G. P. Bowser or Marshall Keeble. I framed our conversation by stating, "I'm collecting narratives about how preachers learn to preach. In the framework of learning to preach, tell me the story of your life." I followed their narratives with appropriate questions such as: "Where did your values about preaching come from?" "Tell me more about that." "What was that experience like?" "Give me some examples of that." Their stories needed to be heard and preserved. My primary conclusion described a pedagogy of imitation that allowed these expert practical theologians to tacitly pass on the tradition of preaching through a series of apprenticeships and mentoring relationships.

Finally, I interviewed professors of preaching, asking them to tell me stories about teaching preaching.[45] I framed our conversation by stating, "I'm collecting narratives from teachers of preaching. Would you tell me your life story?" I remained silent throughout the conversation until the teacher reached the denouement of his or her life story. I followed their narratives with appropriate responses such as: "Where did your values

43. Bullough and Stokes, "Analyzing Personal Teaching Metaphors."
44. Sensing, *African American Preaching*.
45. Sensing, *Pedagogies of Preaching*.

about preaching come from?" "Tell me more about how you learned to preach." "What was that experience like?" "Give me some examples of . . ." I was seeking to answer the following questions:

- What constitutes the discourse(s) of selected professors, and what implications do these perceptions have for the instructional practice of a novice professor?

- How do these professors identify themselves within a larger interpretive community?

- What metaphors do these discourse communities use to describe practical theologians and teaching?

- What are some of the patterns, slippages, and silences, found within an intra- and inter-textual analysis of these discourses?

Therefore, in each case, we talked about their metaphors for preachers and preaching. Metaphors embody a large part of self-understanding. Metaphors are useful in narratives by lending form and structure to stories and by simplifying, clarifying, and summarizing our lives at a high level of abstraction.[46] Further, "a change in metaphor may indicate a change in how the world of teaching is conceived, a change in the evolving story of self."[47] Identifying metaphors contributes to the reflection needed to better understand the constructs that form identities. Similarly, by using the narrative research methodology, I identified themes and patterns in the discourse of these practical theologians, giving me rich data for detailed reflection and interpretation.

Narrative analysis is a flexible and multi-adaptable tool because it is rooted in a basic ontological understanding of how people construct their lived experiences. Patton notes, "The language of story carries a connotation different from that of case study. For example, in program evaluations, people may be invited to share their stories instead of being asked to participate in case studies. The central idea of narrative analysis is that stories and narratives offer especially translucent windows into cultural and social meanings."[48]

Stephen Johnson used a narrative approach as part of his DMin intervention and as one angle of his interpretation. He states that the

46. Bullough and Stokes, "Analyzing Personal Teaching Metaphors," 200.
47. Ibid.
48. Patton, *Qualitative Research*, 116.

problem he is investigating is "the lack of intentional formation of elders for roles of pastoral leadership that is distinctively Christian."[49] After introducing them to the narrative nature of Scripture, he led them through five sessions intended to integrate their personal stories with the story of God. Exercises included using a case study that asked the participants to respond pastorally using the acquired narrative skills. One exercise asked the participants to author "life story conversations" by writing "templates" that could be utilized in pastoral engagements. Finally, as an insider angle of evaluation, the elders were asked to participate in a "Group 'Reauthoring' Exercise." An abbreviated version of the instructions for the exercise were: "To close out our time together, I would like to ask you to think of your life together as a group of pastors. Discuss your life together as elders in terms of an unfolding story. What would the opening chapters of your life together tell? Describe the 'next chapter' in your life together. Where is your story headed?"[50]

APPRECIATIVE INQUIRY

Appreciative Inquiry (AI) has garnered a favorable following in organizational development and is heralded as the most important advance in action research in the past decade.[51] David Cooperrider at Case Western Reserve's School of Organizational Behavior is recognized as the primary theorist advocating AI approaches. AI is a collaborative and generative process of organizational learning and change emphasizing building on an organization's assets rather than focusing on problems. Emerging from the field of organizational development and rooted in

49. Johnson, "Narrative Model," 6.

50. Ibid., 56.

51. Holman and Devange, *Change Handbook*; Hammond, *Thin Book*; Kelm, "Introducing the AI Philosophy"; Whitney and Cooperrider, "Appreciative Inquiry Summit." For a more theoretical understanding of AI, see Cooperrider and Srivastva "Appreciative Inquiry." The abstract states, "This chapter presents a conceptual refiguration of action-research based on a 'sociorationalist' view of science. The position that is developed can be summarized as follows: For action-research to reach its potential as a vehicle for social innovation it needs to begin advancing theoretical knowledge of consequence; that good theory may be one of the best means human beings have for affecting change in a postindustrial world; that the discipline's steadfast commitment to a problem-solving view of the world acts as a primary constraint on its imagination and contribution to knowledge; that appreciative inquiry represents a viable complement to conventional forms of action-research; and finally, that through our assumptions and choice of method we largely create the world we later discover."

theories of social constructionism, AI seeks to structure positively the shared language and images of a group in the conviction that organizations and communities originate in language and construct their reality from common language and imagery.[52] Simply, change follows the type of questions you ask. Whitney and Trosten-Bloom give a complete listing of the principles of AI that pervade the literature.

1. The Constructionist Principle: Words Create Worlds. Reality, as we know it, is a subjective vs. objective state. It is socially constructed, through language and conversations.

2. The Simultaneity Principle: Inquiry Creates Change. Inquiry is intervention. The moment we ask a question, we begin to create a change.

3. The Poetic Principle: We Can Choose What We Study. What we choose to study makes a difference. It describes—even creates—the world as we know it.

4. The Anticipatory Principle: Images Inspire Action. Human systems move in the direction of their images of the future. The more positive and hopeful the image of the future, the more positive the present-day action.

5. The Positive Principle: Positive Questions Lead to Positive Change. Momentum for large-scale change requires large amounts of positive affect and social bonding. This momentum is best generated through positive questions that amplify the positive core.

6. The Wholeness Principle: Wholeness Brings Out the Best. Wholeness brings out the best in people and organizations. Bringing all stakeholders together in large group forums stimulates creativity and builds collective capacity.

7. The Enactment Principle: Acting "As If" Is Self-Fulfilling. To really make a change, we must "be the change we want to see." Positive change occurs when the process used to create the change is a living model of the ideal future.

8. The Free Choice Principle: Free Choice Liberates Power. People perform better and are more committed when they have freedom

52. Whitney and Trosten-Bloom, *Power of Appreciative Inquiry*, 56–57.

to choose how and what they contribute. Free choice stimulates organizational excellence and positive change.[53]

AI's most powerful tool is the appreciative interview that seeks to "uncover what gives life to an organization, department, or community when at its best."[54] Before beginning an AI interview, an affirmative topic or theme must be chosen as the organizing principle. AI does not ignore problems. It simply restates problems as inquiry into possibility. The shift of attention from problem to possibility is an option for all organizational issues.

Once the topic is chosen, the "4-D Cycle" is followed. During the discovery phase, appreciative interviews are conducted with participants in the study. Afterwards, in the dream phase, the group is gathered together to share the dreams that emerged in the interviews. The design phase identifies and drafts provocative propositions that will impact the organization for positive change. Finally, the destiny phase invites action and plans the next steps.[55]

Utilizing the entire 4-D Cycle requires you to go beyond the brief descriptions in this book. If you choose this route, the 4-D Cycle of AI becomes your intervention. Choosing the affirmative topic parallels the writing of the problem and purpose statement. Discovery, Dream, Design, and Destiny phases of AI parallel the project's intervention.[56] A second Discovery phase where AI interviews are used with the participants closes the evaluation loop. During the evaluation, you are asking key questions from the insiders about the positive aspects of the Design

53. Ibid., 54–55.

54. Cooperrider and Whitney, *Appreciative Inquiry*, 11.

55. Ibid., 17.

56. When choosing AI as the primary method of investigation, the tools described in chapter 4 would need to be modified in order to conform to the principles of AI. For example, crafting AI questions will be different. Whitney and Trosten-Bloom, *Power of Appreciative Inquiry*, 152–3, describe three basic AI questions. "*Backward questions* generally come first. They invite us to remember high-point experiences—times when we have experienced the Affirmative Topic to be most alive and most present. . . . *Inward questions* generally follow backward questions. They refer back to the high-point experiences, asking us to make meaning of those peak experiences, and to extrapolate learnings about their root causes of success. . . . *Forward questions* generally come last. At their best, they solicit our hopes, dreams, and inspirations. They encourage us to imagine futures in which the Affirmative Topic is the best it can possibly be. . . . *Transition questions* are often embedded within the forward questions. They are retrospective reflections from the imagined future state—an opportunity for the interviewee to consider first steps and transitions from the current reality to the imagined future."

and Destiny phases of the AI intervention. Your primary advisor might ask you to add your own angle of interpretation and that of an independent expert in order to achieve triangulation. If so, the protocols of the other two angles will be crafted according to AI principles. For example, the independent expert can be asked to analyze the provocative propositions and the plan for next steps. The analysis the expert provides would be guided by questions like, "What positive contributions will these provocative propositions make in the life of the church?" "What blessings would the church experience if the next steps were fully implemented?"

Figure 10: The Appreciative Inquiry 4-D Cycle[57]

AI research on AI itself by Whitney and Trosten-Bloom indicated the following assets for using AI.

1. It builds relationships enabling people to be known in relationship, rather than in role.

2. It creates an opportunity for people to be heard.

3. It generates opportunities for people to dream, and to share their dreams.

4. It creates an environment in which people are able to choose how they contribute.

5. It gives people both discretion and support to act.

6. It encourages and enables people to be positive.[58]

57. Cooperrider and Whitney, *Appreciative Inquiry*, 11.

58. Whitney and Trosten-Bloom, *Power of Appreciative Inquiry*, 20–21.

Furthermore, their research into whole-system organizational change revealed seven agendas suited for AI inquiry. DMin projects similarly address many of these same issues:

1. Organizational Change: Strategic Planning, Culture Transformation, Customer Satisfaction, Morale and Retention, Organization Design, Leadership Development, and Business Improvement.

2. Inter-Organizational Capacity Building: Merger Integration, Alliance Building, Union-Management Partnership, and Strategic Resource Sharing.

3. Community Development: Participatory Planning, Asset Mapping, Economic Development, Educational Reform, and Peace Building.

4. Global Transformation: Global Organizing, Multi-Local Planning, and Consciousness Raising.

5. Small Group Development: Team Development, Business Development, Meeting Management, and Instructional Design.

6. Inter-Group Change: Conflict Resolution and Process Improvement.

7. Personal/Relational Transformation: Leadership Development, Performance Appraisal, Employee Orientation, Career Planning, Relationship Enrichment, and Spiritual Development.[59]

In my second semester service learning class, I give students the following handout, "Appreciative Inquiry (AI) Assignment," as a summary of AI. At the bottom of the page is an in-class assignment that lets the students experience AI firsthand. After class, I assign an AI project for students to implement in their service learning ministry or social justice setting. Step 1: Write three 100-word abstracts on articles describing AI. Find the articles by using the library database or the Internet. Step 2: Write an interview guide based upon the principles of AI. Step 3: Interview at least five people connected to your setting. Step 4: Write a one-page essay describing what themes emerged from your interviews. The assignment aims at generating specific examples, stories, and metaphors about the positive aspects of being involved in the setting under investigation.

59. Ibid., 26–30.

AI Assignment 1

4-D CYCLE:

1. Discovery: Appreciating and Valuing the Best of "What Is"

2. Dream: Envisioning "What Might Be"

3. Design: Dialoguing "What Should Be"

4. Destiny: Innovating "What Will Be"

AI principles are adapted and customized to each individual situation; the full AI process typically includes:

1. Selecting a focus area or topic(s) of interest

2. Interviews designed to discover strengths, passions, unique attributes

3. Identifying patterns, themes and/or intriguing possibilities

4. Creating bold statements of ideal possibilities ("Provocative Propositions")

5. Co-determining "what should be" (consensus re: principles and priorities)

6. Taking and sustaining action

At the heart of any AI process are positive questions that assume health and vitality in the system. Common appreciative questions include variations on the following:

1. High point experiences: Describe a time in your life when you felt alive and engaged. What experience with this organization made you feel most fulfilled?

2. Valuing: What do you value most about yourself, your work, or your organization?

3. Core life-giving factors: What are the core factors that give life to this organization? What are the unique attributes of this system, without which it would not be the same?

4. Wishes for/images of the future: (1) What three wishes do you have to enhance the vitality of this system? (2) Imagine this organization five years from now, healthy and vibrant—What does it look like?

AI Assignment 2

THE FOUR INITIAL QUESTIONS FOR AN APPRECIATIVE INQUIRY INTERVIEW AS APPLIED TO PERSONAL MINISTRY EXPERIENCE

Instructions: In pairs take time to interview one another using the following questions. Be a generous listener. Do not dialogue; rather take turns to actually conduct an interview. If you need more information or clarification, ask additional follow-up questions. Record the results of your interview. When your interviews are completed, you will present the results to the wider group. Before you conduct the interview, take a minute to read the questions and decide how you will personally answer each question and make a mental note of your response. Now proceed with the interviews, paying full attention to the interviewee rather than to your story.

1. **Best Experience:** Reflect on your entire experience of your ministry. Recall a time when you felt most alive, most involved, spiritually moved, or most excited about your ministry. Tell me about this memorable experience that you have had with the church. Describe the event in detail. What made it an exciting experience? Who was involved? Describe how you felt. Describe what you did as a result of the experience.

2. **Values:** What are the things that you deeply value: specifically, the things you value about yourself and your church? (1) Yourself: Without being humble, what do you value most about yourself? (2) Being in ministry: When you feel best about being in ministry, what about yourself do you value? (3) Your church: What is it about your church (or place of ministry) that you value? What is the single most important thing that your church has contributed to your life? (4) Your denomination: What is it about being an Episcopalian/Lutheran/Methodist etc. that you value? What is the single most important thing that being an Episcopalian/Lutheran/Methodist etc. has contributed to your life?

3. **Core Values:** What do you think is the core value of your ministry? What values give life to your ministry? What is it that, if it did not exist, would make your ministry totally different than it currently is?

4. **Three Wishes:** If you had three wishes for your ministry, what would they be?

References Relating Ministry & AI

1. Branson, Mark Lau. *Memories, Hopes, and Conversations: Appreciative Inquiry and Congregational Change*. Herndon, VA: Alban, 2004.

2. Rendle, Gil, and Alice Mann. *Holy Conversations: Strategic Planning as a Spiritual Practice for Congregations*. Herndon, VA: Alban, 2003.

3. Snow, Luther K. *The Power of Asset Mapping: How Your Congregation Can Act on Its Gifts*. Herndon, VA: Alban, 2004.

Since Appreciative Inquiry is fundamentally not a problem-solving form of inquiry, it requires re-conceptualizing the purpose of the DMin project thesis. Savage and Presnell, in *Narrative Research in Ministry: A Postmodern Research Approach for Faith Communities*, advocate collecting participants' narratives as a way to re-imagine the congregation's future story. Although they do not cite AI principles, their approach is distinctly bent toward the same goals. Their participatory approach begins with listening to stories of a "lay-advisory" team at the outset in order to discern the focus of the investigation. The word "concerns" is substituted for the term "problems" in order to find hopeful places of opportunities rather than issues that need fixing. Next, the investigation seeks intersections between the emerging congregational stories and the biblical story. As part of the investigation, you are to explore ways the stories told are correlated with other sources of data. Begin to differentiate between the congregation's stories of concern with a new and possible future story. Finally, co-author a preferred story for the congregation that draws them into new ways of being.[60]

Appreciative Inquiry in Practice

Diana Butler Bass in *Christianity for the Rest of Us*[61] uses principles of AI in her Lilly endowed research investigating revitalized churches. AI theoretically correlated with her stated purpose of finding a "common pattern, language, and spiritual logic" within the practices of thriving congregations.[62] She states, "For the purposes of our research, we de-

60. Savage and Presnell, *Narrative Research in Ministry*, 86–90.
61. Bass, *Christianity for the Rest of Us*.
62. Ibid., 4. She examined fifty churches in various denominations. Ten churches

fined 'practicing congregation' as 'a congregation which has experienced renewed vitality through intentionally and creatively embracing one or more traditional Christian practices.'"[63]

Her research involved multiple methods such as participant observation and interviews. Over a period of time, researchers participated in various activities of the congregations giving them ample opportunities to see the ongoing life of the people in the midst of their religious engagements. Field notes, transcripts of interviews, and focus group sessions were carefully recorded. Secondary sources that included bulletins, documents, brochures, newsletters, and videos were collected as cultural artifacts.[64] The multiple methods employed exemplify the use of triangulation in data collection.

Overall, the project's orientation was controlled by appreciative inquiry. She states, "As we collected qualitative data, we assumed a stance of appreciative inquiry, looking for language of success—especially stories—that could be analyzed and shared with others. Consequently, we chose not to focus our data collection on diagnosing dysfunction or conflict, although we remained open to identifying challenges in our conversations and observations."[65]

Analysis of internal and external validity also illustrates the use of the terms within qualitative more than quantitative research. She employed the concepts of "content saturation," "validation group," and "member checking." She notes the limitations of the research in making broad generalizations applicable to other locations or that her findings are inclusive of all possible practices of thriving churches.[66] Specifically, she notes the limits to the use of appreciative inquiry that focus on "sto-

---

became the subject of extensive in-depth studies. While her research is more comprehensive than any single DMin project, a student could easily replicate her method for a single congregation thus constituting a viable project/thesis.

63. Ibid., 296. The appendix describes in detail her methodology. They desired to look at congregations that were "becoming—more intentional … about their practices in community." She defined vitality on pg. 297 as "coherence of practice, authenticity of practices, and transformation through practice." These "markers" were defined in a way that the data could easily be coded using computer-assisted analysis NVIVO. She also describes the protocol for the use of key informants on pg. 298.

64. Ibid., 303.

65. Ibid. While she does not include an AI interview guide, many of the questions asked can be inferred within the context of the book and the supplemental study guide pgs. 289-94.

66. Ibid., 304.

ries of success" and not examining "stories of conflict and failure." She concludes that the limitations were acceptable due to the fulfillment of the primary purpose of the study, to locate "instructive stories from practicing congregations."[67]

A second example of incorporating AI within the structures provided in this textbook is found in John Ogren's thesis, "Discerning Missional Criteria for the Practice of Church Planting by the South MacArthur Church of Christ." Ogren used AI as part of his intervention as he explored criteria for planting a missional congregation. He conformed to the conventions of the DMin project thesis by stating the following problem and purpose statements: "The problem was a lack of missional criteria to inform and guide our practice of church planting. . . . Accordingly, the purpose of the ministry intervention was to introduce theological categories for considering church planting as a missional practice and to discern communally a set of missional criteria that would inform and guide South MacArther's practice of church planting."[68] Although Ogren stated a problem for his project thesis, his purpose was not to solve an organizational problem but to creatively cast a positive vision for the future. Ogren's use of AI began with the five basic processes of AI, namely: 1) Choose the positive as the focus of inquiry; 2) Inquire into stories of life-giving focus; 3) Locate themes that appear in the stories and select topics for further inquiry; 4) Create shared images for a preferred future; 5) Find innovative ways to create that future. The five processes are characterized by four actions: Initiate, Inquire, Imagine, and Innovate.[69] Ogren did not engage in the final action of "innovate" given his project's delimitations, which were informed by his purpose. It was determined that innovation was an act to be finished by a subsequent church planting team.

In leading the participants to author a set of missional criteria, he utilized a theological reflection model that emerged from his theology section, and he relied upon the practice of *lectio divina*. At the end of each of the four sessions, he concluded by asking the following questions:[70]

---

67. Ibid.

68. Ogren, "Discerning Missional Criteria," 13–14.

69. Branson, *Memories*, 29.

70. Ogren, "Discerning Missional Criteria," 132, 139, 143, 148.

1. When has our fellowship with the Triune God empowered us to experience and practice unity amid diversity? What themes or images emerge from these stories? How do these experiences of God help us to imagine church planting as an expression of the communal life of God?

2. What themes or images emerge from these stories? How do these experiences of God help us to imagine church planting as a creative partnering with God who is at work in the world and in culture?

3. When have we experienced God's salvation in terms of his transforming power in our relationships in community? What themes or images emerge from these stories? How do these experiences of God help us to imagine church planting as an outworking of God's transforming power in human relationships?

4. When have we been incarnational in such a way that our ministry reflected a selfless engagement of culture? What themes or images emerge from these stories? How do these experiences of selfless love help us to imagine church planting as an opportunity to enter fully into the cultural realities of the people we wish to evangelize?

Following the four sessions, the participants met for a retreat. They used the themes and images from the earlier sessions to write a "provocative proposal" based on Branson's categories:[71]

1. are stated in the affirmative, as if already happening

2. point to real desired possibilities

3. are based on the data

4. create new relationships, including intergenerational partnerships

5. bridge the best of "what is" toward "what might be"

6. require sanctified imaginations, stretching the status quo by pushing boundaries

7. necessitate new learning

8. challenge organizational assumptions and routines

During the sessions and the final retreat, Ogren's participants authored a detailed missional criteria centered around the categories of

---

71. Ogren, "Discerning Missional Criteria," 65, quoting Branson, *Memories*, 86–87.

"God, Gospel, and Culture."[72] To evaluate the project, Ogren returned to the conventions set out in the research methodologies course and used a multi-method of triangulation. Although he explored using the criteria of AI for his evaluation, he chose to return to safe ground. But the possibility remains to implement AI throughout the process.

CHOOSING THE BEST FIT

After considering the tools and techniques discussed in chapters 4 and 5, you will need to decide which tool to use and for what purpose. Some of the tools seem to fit one angle of vision better than another. However, any of the tools can be adapted to gather data from any of the three angles. Students often surprise me when they use their imagination in the context of their particular intervention. They often fit the tools with their participants in insightful ways. For example, a survey could be used to gather information from the participants about the project. The researcher could use a survey to gather data from the larger congregation and use the information as the outsider's perspective. In this example, the congregation is functioning as outsiders because they were not directly involved as participants in the project. Below is a chart exemplifying common uses of various tools.

Tool	Insider	Researcher	Outsider
Observation		x	x
Interview	x		x
Questionnaire	x		x
Focus Group	x		
Scales or Instruments	x		
Demographic Data	x		
Feedback Instruments	x		
Participant's Homework	x		
Case Study	x		x
Survey	x		
Independent Expert			x
Narrative	x	x	
Appreciative Inquiry	x		
Field Notes	x	x	

72. Ibid., 70.

6

Taking Note

FIELD NOTES ARE USED in connection with the various tools described in chapter 4. Participant observers, interviewers, focus group facilitators, and the researcher are some of the people who will be taking notes throughout the process. "Field notes . . . contain the ongoing data that are being collected. They consist of descriptions of what is being experienced and observed, quotations from the people observed, the observer's feelings and reactions to what is observed, and field-generated insights and interpretations. Field notes are the fundamental database for constructing case studies and carrying out thematic cross-case analysis in qualitative research."[1]

NOTES FROM THE FIELD

Researchers often find taking field notes (or asking a trained participant observer to take notes) the most efficient way to gather their angle of evaluation. Patton states that the "foundational question" for a heuristic inquiry is "What is my experience of this phenomenon and the essential experience of others who also experience this phenomenon intensely?"[2] He defines *heuristics* as "a form of phenomenological inquiry that brings to the fore the personal experience and insights of the researcher. . . . Heuristic research epitomizes the phenomenological emphasis on means and knowing through personal experience; it exemplifies and places at the fore the way in which the researcher is the primary instrument in qualitative inquiry."[3]

---

1. Patton, *Qualitative Research*, 305. See also Emerson, Fretz, and Shaw, "Participant Observation."

2. Patton, *Qualitative Research*, 107.

3. Ibid., 107, 109.

It is difficult to define and sequence the internal intellectual process involved in a heuristic inquiry. The mysterious path of induction, abduction, and deduction, convergence and divergence, taking apart and putting the whole together again, etc., is a path that is impossible to replicate and different for every researcher. Patton summarizes five basic processes of a heuristic analysis as "immersion, incubation, illumination, explication, and creative synthesis."[4] Immersion occurs when you fully engage the life of your project and the experiences of the participants. Incubation involves deep reflection that allows the experiences of the project to take shape in thought. Illumination comes from moments of epiphany and growing awareness and clarity about the meaning of your project; themes and patterns emerge. Explication involves making understandings concrete and refining explanations. Creative synthesis brings all the pieces together in a holistic fashion. Throughout the heuristic analysis, field notes facilitate the process by bringing order to your understandings and interpretations. A theoretical and rigorous process that can be examined, audited, and judged now controls your angle of evaluation of the project.

Taking notes before, during, and after the ministry intervention collects your observations and initial interpretations. Protocols will specify what should be recorded when. Whether it is a lesson presented, an interview conducted, an activity observed, or some other project-related engagement, you will sit down as soon as possible and record a note on the event. Such comprehensive note-taking emphasizes the longitudinal value of the data. "Field notes contain the descriptive information that will permit you to return to an observation later during analysis and, eventually, permit the reader of the study's findings to experience the activity observed through your report."[5]

Some object that these notes are merely subjective reflections and have little evaluative value. However, if the note taking follows a disciplined protocol, the final collection of notes represents a data set that can be examined, analyzed, and interpreted by other investigators later. The researcher's notes are subject to the same standards of documentary analysis and interpretation that are employed when examining other data sets. Likewise, the researcher's notes will be triangulated with the other two angles of evaluation, providing the requisite checks and balances in the interpretive process.

4. Ibid., 486.
5. Ibid., 303.

Field notes are not merely journal entries. Field notes provide a straightforward description of what selectively took place. The process is considered "selective" because it is impossible to record everything that took place. The protocol in your methodology chapter should clearly state what data should be gathered for a particular observation. The decision of what to observe is dictated by the problem and purpose statement of the project. Some things that occur might be interesting, but if those tidbits fall outside the scope of your project, then let them fall by the wayside. At the time of the observation, it might be difficult to know if something is meaningful or not. In those cases, make a note, then use discretion about whether or not the happening makes the cut in the final analysis.

Field notes are running descriptions of settings, people, activities, and sounds. Field notes may include drawings or maps. The intent of taking notes is to collect data that will aid you in writing a descriptive narrative of a given experience. Notes give the advantage of capturing what is going on in a given setting at a specific moment. Field notes work because implications for theory only become visible as one observes and records, over time, particular practices of ministry. Although you will anticipate what you might observe as noted above, it is important to document what is actually taking place rather than what you were expecting to see or not see. Do not let your expectations hamper your observations. Although confirmations of what you already know will often occur, your research is an exercise in DISCOVERY.

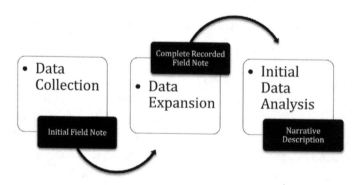

Figure 11: Note-Taking Process

It may be difficult to record everything as it occurs. Data reduction protocols will be determined by the project's purpose. Once the note-taker knows what is being observed, it still is difficult to record every act or quote that is relevant. Instead, jot down notes that will serve to prompt your memory later. As soon as possible, elaborate on your notes by giving details of what was observed earlier. It is easy to think you will fill in the gaps in your notes later, but memories are prone to fail, and details may fade quickly after a good night of sleep. Failure to expand field notes into a narrative account of the event can lead to loss or inaccurate recording and subsequent interpreting of data.

Project proposals state the occasions during which such field notes will be taken and for what reason. The problem and purpose of the project determines the answer to the question, "How will these notes be used?" For example, say the problem statement identifies the lack of incorporating spiritual disciplines in the lives of the identified church leaders. The pastor decides to make a presentation on spiritual disciplines in session 2 of the intervention. The lesson plan has 15 minutes set aside for a mini-lecture, 10 minutes for round-table discussions, 10 minutes for Q & A, and 20 minutes for a spiritual discipline exercise. The protocol describes how the pastor has invited and trained a participant observer to attend the session in order to take field notes. The protocol should identify what the observer should record. The pastor's ability to present a mini-lecture, facilitate a discussion, and lead a spiritual exercise is not recorded. Why? Neither pedagogy nor leadership is connected to the problem and purpose. Instead, the protocol delineates items directly related to the participants engaging and developing spiritual disciplines in this one setting. This is an example of data reduction. The note-taker selects, focuses, and narrows the gaze of observation to those items pertinent to the project's focus.

What does the note-taker observe? Some suggestions include the following possibilities:

1. The setting. Arrive early so that you can describe the overall setting before you begin. How are objects arranged? Likewise, you will note when people arrive, who they arrive with, and certain interpersonal dynamics that exist before the event even begins. Where do people sit? Next to whom? Take note of dress, non-verbal clues, normal and abnormal actions taken by the participants, etc.

2. Activities and interactions that occur in the setting. Who is doing what? Sometimes, it is not what a person says but how they interact that is important. Making things happen even if words are not spoken can convey power.

3. Activities and interactions outside the official setting. Note who is checking out early, who leaves early, who stays late. Sometimes, conversations that occur after the event are crucial. Decisions are sometimes made in the parking lot. People will debrief over coffee afterwards and say things that they would have never said during the official meeting.

4. Frequency and duration of certain behaviors.

5. Conversations.

6. Your own behaviors.

7. What does not happen?

The field notes you take as a reflexive angle of interpretation provide a framework for analysis and for writing the final chapter of your thesis. You will include in your interpretations how your heuristic journey informed your reflections and findings. Patton offers several reflexive questions to help you in the process: "What do I know? How do I know what I know? What shapes and has shaped my perspective? How have my perceptions and my background affected the data I have collected and my analysis of those data? How do I perceive those I have studied? With what voice do I share my perspective? . . . What do I do with what I have found? . . . How do those studied know what they know? What shapes and has shaped their worldview? How do they perceive me, the inquirer? Why? How do I know?"[6]

Field notes are an interpretation, a selected set of perceptions, from one vantage point. As noted above, it is a selective process as to what to record. It is not practical or possible to record it all (even all the interesting stuff). A two-column technique might be helpful in certain situations. In one column, record the field notes. In a parallel column, record your initial reactions, feelings, and interpretations. By recording your initial reactions and hunches, you will begin the interpretation process. You may find this material to be ideal for writing subsequent interview questions. According to Miles and Huberman, possible reflections include:

- what the relationship with informants feels like, now that you are off the site

- second thoughts on the meaning of what a key informant was "really" saying during an exchange that seemed somehow important

6. Ibid., 495.

- doubts about the quality of some of the data; second thoughts about some of the interview questions and observation protocol

- a new hypothesis that might explain some puzzling observations

- a mental note to pursue an issue further in the next contact

- cross-allusions to material in another part of the data set

- personal reactions to some informants' remarks or actions

- elaboration or clarification of a prior incident or event that now seems of possible significance[7]

Tips For Taking Field Notes[8]

- Begin each notebook entry with the date, time, place, and type of data collection event. Leave space on the page for expanding your notes, or plan to expand them on a separate page.

- Take notes strategically. It is usually practical to make only brief notes during data collection. Direct quotes can be especially hard to write down accurately. Rather than try to document every detail or quote, write down key words and phrases that will trigger your memory when you expand notes.

- Use shorthand. Because you will expand and type your notes soon after you write them, it does not matter if you are the only person who can understand your shorthand system. Use abbreviations and acronyms to quickly note what is happening and being said.

- Cover a range of observations. In addition to documenting events and informal conversations, note people's body language, moods, or attitudes; the general environment; interactions among participants; ambiance; and other information that could be relevant.

- Add a second column or use the other side of the page to record your own perspectives or initial interpretations.

The participant observer might not be able to record the observations by taking notes. Sometimes a voice recorder or videotape might be preferred. But whether written, typed, or recorded, the observations should concern what has occurred in specific settings within the context

---

7. Miles and Huberman, *Qualitative Data Analysis*, 66.

8. Adapted and supplemented from Mack et al., *Qualitative Research Methods*, 24.

of the project. When recording, transcriptions of the tapes will be necessary.[9] Possibly, the researcher can listen to the tapes and take notes at the same time. Advantages of taking notes during the actual event include being able to notice aspects that otherwise fall outside the range of the recording device. Advantages of a recording device include the details it will record. You will not miss the next sentence because you are busy writing down something previously said. A video recorder also will capture gestures and facial expressions that a voice recorder will miss.

Merriam cautions,

> Ideally, verbatim transcription of recorded interviews provides the best database for analysis. Be forewarned, however, that even with good keyboard skills, transcribing interview is a tedious and time-consuming project. You can of course hire someone to transcribe tapes for you. This can be expensive, and there are trade-offs in doing it. You do not get the intimate familiarity with your data that doing your own transcribing affords. Also, a transcriber is likely to be unfamiliar with terminology and, not having conducted the interview, will not be able to fill in places where the tape is of poor quality. If someone else has transcribed your tape, it is a good idea to read through the interview while listening to it in order to correct errors and fill in blanks. However, hiring someone to transcribe allows you to spend time analyzing your data instead of transcribing.[10]

Immediately after the event, you may be tired and need to go home, but this is the best time to assess your notes and fill in the gaps. Do not trust your memory to somehow hold onto vital information through the night. At this time, expand your shorthand notes into complete sentences so that anyone who reads them will understand your notes. Identify questions that are still unanswered and require follow-up. Save your notes, preferably as a computer file, in a safe and secure place. Make a copy. Label the notes for easy access and filing. These notes are now a data set. Anyone should be able to come and interpret or audit your interpretations from this data set.

Below is a fictive example of a partial field note that emerges from past experiences. In the note, the observer used "MO" ("my observation") to indicate her initial interpretations. She could easily use her

9. See Patton, *Qualitative Research*, 382, Exhibit 7.4, for tips for tape-recording interviews.

10. Merriam, *Qualitative Research*, 88.

initials instead. In my opinion, the two-column method is clearer to understand and would facilitate moving from note to a fuller description. The following example is difficult to interpret. Even the author may have difficulty understanding the inscriptions if she does not elaborate the notes shortly after the event.

---

p.2
teens down hall
RT in wc/Ø write//OT doing it//watch OT ✱
??room dark, lites ON//OK   ---MO//not not
---Teen parents 2
--bleeding markers!✱?
no one distracted, all involved
TS - cell arghhh
--he left!! MO//maybe a prob/other reason?

The following digital file represents the typed notes recorded one hour after the event. Helpfully, the researcher converted the note to the two-column method. The two columns allow the note-taker to distinguish clearly between participant comments and actions and the researcher's initial interpretations. From this digital file, the researcher can easily move to narrative description even weeks after the event. The following exercise is adapted from Ammerman:[11]

---

11. Ammerman, et al., *Studying Congregations*, 209–10.

Observation of Congregational Timeline Exercise

Date: Sunday, 9/13/09
Time: 7 pm–9 pm
Place: Maple Street Place: A Community Devoted to God
Occasion: The study took place during the month of September marking the congregation's Jubilee Celebration. The congregation started in September 1959 after a divisive split with St. John Lutheran Church.

The DMin project participation team was asked to informally interview the others during the exercise. The question: "How does this exercise make you feel?"

Facts about the congregation were recorded using markers above the timeline. Everyone was invited to go to the wall and write their memories of events. Below the line, other community facts were recorded including regional and national events. SJ, who brought her laptop and works at the local library, assisted anyone with dates and details about community, regional, and national events. SJ did not prompt anyone's memory, only responded when asked. People were encouraged to check with SJ about the exact date.

At 7:05, pastor LM explained how the exercise would work, how it fit with the congregation's Jubilee celebration, and how the information would be used to facilitate her DMin project. Everyone was asked to mark the date when they joined the congregation or record their earliest memory in their life at the church. Each person added their initials to all their entries. They were asked to recall any important events in the life of the church especially those happenings that brought them personal blessings.

Initial Observations

Singles group planned an outing. Communication problem??? 2 board members out of town. ZT uneasy about project stayed. The whole DMin participation group is here. They were prompt. I arrived ten minutes early to make sure all was in order and to make sure I was relaxed.

Observation of Congregational Timeline Exercise

If persons added to someone else's entry, they were to use a different color pen and initial the addition. Each person was encouraged to share their valuable experiences in the life of the community.

It took about 10 minutes before everyone became fully engaged in the process. 5 sub-groups seemed to be working as a team, 2 couples worked together, everyone else worked independently or occasionally engaged in conversation.

Laughter or loud comments interpreted as jest were recorded 27 times.

The back of the sanctuary is not well lit. The architect's design depended upon the skylights.

LY's eyes were wet and red as she worked alone.

SJ noted that only 7 people asked for her assistance.

The 3 teens escaped down the hallway by 7:20. They did not return.

RT, in a wheelchair depended upon OT to write.

AW twice went to the back pew to sit and watch.

Only one table with markers. Maybe too far away.

TS received a cell phone call and left the room for about 15 minutes.

. . .

Although 3 couples remained after the exercise to talk for another half hour, the rest of the group left around 9:15 pm.

EE & JY talked in the parking lot. It was not observed as to the content of these conversations.

Initial Observations

Everyone seems happy and engaged.
Good hearted teasing.

LY is crying. Not allergies. Seems to be recalling a sad experience. Not tears of joy.

. . .

Only 3 seem to be asking questions. The others are seemingly too involved with the timeline themselves. Keep watching this.

Teens stayed longer than I anticipated. Parents made them stay I guess.

Accessibility issue. Does anyone else notice the problem? Doesn't appear so. Are they too familiar? What if this were a visitor?

OT not writing own reflections— only a recorder for RT.

. . .

Lighting an issue for older folk???

Didn't check to see if markers bleed through!!!

Everyone appears to be taking the project seriously.

TS left. Hope there is not a problem.

AW—thoughtful? Tired? What? Seems to be content.

The timeline is filling up nicely. Most stuff during the last decade of course. RT spending lots of time on the founding. Wonder if she remembers the split?

TS is back. Now asking people the interview question.

Observation of Congregational Timeline Exercise

The timeline was left on the wall throughout September and October so that anyone could add or elaborate. 14 people not in the original group added 17 comments. From the original group, 27 additional comments were added. After a fellowship meal on Sunday, November 8, 2009, people were asked to post stickers on the timeline that identified red—the most significant event in the life of the church, green—second, yellow—third. One sticker of each color per person. Anyone in the congregation was allowed to participate. It happened quickly and demographic information was not recorded. 51 red stickers, 49 green stickers, and 40 yellow stickers were attached to the timeline.

If you take the time now to convert your notes into a descriptive narrative, it will save you time when writing the chapter that reports your results. By describing now what happened and what you learned during the observation, interview, activity, or focus group, your first draft of your thesis will be fresher and more accurately reflect the people and activities of the setting.

VERBATIM: A SPECIFIC TYPE OF FIELD NOTE

Verbatim reports differ from case studies by being an exact recall of a conversation in context. Clinical Pastoral Education (CPE) programs and similar pastoral settings often utilize verbatims. They are excellent tools in analyzing motivations and behaviors, and they can help you in learning to be more sensitive and responsive to the needs of people. The verbatim permits you to discover the meanings of theological terms and categories in the lives of persons with whom you are working. The verbatim helps anchor reflections in concrete experiences. A verbatim contains information on backgrounds, actual experience, interpretations, plans for further action and responses. It is a report on conversations and meta-communications of a particular ministry encounter. It is a transcript from memory. The format of a verbatim is:

INTRODUCTION

Time, place, brief description of the person (maintain confidentiality), your relationship to the person (how you got to talk with the person; how long you have known him or her, and in what capacity), the context of the conversation including the purpose for the meeting (what you thought of and felt about them and their situation before this conversation), and any other details or circumstances that are relevant.

TRANSCRIPT

Words, body language, emotions felt and perceived, actions. The way the event is remembered is fertile ground for interpretation. Be as exact as possible (e.g., make notes as soon as possible after the encounter). Record the conversation, including pauses, non-verbal communications, facial expressions, etc., insofar as they help catch the "tone" of the experience. If the conversation is longer than can be conveniently reported, give highlights, being sure to indicate where breaks occur, and summarize missing parts. The effort in this section of the verbatim is to be purely descriptive, omitting explanation of why you did what you did. This effort calls for candor that will be difficult to achieve at times. An example of a verbatim: (Number the responses. Disguise names. Don't try to "doctor" your report to make it look better. Rather, in the analysis section indicate changes you would make.) S1: How are you today, Mrs. Doe? (intern) D1: Fine, how are you? (Mrs. Doe) S2: We missed you in church Sunday. D2: I missed being there (blushing) . . . etc.

REFLECTION

What is happening? What rubs you wrong? What makes you uncomfortable? Uncertain? Frustrated? Angry? What issues are unresolved?

ASSESSMENT

The following list of questions can enable you to examine your angle of interpretation during the evaluation stage of the project: (1) What took place? Summarize your experience during this encounter, including a description of the feelings, turning points, and/or tensions you had during the dialogue. (2) Where do you and the person now stand in your relationship? (3) What was effective? What would you do differently? Compare and contrast your intention when you entered the room with the outcome (discrepancy between intention and performance, shift in expectations, etc.) (4) What were your responses? An evaluation of your responses, trying to identify your dominant feelings during the conversations, is not an invitation to probe the depths of your unconscious, but a simple effort to catch the feelings on or near the surface (i.e., is this a person who makes you feel angry, happy, frustrated?). What did you see as the person's needs, and did your responses get at these needs? Are there any points that strike you as particularly significant now; any responses you would certainly want to omit or do differently (indicate by your coding scheme, e.g., D2)? Present alternatives: What other ways of responding were available? (5) What does this interview reveal about the person and about you? What kind of person are you in this interview? (6) What effect did this interview have on the person? How did he/she feel when it was over, and why?

GOALS, LEARNINGS, AND FUTURE INVOLVEMENT

What goals and plans will you have for your next meeting? What did you learn by studying this relationship?

THEOLOGICAL ANALYSIS AND EVALUATION

(1) What theological doctrine, problem, question, principle, issue, etc., is demonstrated or suggested in this verbatim? Where was God present?(2) What are the theological dynamics of the actual situation (grace, redemption, forgiveness, salvation, hope, etc.)? Reflect theologically on the encounter, identifying implied or explicit theological themes that emerged. (3) How has this report helped you integrate your experience and theological understanding? State the questions or learning issues that emerge for you from this ministry encounter, and your reflections upon it. How does this relate to your Learning Covenant?[12] (4) What are you learning about self and style of ministry? As a tool for the discovery of your ministerial style, strengths, and weaknesses, the verbatim focuses on one specific, concrete example of your style. Describe your functioning as a minister, noting whether you identified and followed the person's feelings and responded pastorally to her/his needs. The ver-

---

12. A Learning Covenant is a document that details a social contract between a teacher, student, and participants in a contextual education environment. For example, student interns working for churches who are allowing their ministerial activities to be counted as field education will write a document that governs all the expectations and requirements of the parties involved. See, Wickett, *How to Use.*

batim indicates what you did, in fact, not what you would have liked to have done. It is a powerful weapon against wishful thinking.

When describing triangulation, observation is the only tool I listed for the researcher's perspective. While there are other ways to gauge your own understanding of the project as it develops, the primary way to do this is to take extensive field notes about the process. The field notes become a data set. You will analyze your observation notes (sometimes called a field journal) the same way you would analyze any other field note, document, transcript, questionnaire result, or interview data.

7

Analyze This

I T IS DIFFICULT TO separate the activities of data collection and data interpretation. Data interpretation begins the first day you begin gathering data. For the DMin researcher, that first day occurred before the DMin project was even conceived; the pastor-student was already striving to understand the context through the course of ministerial activities and practices. The previous chapters indicated ways to begin the interpretive process even in the midst of the data collection phase of the project. To separate the processes is messy and ambiguous. But the processes are formally described here as distinct actions.

Once you have gathered your data, how will you analyze the data? "Data analysis is the process of bringing order, structure, and meaning to the complicated mass of qualitative data that the researcher generates during the research process."[1] Qualitative analysis requires some creativity, for the challenge is to place the raw data into logical, meaningful categories, to examine data in a holistic fashion, and to find a way to communicate the interpretation to others. Sitting down in front of a pile of notes and transcriptions can be a daunting task. It can involve hundreds of pages. Each of the tools above will generate several pages of field notes, transcripts, and archival documents. Some mechanism for storing, organizing, and summarizing large amounts of data needs to be pre-determined before the data is ever collected.

Data sources are often seen as texts. Whether the data source is a set of observations, artifacts, transcripts, or something else, analysts often act as translators and exegetes. A hermeneutical spiral of inquiry

1. Swinton and Mowat, *Practical Theology*, 57. The most comprehensive book on qualitative data analysis I have found is Miles and Huberman, *Qualitative Data Analysis*.

is utilized to examine the parts in light of the whole and back again. Oscillating between the bits of data and the whole context allows a process of updating, refining, and modifying interpretations as an ongoing process.

Be specific in your methodology section about assessing the worth of the set of activities or project according to its impacts on the primary audience for whom the project was formulated. You will begin by locating yourself within the larger framework of the project. Next, you will describe and organize the data in a way that facilitates interpretation.

Finally, you must exercise caution in claiming too much. Recall the limitations and delimitations set forth in your design of the project. Tentative language is best when offering conclusions and making assessments about the results of the project.

THICK DESCRIPTION

Thick description is a term made popular by anthropologist Clifford Geertz in his classic work *The Interpretation of Cultures*.[2] A thick description takes the data you have collected and gives a detailed interpretation of those data through your three angles of evaluation, taking the reader into the setting being described. A thick description goes beyond a simple narration that merely delineates the information ("thin" description), but explores the deeper and often hidden meanings behind the words, gestures, actions, and practices observed during the project. A thick description explores the possible meanings of a sign. For example, if someone tells me, "the door is open," I have to make an interpretation of its meaning. Is she telling me to close the door behind me, to be quiet because someone outside might hear me, or that she is receptive to my inquiry? Context determines the meaning. A thick description will make explicit the fullness of your understanding of the implied range of meaning of the social settings, actions, or words.

The research process you engaged in produced a voluminous amount of information. Your next task involves capturing the data using patterns, categories, or themes, and then interpreting this information by using some schema. As you are writing and reflecting on the large data sets, you can step back and consider what you have learned. Were

---

2. Geertz, *Interpretation of Cultures*. Lindbeck, *Church*, also uses the term "thick description" when describing his cultural-linguistic approach to hermeneutics.

there repeated concerns, topics, expressions, stories, or claims? Were there contradictions between the data sources? Do the words and actions of the participants correlate? Your description of the data not only helps you manage the stacks of paper on your desk, but also leads you to analysis and interpretation. Your descriptions of the data allow the reader to understand the basis for your analysis and interpretation.

DOCUMENTARY ANALYSIS[3]

Documents such as field notes, verbatim, transcriptions, and interview data all need to be unpacked and analyzed. Before you begin organizing the data, read and re-read the data multiple times on different occasions. Becoming familiar with the data will enable you to take the next steps more easily. Also, understand the context in which the document was formed. What can be claimed based on a particular document? If too much is claimed by over-reliance upon a particular document, interpretation is skewed. What do the data mean? Are they relevant to the case under consideration? Do the data complement or challenge themes that emerge from interviews, field observations, and other tools?

Moschella suggests three ways to read the data.[4] A literal reading will highlight particular words, phrases, language, interruptions, and gestures. An interpretive reading of the data allows you to select and organize the document according to "implied or inferred meanings." Finally, she suggests a reflexive reading that brings to bear your per-

---

3. There are several software packages available that facilitate documentary analysis. The most popular is QSR's Nvivo at http://www.qsrinternational.com/. Other common programs are ETHNOGRAPH at http://www.QualisResearch.com, and ATLAS at http://www.atlasti.com/index.html (accessed October 29, 2009). See also, Lewins and Silver, *Using Software*, and Fielding, "Computer Applications."

Patton, *Qualitative Research*, 443, lists "three basic types of qualitative analysis software: Text retrievers, code-and-retrieve packages, and theory-builders."

The limitations for DMin students are two-fold. First, most ministers do not have the experience setting up the software to make it an efficient use of time. The software is only as good as the person who sets up the analysis. Secondly, although there are licenses available from schools or from QSR for only one semester, the cost of buying the program is usually prohibitive for most ministers. For most ministers, a word processing program will be able to handle most tasks like searching for strings of text, creating macros, and using MS Word's "spike" feature. Embedding code words within the file enables word processors to operate more efficiently when coding data.

4. Moschella, *Ethnography*, 172–3. See also Mason, *Qualitative Researching*, who utilizes these same three categories by making specific applications to each method she discusses.

sonal feelings and understandings of the data. These categories might be suggestive of how you organize your data. A literal reading of the data would gather quotes, the sequence of an interaction, and other formal structures. Since a literal reading of the data may not be possible, you will need to indicate how your interpretive reading of the data fits into the overall schema. You will note what you think the data means and represents. You will indicate what inferences you think the data is making. Finally, the reflexive reading will help you locate your role as researcher in the generation and interpretation of the data.[5]

You will need to be cautious when unpacking large volumes of data. Two problems that often occur involve multiple meanings and imposed meanings. As you make sense of the emerging themes from the data, another set of eyes will prove helpful. They may be able to see that an event or an expression might signify more than the surface meaning. Likewise, a second person looking at the raw data might realize that you are imposing your own biases upon the interpretation rather than letting the data speak for itself. Using peer researchers, performing member checking by participants, and triangulating your analysis with the other angles of interpretation will help you avoid these snares.

Three Analytical Frames: Themes, Slippage, Silences

I have recommended a multi-methods approach of evaluation that allows triangulation. Three analytical frames of reference will emerge from your triangulating the data, namely, the insider's, outsider's, and yours. As you compare and contrast the angles, you will find areas of agreement and disagreement. Your analysis must account for both the convergence and divergence in the data. One way to organize the data is to discuss the areas of significant overlap as themes or patterns, the areas of disagreement as slippage, and the "realities" not represented in your findings as silences.

"The principle of convergence suggests that when things fit together they will lead to a classification system for the data. What begins to emerge is a 'manageable and accessible package' in which emergent themes move to the forefront. Such themes can be judged by two criteria: Internal Homogeneity (the extent to which the data that belong in a certain category hold together); External Heterogeneity (the extent to

5. Mason, *Qualitative Researching*, 115.

which differences among categories are distinct and clear."[6] The greater degree of convergence attained through the triangulation of multiple data sources, methods, investigators, or theories, the greater the confidence in the observed findings. Similarly, if you find disconfirming evidence or slippage, then you will need to openly describe and interpret the divergent paths the data suggests.

The most common and easiest part of the process is generating themes, categories, and patterns. This is the first step where you impose meaning and generate an emerging theory. Data theme analysis involves a sorting, organizing, and indexing of the material that enables you to locate internally consistent patterns that often fit within existing knowledge. Creswell states that pattern theory contains an interconnected set of concepts and relationships, but it does not require causal statements.[7] The fact that something correlates with something else does not mean the first caused the second or vice versa. Causal assumptions may be tentatively asserted, but further proofs will be warranted.

Describing categories, Merriam notes that

> Categories should *reflect the purpose of the research.* . . . Categories should be *exhaustive*; that is, you should be able to place all data that you decided were important or relevant to the study in a category or subcategory. Categories should be *mutually exclusive.* A particular unit of data should fit into only one category. If the exact same unit of data can be placed into more than one category, more conceptual work needs to be done to refine your categories. Categories should be *sensitizing.* The naming of the category should be as sensitive as possible to what is in the data. An outsider should be able to read the categories and gain some sense of their nature. . . . Categories should be *conceptually congruent.* This means that the same level of abstraction should characterize all categories at the same level.[8]

Van Manen offers three approaches for identifying themes, which he describes as "the structures of experience."[9] (1) Find the phrase that communicates the fundamental meaning of the text as a whole. (2) Select the statements that are particularly essential and revealing about the

6. Miller-McLemore and Myers, "Doctorate of Ministry," 18.

7. Creswell, *Research Design,* 94.

8. Merriam, *Qualitative Research,* 183–84.

9. Van Manen, *Researching Lived Experience,* 79. On pages 87–88, he gives a detailed definition of theme from a phenomenological perspective.

phenomenon being described. (3) Examine every sentence's contribution to the phenomenon being described.[10] The identified themes need to remain true to the essential quality of the experience described. If the phenomenon would change by deleting a theme from the experience, then we know that such a theme is essential to the meaning of the phenomenon described. Van Manen also lists four aspects by which people experience the world, namely, spatiality, corporeality, temporality, and relationality.[11] These four aspects together form a unity of experience and might prove useful when assessing your data. Van Manen emphasizes how the central meaning of something is often multi-layered and multi-dimensional, which invites continued reflective analysis of the structural and thematic aspects of experience.[12] Therefore, thick description is employed as a point of entry into the layers of meaning that are present within the narratives.

One common theme found in most research projects is "Rival Interpretations." For example, when studying the effectiveness of a new liturgical style, supporting data emerges from the focus groups, your field notes, and the opinions from your independent expert. The supporting data substantiates what you anticipated to see. Concurrently, you also hear alternative explanations that may contradict what you expected or may at least explain the event differently. Several bits of data may support one or more differing theories. These rival interpretations must be gathered and interpreted.

Finally, pattern analysis seeks to avoid the common pitfalls of seeking precise measurements to determine definitions and "linguistic arbitrariness."[13] Therefore, definitions are loosely delineated and are not intended to replace complex concepts. Consequently, interpretation involves analogies, paradigmatic examples of what the concepts are and are not, and plausible generalizations from particular instances employed in the analysis.[14] The distillation of themes always falls short of the goal and is at best a simplification or a reduction of the deeper meanings embedded in the texts. Formulating themes and patterns is just one way of capturing, make sense of, and communicating the phenomenon being analyzed.

10. Ibid., 92–93.
11. Ibid., 101.
12. Ibid., 78.
13. Scriven, "Philosophical Inquiry Methods," 136.
14. Ibid.

Slippage asks, "What is not congruent in the data?" "What is contradictory in nature?" Slippage seeks disconfirmation of findings. The search for rival explanations involves looking for other ways of organizing the data that might lead to different findings. It is a matter of considering the weight of evidence and looking for the best fit between data and analysis. It is important to report whatever alternative explanations are considered and tested during data analysis. Considering the instances and cases that do not fit the pattern increases understanding of qualitative patterns. These are the "exceptions that prove the rule," or for evaluation purposes, cases that elucidate the findings. Examples that do not fit help clarify the limits and meaning of the primary patterns.

The readers of your report will be able to make their own decisions about the plausibility of alternate explanations and the reasons that deviant cases do not fit within dominant patterns.[15] Patton states elsewhere,

> A common misunderstanding about triangulation is that the point is to demonstrate that different data sources or inquiry approaches yield essentially the same result. But the point is really to *test for* such consistency. Different kinds of data may yield somewhat different results because different types of inquiry are sensitive to different real-world nuances. Thus, understanding inconsistencies in findings across different kinds of data can be illuminative. Finding such inconsistencies ought not be viewed as weakening the credibility of results, but rather as offering opportunities for deeper insight into the relationship between inquiry approach and the phenomenon under study.[16]

Intertextual methods within discourse communities also allow for the analysis of slippage by looking for internal coherence, patterns, contrasts, and intersections. The significance of a speaker's slippages is a subject for later interpretation. A secondary analysis could also be conducted by asking the interviewee to verify the researcher's interpretations. Van Manen uses slippage as a springboard into a second interview.[17] He encourages continued conversations and interviews until the participants are satisfied with your analysis of their perspectives.

The question that silence asks is "What is left unsaid that needs to be examined?" Van Manen states that nothing is more silent than that

---

15. Patton, *How to Use*, 159.

16. Patton, *Qualitative Research*, 248.

17. Van Manen, *Researching Lived Experience*, 114.

which is taken for granted or self-evident.[18] He notes how silences fall into different categories. People just do not speak about something for various reasons. Sometimes silence is part of who we are. Some silences are epistemological. These unspeakable silences are the beginning of interpretation. Epistemological silences may occur because of the linguistic ability of the speaker, the form of the discourse, or the setting and timing of the discourse. Others may be able to give voice to these silences. Maybe, at another time and place, the participant can also give voice to these silences.

Omissions are also silences. The gaps in the story may prove to be the most significant aspect of the narrative. Other silences occur when only one side of an argument is being told or a narrative is being reinterpreted in such a way as to silence other voices. Bringing the data into conversation with other data sets helps fill in the gaps. In an unpublished pilot study, I interviewed 17 preachers using a narrative approach. I asked one question, "Tell me the story of your life." All the preachers interviewed engaged their narratives seemingly eager to share their lives. During the last days of the data collection process, I became aware that one of the preachers was telling me something new. He was describing his family, his relationship with his wife, and telling the history of his two daughters. After all the interviews were collected, I reviewed the other 16 interviews listening for any mention of family. Although all 17 preachers were married with children, only one brought up the subject. That silence was deafening. The purpose of my study did not relate to family systems and dynamics, but a thesis is waiting for someone to explore the silence in my data.[19]

Olson describes silences as what occurs when we tell "cover stories."[20] A cover story is one we believe will be acceptable to society. We often silence the stories we believe will be unacceptable even when they are deemed more "real" or authentic to our experiences. We discount what experience teaches and tell the cover stories instead.

In the new world of social networking, we see avatars, second world, and plastic identities becoming commonplace. However, virtual identities only highlight what has been true in human societies for millennia. People often create public personas that hide their private selves.

18. Ibid., 112–4.
19. Sensing, *African American Preaching*.
20. Olson, "Conceptualizing Narrative Authority," 128.

There is a plethora of reasons, some honorable and others not. These plastic identities contribute to the silences in people's stories. For example, preachers often tell their stories, especially call stories, as a witness from the pulpit and in public. Their personal stories become rhetorical devices with homiletical aims. In one sense, they are cover stories. The public story overshadows the actual event, even if the preacher is asked in private during a research session.

As a segue into the next section, note that coding your data introduces silences in your research. This is an inherent limitation to all coding methods (even when software is used).[21] By imposing a particular way of seeing the data, categorizing the themes, you are framing the data in a particular way.[22] It becomes difficult to see the data outside the frame. By utilizing one framing lens, you have imposed a powerful conceptual grid that is difficult to escape. The grid is necessary to organize the data, but it also deflects attention away from uncategorized words and actions that become silences in your analysis. Therefore, secondary analysis of the data that looks for uncategorized activities and themes is needed. Ways to approach the secondary analysis include examining the literature for a different theoretical perspective, seeking counsel from another researcher or advisor, and re-examining the data for large sections that have minimal codes applied. Secondary analysis of this sort is similar to looking for deviant cases.

Coding Data

Collecting and identifying themes is the primary way qualitative researchers process and analyze data.[23] The researcher has collected data from three angles of evaluation. That data has been recorded or transferred to field notes, transcripts, and interpretive summaries. Coding (sometimes

21. Patton, *Qualitative Research*, 57, warns, "Although software programs now exist to facilitate working with large amounts of narrative data and substantial guidance can be offered about the steps and processes of content analysis, making sense of multiple interview transcripts and pages of field notes cannot be reduced to a formula or even a standard series of steps. There is no equivalent of a statistical significance test or factor score to tell the analyst when results are important or what quotations fit together under the same theme. Finding a way to *creatively synthesize* and present findings is one of the challenges of qualitative analysis."

22. The oft-quoted phrase, "a way of seeing is always a way of not seeing" is an axiom from Burke, *Permanence and Change*, 49.

23. See Berg, *Qualitative Research Methods*, chapter 11 for an extensive description of coding.

called "indexing," "tagging," or "labeling") is a way to get a handle on the raw data so that it is more accessible for interpretation. Coding assigns units of meaning to descriptions, quotes, texts, etc. Always keep in mind that you are preparing the data in such a way as to facilitate its use in addressing your project's problem and purpose. Additionally, do not let your coding system oversimplify your data. Complex social dynamics and interactions cannot be reduced to simple terms without a loss of meaning and significance. It is not the words or sentences that count but the meaning of the words in a specific context. While the coding process enhances your ability to manage the data, keep the complexity of your context in full view before, during, and after your detailed analysis.[24]

To begin with, store and protect your data carefully. Choose a method that allows someone else to locate and describe each piece of data filed in your system. Ideally, the data is coded and stored in such a way that you can retrieve information in the raw data that otherwise is not accessible.

You will want to start by getting a systematic overview of your data so that you have a clear and comprehensive idea of its coverage and scope. A first attempt at determining the codes you will use begins during the writing of your theoretical and theological constructs chapter, or when writing the problem and purpose statements. Do not hesitate to re-categorize more than once. Your data will be the primary place codes emerge. Do not force a coding system onto the data that somehow bends it to fit your presuppositions. "The analyst should be ready to redefine or discard codes when they look inapplicable, overbuilt, empirically ill-fitting, or overly abstract."[25] Being creative and playing with the data may highlight associations that would remain hidden at first glance.

Determine the main themes that emerge from the categories. Words, phrases, or events that appear to be similar can be grouped into the same category. These categories may be modified or replaced during subsequent stages of analysis. Even when you have narrowly defined categories, some items may find a place in multiple locations. You will want to code your data as soon as possible, maybe as early as the next day after the field note or transcript is taken. If you wait until all the data is gathered before you go back, the mountains of paper will be discour-

---

24. For a detailed example of coding see Miles and Huberman, *Qualitative Data Analysis*, 57–65.

25. Ibid., 65.

aging. One caution—be careful not to allow a decision made during the first rounds of data generation to overpower the possible insights that are generated in the last stages of data collection.

Code the themes into sub-themes (second level coding). Miles and Huberman call this "pattern coding" and suggest four important functions: "1) It reduces large amounts of data into a smaller number of analytic units. 2) It gets the researcher into analysis during data collection, so that later fieldwork can be more focused. 3) It helps the researcher elaborate a cognitive map, an evolving, more integrated schema for understanding local incidents and interactions. 4) For multicase studies, it lays the groundwork for cross-case analysis by surfacing common themes and directional processes."[26]

As you read your data, apply your code in the appropriate places, maybe in the margin of the document. At the same time, record that code in an index. You might use identifiers like document name, date, page number, paragraph number, line number. The coding system also makes cross-referencing possible. The index becomes the primary way you can retrieve data.

Tesch provides eight steps to consider:[27]

1. Get a sense of the whole. Read all of the transcriptions carefully. Perhaps jot down some ideas as they come to mind.

2. Pick one document (one interview)—the most interesting, the shortest, the one on the top of the pile. Go through it, asking yourself, What is this about? Do not think about the "substance" of the information, but rather its underlying meaning. Write thoughts in the margin.

3. When you have completed this task for several informants, make a list of all topics. Cluster together similar topics. Form these topics into columns that might be arrayed as major topics, unique topics, and leftovers.

4. Now take this list and go back to your data. Abbreviate the topics as codes and write the codes next to the appropriate segments of the text. Try out this preliminary organizing scheme to see whether new categories and codes emerge.

---

26. Ibid., 69.

27. As quoted in Creswell, *Research Design*, 192.

5. Find the most descriptive wording for your topics and turn them into categories. Look for reducing your total list of categories by grouping topics that relate to each other. Perhaps draw lines between your categories to show interrelationships.

6. Make a final decision on the abbreviation for each category and alphabetize these codes.

7. Assemble the data material belonging to each category in one place and perform a preliminary analysis.

8. If necessary, recode your existing data.

Finally, when you report your data, various ways exist to display your codes to enhance the reader's access. Graphs, charts, tables, and matrices are commonly employed. Clearly label your exhibits. Describe the nature and function of the exhibit in the body of the chapter. Remember, the only reason you are using an exhibit is to increase communication. Overuse of exhibits clutters your writing and detracts from your purpose.

Camp, in his thesis "Bridging the Generation Gap," took extensive field notes as a participant observer. He cited Merriam, *Qualitative Research and Case Study Applications in Education*, as a theoretical source for his protocol, and Barney Glasser and William Strauss, *The Discovery of Grounded Theory*, as the theoretical basis for his coding method.[28] He describes his note-taking as follows:

> Immediately after each session, I wrote careful field notes, recording my observations about the characteristics of the participants, their style of interacting with each other, the content and manner of their conversations, as well as more subtle factors, such as silences, body language, and tone of voice. In addition, after each session I recorded observations of my own behavior, to practice the reflexive awareness that my participation changes that which I am observing. I dated and typed all of my field notes, following a standard format, and saved them in an electronic file. These field notes served as a data set for constructing an interpretation of what was happening within the group over time as a result of my project.... In the process of writing and reflecting on my field notes, I began developing a coding scheme, the final iteration of which is represented in table 1:

28. Merriam, *Qualitative Research*, 94–104, and Glasser and Strauss, *Discovery of Grounded Theory*.

TABLE 1. CODING SCHEME FOR FIELD NOTES	
1.	New understanding can lead to greater intergenerational respect.
1.1	Explicit statements relating to new understanding leading to greater respect
1.2	Stereotypes: how one generation speaks about the other
1.3	Story-telling: references to the power of story telling, or sharing through stories per se
1.4	Responses to teaching: which themes from the session content resonate with the group
1.4.1	Ephesians 2
1.4.2	Generational Patterns
1.4.3	"Myth" of White Station as a loving congregation
2.	Impacting the larger congregation
2.1	Expression of desire for project to impact church
2.2	Replicating interaction from project sessions in other small groups
2.3	Promoting the project "up front"

From these categories, I generated an interpretation of my project's effectiveness and compared that interpretation with the other two methods of evaluation.[29]

Concept mapping is another way to graphically display your data.[30] "Concept maps are graphical tools for organizing and representing knowledge. They include concepts, usually enclosed in circles or boxes of some type, and relationships between concepts indicated by a connecting line linking two concepts. . . . Another characteristic of concept maps is that the concepts are represented in a hierarchical fashion with the most inclusive, most general concepts at the top of the map and the more specific, less general concepts arranged hierarchically below."[31]

As categories develop, devise an "audit trail" that identifies the data as it is moved and relocated from place to place. An audit trail provides

29. Camp, "Bridging the Generation Gap," 47–48.

30. *Cmap* is a free access web site that assists in constructing concept maps. Florida Institute, "Cmap Tools."

31. Novak and Cañas, "Theory Underlying," 1.

your reader a path for evaluating your process and clarifying your conclusions, thus increasing the project's face validity. Likewise, an audit trail enables you to recall your own decision-making process. Often, projects occur over several months. Decisions made early in the research will more aptly cohere with your later work when you can verify your analysis.

Recognize that various approaches (grounded theory, case study, ethnography, etc.) will have domain-specific ways that data analysis is routinely accomplished and therefore accepted by the research community. For example, grounded theory demonstrates how analysis is the interplay between researchers and data. Therefore, grounded theory offers a framework for coding procedures that enhances standardization and rigor in the analytical process. "Grounded theory is meant to 'build theory rather than test theory.' It seeks to 'provide researchers with analytical tools for handling masses of raw data.' It strives to help qualitative analysts 'consider alternative meanings of phenomenon.' It emphasizes being 'systematic and creative simultaneously.' Finally, it elucidates 'the concepts that are the building blocks of theory.'"[32] Therefore, your particular approach may have domain-specific ways to code data, and it behooves you to abide by the rules.

STEPS IN DOCUMENT CONTENT ANALYSIS[33]

1. *Determine which types of documents would be the most valuable for your research question.* Would an analysis of sermon transcripts help understand the church's or synagogue's character and identity? Do the financial records adequately describe the congregation's resources? Can an examination of church photo albums help uncover its present dysfunctional relationships?

2. *Identify which items are indicators of the themes and questions you are exploring.* Does the way the senior minister is addressed in worship services indicate how the church perceives her? Would counting the number of times a lay leader speaks or is present in front of the congregation define his power in the group? Can you compare records of membership, contributions, and participation in missions to determine the congregation's level of commitment?

---

32. Patton, *Qualitative Research*, 127, citing Corbin and Strauss, *Basics of Qualitative Research*.

33. Ammerman, et al., *Studying Congregations*, 211.

Do you need to look or listen for the exact words such as "love" and "family," or will you count how often a statement refers to these ideas without using the words explicitly?

3. *Decide how you will select the specific documents to be analyzed.* Will you look at every record, pamphlet, or newsletter issue? Should you randomly select a number of documents from each month or each year? Would it be best to examine only the committee notes from the groups most involved in the issue at hand? Think about what group of documents will give you a fair picture of the congregation, and be careful not to select in such a way as to skew your results (for instance, analyzing orders of worship only for first Sundays in a church that has Communion each first Sunday).

4. *Construct a set form, questionnaire, or code book to record the items you are tracking.* If you are looking for items that indicate a congregation's theology, for instance, you might want to start with a list of the major themes you recall. Then as you read or listen, you can add to your list. Each time you encounter a reference to a given theme, note what was said, what kind of reference it was (Bible verse, story, testimony, and so forth), when it occurred (date), in what context (Sunday morning, special occasion, and the like), and other information you think might be relevant. Your form may have a line for each occurrence, with columns for theme, date, type of reference, and so forth.

5. *Once the form is constructed, do a "test run" of your instrument on a document or tape to see how it works.* Does the form allow enough room for your written comments? Are there other key words or ideas you want to include on the form? Do you need to be more specific in what you are looking for? For instance, when examining how often a hymn appeared in old worship bulletins, would a simple yes/no checklist of the top forty favorite hymns identified by the congregation be adequate, or would you want to list every title?

6. *After you, or members of the study team, have examined a document, you may want to ask another person to perform the same task and then compare the results for greater accuracy.* Have you interpreted certain statements or figures as another person would? Are your criteria for coding and assigning a particular item to one category

clear and well defined, so others can duplicate your work? If there are differences, you may need to discuss and revise the criteria of your content analysis.

7. *Finally, construct a table of results to summarize your findings.* The goal will be to quantify, to count or give a number value to, the occurrences of various events, ideas, or themes related to your research interest. How many references to God's justice have you counted, for instance, and has that number increased or decreased over time? How many announcements of events for children are contained in the newsletters you analyzed, and did that number change over time? Hints for strategies of analysis are found later in this chapter.

REPORTING DATA

After you have analyzed your data, you will report it in chapter 4 of your thesis. Although raw data might appear in an appendix, this chapter will organized the data in a readable format. Tough decisions about selection and sequence will determine if chapter 4 is drudgery or enlightening. Decisions about omitting your favorite quote will create doubt even years after your thesis has collected dust in the library. Oftentimes, the best time for figuring out what you should include occurs—to your dismay—the week after your oral defense. The same wonder happens to the preacher when recalling the sermon during Sunday's lunch. Do not fret. Monday quarterbacking is a common phenomenon.

Description and quoting from interviews, questionnaires, and transcripts is the foundation of qualitative research. Patton advises, "Sufficient description and direct quotations should be included to allow the reader to enter into the situation and thoughts of the people represented in the report. Description should stop short, however, of becoming trivial and mundane. The reader does not have to know everything that was done or said. Focus comes from having determined what's substantively significant and providing enough detail and evidence to illuminate and make the case. . . . Yet, the description must not be so 'thin' as to remove context or meaning."[34]

The most common reporting scheme I have seen in DMin theses reports the data in a dry delineation corresponding to the angles of triangulation. These waterless descriptions pedantically state, "The following

34. Patton, *Qualitative Research*, 503.

themes emerge from my field notes . . . The independent expert reported . . . From the questionnaire given in the final session, the participants reported that . . ." Patton, after describing narrative and case study approaches for reporting data, provides the following list of options for organizing and reporting qualitative data that may refresh your work:

Analytical Framework Approaches

- Processes: Qualitative data may be organized to describe important processes. For example, an evaluation of a program may describe recruitment processes, socialization processes, decision-making and communication processes, and so on. Distinguishing important processes becomes the analytical framework for organizing qualitative descriptions.

- Issues: An analysis can be organized to illuminate key issues, often the equivalent of the primary evaluation questions, for example, variations in how participants changed as a result of the program. In a study of leadership training, we organized the qualitative report around such key issues as conflict management, negotiation skills, enhancing creativity, and effective communications—all important training issues.

- Questions: Responses to interviews can be organized question by question, especially where a standardized interviewing format was used. For example, if an evaluation includes questions about perceived strengths and perceived weaknesses, responses to these questions would be grouped together.

- Sensitizing Concepts: When sensitizing concepts such as "leadership" versus "followership" have played an important preordinate role in guiding fieldwork, the data can be organized and described through those sensitizing concepts.[35]

For example, my PhD dissertation on the topic of preaching pedagogies organized the data around the emerging metaphors and themes I uncovered.[36]

- Faith Seeking Understanding (Herald, Teacher, Bridge and Vessel, Dialogue Partner, Witness, Servant, Personal Relationship With God).

---

35. Ibid., 439

36. Sensing, *Pedagogies of Preaching.*

- Faith Relating To One Another In Community (Family, The Congregation as a Community of Faith, Marriage, Fellow Struggler, The Classroom as a Community of Faith.

- Faith Expressing Itself In The Classroom (Past Influences: Former Teachers and Preachers, Past Influences: Homiletic Literature, A Technical Pedagogy, A Developmental Pedagogy, Classroom Practices, Mentoring).

If I were to reorganize the chapter above, I would use only metaphors in a parallel construction for each of the subsections. In the final chapter of my dissertation, I interpreted this data by proposing that pedagogies of preaching are communal, formative, critical, and public activities.

Data analysis involves thick description of themes, slippages, and silences. Documentary analysis is the primary way large quantities of data are summarized, categorized, and assessed. Coding data allows you easy access to your findings so that the materials are manageable. Finally, you will want to report the data in a way that both holds your reader's attention and increases the data's credibility. In the next chapter, credibility will be discussed in detail.

8

So What?

THE QUESTION, "So WHAT?" indicts the speaker, the author, and each of us who has tried to communicate to others. It is a question of relevance. To be asked is to be judged. All of us want our words to be clear and persuasive. It helps if those words are also concise. None of us wants to be in the church boardroom defending our DMin project's relevance. Instead, we want to hear words of recognition, acceptance, gratitude, and anticipation. If a stranger asks us about our ministries on the street, we hope for an immediate nod of recognition. If our peers ask us about our projects at a conference, we desire longing looks of jealousy. When our grandchildren tell stories about us, we want our legacy to echo loudly even for the next generation. On the other end of the extreme, the question of "So what?" leads us to dream about our theses gathering dust mites and turning yellow in the lost closet of the library's archives. Or, as happened in a recent research seminar, being used as the example of "what not to do!" Shudder the thought.

At the DMin defense, the question of "So what?" is obligatory. In the last chapter of your thesis, you will anticipate the question by providing your interpretations as pragmatic articulations of the significance of your research. When your committee reads your final chapter, I foresee them saying, "Well done my good and faithful student. Here are the keys to your terminal degree." The final chapter's purpose is to answer the question, "So what?" so that you can avoid other definitions of "terminal" that sometimes find their way into the oral defense.

INTERPRETATIONS

Your interpretations will start with the description of your analysis from chapter 4 and lead you to implications, significances, and inferences for future pastoral practices. Patton defines interpretation as "going beyond the descriptive data. Interpretation means attaching significance to what was found, making sense of findings, offering explanations, drawing conclusions, extrapolating lessons, making inferences, considering meanings, and otherwise imposing order on an unruly but surely patterned world."[1] The definition is daunting. The final chapter in many theses is often the shortest because students are ill equipped and not prepared to provide interpretations to a pastoral intervention or project. Students are prepared to interpret texts, contexts, pastoral dilemmas, conflicts, and a host of other related pastoral practices, but the MDiv degree often neglects the social science methods that the DMin project thesis has employed.

Before you make your interpretations final, reflect over the whole project. Make sure all parts are in place before locking your conclusions into place. Wolcott uses the illustration of tightening the nuts and bolts on a wheelbarrow.[2] While not reading the instructions is supposedly a sign of strength, reading through all the instructions before beginning often saves time and frustration later. While the wheelbarrow is still wobbly, tighten all the screws finger tight before you apply the wrench. Tightening one bolt too tight will skew the whole and make other parts not fit precisely. The misalignment of one handle will affect how the whole functions. A wheel may look more like an ellipse than a circle. Likewise, locking into one conclusion may make other details appear eccentric, out of line, or inappropriate. Therefore, reflect over the whole before tightening your conclusions into place. Additionally, as a wheelbarrow will need to have the bolts retightened after the first few uses, so your thesis will need to re-examine its conclusions during the final editing process.

When presenting your interpretations, invite your readers into the interpretive act by granting them access to your primary data, your thought processes, and your rationales for making your conclusions. Your thesis becomes one partner in a larger conversation. Other dialogue partners include the DMin committee, the participants in your project, the local congregation where you conducted your project, future leaders and pastors who may turn to your thesis for guidance, and the ongoing literature in the field. Although the committee is the primary reader, keep the larger reading community in mind. Your committee

1. Patton, *Qualitative Research*, 480.
2. Wolcott, *Writing Up*, 47–48.

will require your interpretations to have pragmatic consequences for the larger community so that your project thesis will fulfill the intent of the DMin degree.

Furthermore, you must be careful to delimit your conclusions to situations, time periods, persons, and contexts for which the data are applicable. While you do keep the larger reading audience in mind, you remain tentative about how your interpretations might apply to their situations. (See the discussion on generalizability below.) The delimitations set forth in chapter 1 cannot be ignored. The very nature of qualitative research looks at the depth of a particular context more than the breadth of multiple contexts. Just because you are asked now to extrapolate your findings to other contexts, do not confuse boldness with arrogance.

Trustworthiness

Issues of *generalizability, validity,* and *reliability* are essential to ensure the credibility of the project and the understanding of the experiences being studied. The umbrella term for these issues in qualitative research is *trustworthiness.* The reader can "trust" the findings, and the study is worth paying attention to. Trustworthiness will be elaborated below using the terms *applicability* (and its synonyms), *dependability, credibility* (and its synonyms), and *reflexivity.* Qualitative research does not water down the standards of rigor and precision. Qualitative researchers do not want to misrepresent the people and the phenomena they are studying. While the terms *reliability, generalization,* and *validity* will be used below, the substructures of the functions of these words are being adapted for social science perspectives.[3]

Qualitative research cannot be judged by the same standards as quantitative research. Issues of validity are often talked about in terms of the natural sciences. In actuality, no "truth test" can be applied to

---

3. See Merriam, *Qualitative Research,* 198–212, for a traditional discussion of terms in a qualitative setting. See Altheide and Johnson, "Criteria for Assessing," who compare and contrast five basic positions: positivist, postpositivist, constructivist, postmodernist, and poststructuralist. The basic differences relate to whether there is a standard set of criteria for all research, no standards or criteria at all, to alternative standards and criteria for various qualitative approaches. My approach resembles a modified constructivist approach that emphasizes *trustworthiness* with a nod towards the classical criteria. My rationale for acknowledging the traditional terms is rooted in my anecdotal feel that most folks in the pew will be more familiar with the statistical language of validity and reliability.

either. Researchers and readers of qualitative research will engage in a dialectical process that will establish the value of the qualitative research product. If those to whom it was presented judge the research useful, relevant, and significant, then the research is deemed valid.[4]

Authors of qualitative research are often concerned with legitimization and acceptance of a method that is still viewed as second class by the old guard. However, they are also cautious not to present a methodology that becomes sterile, inflexible, and just as arrogant as the one they perceive has developed among the positivists. Munro suggests that, as an epistemological concept, validity assumes some absolute, fixed, and verifiable truth.[5] If the methodology is deemed appropriate in relationship to the research questions, data collection procedures, and analysis techniques, then validity questions are subservient to the methodology at hand.[6]

Applicability

External validity or *generalizability* is the degree to which findings derived from one context or under one set of conditions may be assumed to apply in other settings or under other conditions. On the one hand, generalizability is not the responsibility of the qualitative researcher, at least according to Lincoln and Guba.[7] Once a rich description is provided, it is up to the reader, secondary researchers, or other practitioners to decide if the models described could be transferable to other contexts. On the other hand, aspects of internal validity addressed below overcome this objection. While the existence of local conditions in a particular context will not be duplicated in any other context, there are degrees of similarity between situations. Practical theologians have been navigating the waters of recontextualization and the hermeneutical issues of interpretation for centuries.

There are many substitute words suggested for generalizability in the qualitative research literature, including *transferability*, *replicability*, *applicability*, *extrapolation*, and *fittingness*. However designated, generalizability ". . . is established by describing the means for applying the

---

4. Patton, *Qualitative Evaluation Methods*, 485.

5. Thomas, "Putting Nature," 7.

6. Munby, "Gazing," 2; See also Howe and Eisenhart, "Standards."

7. Lincoln and Guba, *Naturalistic Enquiry*, 316.

research findings to other contexts. Fundamentally, the possibility of applying findings across settings is established through thickly detailed descriptions that enable audiences to identify similarities of the research setting with other contexts. Put another way, it enables other audiences to see themselves and/or their situation in the accounts presented."[8] Swinton and Mowat recognize a degree of shared experiences that are common to humans and suggest the categories of "identification" and "resonance."[9] Research from a particular context might not be directly transferred in a one-to-one fashion to another, but a degree of resonance can invoke a sense of identification and fittingness. While no context is identical to another, there may be enough similar experiences and phenomena between two settings for someone else to utilize. The purpose of qualitative research is to gather depth of insight about the particulars of a setting. The more you know the intimate details of your particular project, the more the possibility of recognizing those same particulars in another context exists. The purpose of action research is to apply a specific solution to a particular problem. The more you understand how the intervention worked in addressing the issue at hand, the more the possibility of applying that intervention to a new context increases.

Your delimitations in chapter 1 created a box around your conclusions in such a way that your analyses and interpretations were contained to only those items within the box. Now, in this section, you are allowed to venture outside the box and suggest some possible applications that are tentatively proposed as universals (or at least applicable to other contexts). The questions of "How useful?" "Does it apply?" and "To what extent?" help answer questions of significance—is it important or just interesting? Such questions prompt Patton's use of the term *extrapolation*.

> Extrapolation clearly connotes that one has gone beyond the narrow confines of the data to think about other applications of the findings. Extrapolations are modest speculations on the likely applicability of findings to other situations under similar but not identical, conditions. Extrapolations are logical, thoughtful, case derived, and problem oriented rather than statistical and probabilistic. Extrapolations can be particularly useful when based on information-rich samples and designs, that is, studies that pro-

8. Merriam, *Qualitative Research*, 176–7.
9. Swinton and Mowat, *Practical Theology*, 47.

duce relevant information carefully targeted to specific concerns about both the present and the future.[10]

Patton lists five principles of generalization that are appropriate for qualitative research and that find their parallels in the quantitative field:

1. The Principle of Proximal Similarity. We generalize most confidently to applications where treatments, settings, populations, outcomes, and times are most similar to those in the original research.

2. The Principle of Heterogeneity of Irrelevancies. We generalize most confidently when research findings continue to hold over variations in persons, settings, treatments, outcome measures, and times that are presumed to be conceptually irrelevant. The strategy here is identifying irrelevancies, and where possible including a diverse array of them in the research so as to demonstrate generalization over them.

3. The Principle of Discriminate Validity. We generalize most confidently when we can show that it is the target construct, and not something else, that is necessary to produce a research finding.

4. The Principle of Empirical Interpolation and Extrapolation. We generalize most confidently when we can specify the range of persons, settings, treatments, outcomes, and times over which the finding holds more strongly, less strongly, or not at all. The strategy here is empirical exploration of the existing range of instances to discover how that range might generate variability in the finding for instances not studied.

5. The Principle of Explanation. We generalize most confidently when we can specify completely and exactly (a) which parts of one variable (b) are related to which parts of another variable (c) through which mediating processes (d) with which salient interactions, for then we can transfer only those essential components to the new application to which we wish to generalize. The strategy here is breaking down the finding into component parts and processes so as to identify the essential ones.[11]

10. Patton, *Qualitative Research*, 584.

11. Ibid., 581–2, quoting William R. Shadish, "The Logic of Generalization: Five Principles Common to Experiments and Ethnographies," *American Journal of Community Psychology* 23 (3), 1995a, 424–6.

Riessman, discussing narrative research as a subset of qualitative approaches, lists persuasiveness, correspondence, coherence, and pragmatic uses as criteria for the validation of research.[12] However, she emphasizes that there is no set formula. Nor should there be, for each context may require a new or different set of criteria to effectively reach for understanding. The qualitative methods require flexibility. This opens the doors for a host of unscrupulous methods, sloppy work, and invalidated babble to pass as legitimate research. Therefore, Riessman encourages making visible the contexts and methods used in projects so that others may be able to determine for themselves about validity concerns. The reader ultimately determines the validation of this research (*face validity*). Is the interpretation persuasive? Does this research have pragmatic uses (*catalytic validity*)? Is this research believable?

Eisner lists *coherence* (Does the research report or narrative make sense? How have the conclusions been supported? To what extent have multiple data sources been utilized to give credence to the interpretation made?), *consensus* (the condition in which the readers of a work concur that the findings and/or interpretations reported by the investigator are consistent with their own experience or with the evidence presented), and *instrumental utility* (the usefulness of the study).[13]

Generalizability claims, however, are limited. A limitation to qualitative research must be seen in the recognition of not being able to discover some macro-narrative (a more positivist concern). Patterns, metaphors, images, and themes cannot be turned into propositional truths in an attempt to construct utility. Just because you have a hammer, that does not mean everything else is a nail. One pink pill in your medicine bag does not cure all ills. "To the interpretive researcher the purpose of research is to describe and interpret the phenomena of the world in attempts to get shared meanings with others. . . . It is a search for perspectives and theoretical insights. It may offer possibilities but no certainties as to what may be the outcomes of future events."[14] The purpose of qualitative research, and your project in particular, must be the first criteria in deciding if your findings fit another context.

---

12. Riessman, *Narrative Analysis,* 64–68.

13. Eisner, *Enlightened Eye,* 53.

14. Thomas, "Putting Nature," 42.

Dependability

Reliability or dependability are close cousins to generalizability and applicability, asking more pointedly: "Can you trust it?" "Is it believable and credible?" "Does it produce similar results under constant conditions on all occasions?" "Is it replicable?" "Is it stable over time?" Reliability is problematic in the social sciences simply because human behavior is never static. Human behavior is unpredictable in many ways. Measurements, observations, and people can be repeatedly wrong.[15] Therefore, the question is not whether the findings will be found again, but whether the results are consistent with the data collected. It must be possible for an external person to audit the progress of the work and find the path to be sound. The auditor might not agree with the interpretations, but she must agree that the method used to arrive at those interpretations was properly implemented. "Dependability and confirmability are provided through an audit trail that clearly describes the processes of collecting and analyzing data and provides the means by which readers may refer to the raw data."[16]

Credibility

Internal validity or *credibility*:[17] Does the study measure or describe what it is suppose to measure or describe? Can you demonstrate confidence that the conclusions are reasonable and that another researcher facing the same data would reach a conclusion that is generally equivalent or at least consistent? Likewise, the rich "thick" descriptions of the study are deemed credible when they present the experiences of people in such a way that the participants would recognize them as their own. The participants would respond, "This description of my words and experiences is faithful."

Credibility is related to the degree of confidence that others can have in the findings of a particular project. If you recall, chapter 3 cited Merriam's listing of five characteristics that all qualitative research has in common. The second characteristic is that the researcher in qualitative studies is the primary instrument. Patton sees that understanding of your role in the project as a key to understanding validity.

15. Merriam, *Qualitative Research*, 205.
16. Ibid., 177.
17. Creswell, *Research Design*, 121.

Validity in quantitative research depends on careful instrument construction to ensure that the instrument measures what it is supposed to measure. The instrument must then be administered in an appropriate, standardized manner according to prescribed procedures. The focus is on the measuring instrument—the test items, survey questions, or other measurement tools. In qualitative inquiry, *the researcher is the instrument*. The credibility of qualitative methods, therefore, hinges to a great extent on the skill, competence, and rigor of the person doing fieldwork—as well as things going on in a person's life that might prove a distraction.[18]

The following methods are often utilized to ensure internal validity and increase the credibility associated with the research project:[19]

1. Triangulation (review the discussion in chapter 3)—Caution needs to be exercised when using triangulation as a means to secure "objective" truth through validation. Rather, triangulation is a method-appropriate strategy of founding credibility and trustworthiness. The trustworthiness of data and interpretation is enhanced by triangulation, but it should not be assumed that you have met the standards of validity as defined by a positivist researcher. Theoretically, triangulation and the use of multi-methods in research have sometimes come under attack when the goal is to ascertain an empirical "true" account of the setting or activity. Even with multiple lenses, the interpretation is still limited and bounded by the context. Triangulation might produce a fuller picture, but not a more "objective" picture.[20] The "whole picture" is impossible to ascertain. Triangulation allows the researcher to substantiate the picture that is being seen and interpreted, but it is not the pot of gold at the end of the rainbow. Subsequently, the theory of triangulation and multi-methods is not a quick and easy substitute for the positivists' search for validity. To return to the discussion in chapter 3 about method, Fielding and Fielding go on to warn, "Similarly different methods have emerged as a product of

18. Patton, *Qualitative Research*, 14. See 49–54 for a discussion of "empathic neutrality" as a stance taken by the researcher that is contra the debate between "objectivity" and "subjectivity."

19. The list is a compilation between Merriam, *Qualitative Research*, 204–5; Patton, *Qualitative Research*, 552–70; and Cresswell, *Research Design*, 196.

20. Fielding and Fielding, *Linking Data*, 33–34.

different theoretical traditions, and therefore combining them can add range and depth, but not accuracy. . . . What is important is to choose at least one method which is specifically suited to exploring the structural aspects of the problem and at least one which can capture the essential elements of its meaning to those involved."[21]

2. Reflective Confirmation—The researcher should allow insiders to confirm the findings she has assembled as an initial analysis; she should seek a reflective reading from key informants. This process is also referred to as *member checking*—taking data and tentative interpretations back to the people from whom they were derived and asking them if the results are plausible. Member checking gives you another opportunity to hear from your participants and may generate new ideas, patterns, and interpretations that you missed. Your participants are one angle of your triangulation evaluation process. It is not enough merely to gather a questionnaire from your group and conclude that this is sufficient. If your project is action research, then the responsibility of the group being co-interpreters involves taking seriously not only the data you collect, but how you organize, describe, and interpret the data. Member checking may be a time-consuming process, but it will increase the value of your project and may protect you from possible misinterpretations and future problems. Additional dilemmas occur when discrepancies arise between your perceptions and the participants'. Participants may believe you have no right to report certain information even if accurate. Therefore, you will need to answer the question, "Who decides what material can be used?" In the Introduction, I described how practical theology is a communal activity. The participants in the project are functioning as co-authors of the findings, interpretations, and conclusions. Erlandson et al. summarize the literature by offering the following list of the possible places member checking can enhance the credibility of a project: (1) Member checking is conducted continuously and is both formal and informal. Listed below are areas in which member checking is often conducted during a naturalistic inquiry. (2) Member checking may be conducted

---

21. Ibid. See Flick, "Triangulation Revisited," 175–97, for an application of triangulation using the construct of the *structural aspects of the problem* and the *essential elements of its meaning to those involved.*

at the end of an interview by summarizing the data and allowing the respondent to immediately correct errors of fact or challenge interpretations. (3) Member checking may be conducted in interviews by verifying interpretations and data gathered in earlier interviews. (4) Member checking may be conducted in informal conversations with members of the organization. (5) Member checking may be conducted by furnishing copies of various parts of the inquiry report to various stakeholding groups and asking for a written or oral commentary on the contents. (6) Before submission of the final report, a member check should be conducted by furnishing entire copies of the study to a review panel of respondents and other persons in the setting being studied.[22]

3. Thick Descriptions—the more detailed analysis that you provide the reader, the more credible your work. When the reader is able to follow your analysis, your reliance on data, and the paper trail you followed, your ethos as a researcher is enhanced (see chapter 7 for a detailed understanding of thick description).

4. Alternative Themes, Negative Cases, Divergent Patterns, and Rival Explanations—When you present data or themes that run counter to the interpretations presented, this will increase the integrity of your analysis. Describe how you looked for these things and what results you encountered. Alternative explanations increase the reader's acceptance of the study. Failure to consider alternative explanations prompts readers to question other aspects of the research. Therefore, you will have to anticipate as many of the reader's questions as you can and respond with a counterpoint to the most important objections. As Yin states, "To represent different perspectives adequately, an investigator must seek those alternatives that most seriously challenge the design of the case study. These perspectives may be found in alternative cultural views, different theories, variations among the people or decision makers who are part of the case study, or some similar contrasts."[23] A critical listener or the faculty advisor are good sources for seeing beyond the scope of the investigator's preconceived solutions. But if you anticipate these objections and offer alternatives, remain fair to

22. Erlandson, et al., *Doing Naturalistic Inquiry*, 142.
23. Yin, *Case Study Research*, 164.

their positions; then you can argue for their rejection based upon the evidence generated in your study.

5. Peer Debriefing—This allows another perspective that can question and review the account given. Often, no one is closer to the research than a co-laborer or a trusted colleague. They know both your work and your capacities as a researcher. Their opinion, when explicated in your writing, offers your reader an insight into the project that otherwise is not possible.

6. Outsider's Perspective—Judgments from outsiders or an external auditor of the research are helpful. Who can evaluate the raw data, the initial analysis, or the final product? Finding an independent expert is a common choice for DMin researchers who desire an outside angle of evaluation. The independent expert often represents the type of person who would read your completed thesis. The expert represents the intended audience and users of your project's results. The expert does not duplicate the work of your committee but instead focuses on the fulfillment of the intended purpose of the project in application.

7. Long-term Observations—Longitudinal studies are not practical for DMin projects, but prolonged engagement at the ministry site develops deeper understandings of the people and the context of the project. "Credibility is established by prolonged engagement with participants; triangulation of information from multiple data sources; member checking procedures that allow participants to check and verify the accuracy of the information recorded; and peer debriefing processes that enable research facilitators to articulate and reflect on research procedures with a colleague or informed associate."[24] Long term observations also include making raw data available for others to analyze. Given these means by which a researcher can establish credibility for the study, the bottom line relates to whether the findings "ring true" for the participants. However, DMin projects are limited by the amount of time most programs allow for the interventions. A four-month project, for example, does not allow for what the literature describes as

---

24. Stringer, *Action Research*, 2nd ed., 176; 3rd ed., 57–60. See also Lincoln and Guba, *Naturalistic Inquiry*, 313–6, and Erlandson, et al., *Doing Naturalistic Inquiry*, 29–31.

"prolonged engagement." However, because DMin students have already served for months, if not years, in the field of study in question, DMin researchers do meet the criteria and rationale for prolonged engagement by the nature of their relationship with the context in question.

8. Researcher's Biases—clarifying your assumptions, worldview, and theoretical orientation at the outset of the study (see the discussion of reflexivity in chapter 2). Researcher bias is one example of reflexivity.

Reflexivity

In the introductory section of your thesis, you explored how your emotions, perspectives, and identity would influence your research. Now is the time to retrospectively consider how you as a researcher affected your results. In the next section of your thesis, you will explore personal significance, but in this portion, you need to explore the relationship between your identity and the whole project. How do you think your presence influenced your results? Were there any surprises? What touched you or moved you? How did those feelings affect the project? Remember, you are not the subject, the purpose of the thesis is. Therefore, in your reflexive account, do not lose sight of the focus of the thesis.

Your credibility as a researcher is dependent on training, experience, record of accomplishment, status, and presentation of self through reflexivity. One of the primary ways you demonstrate your ability is by being open about the technical rigor you applied to the research process. Provide evidence that the research has been carried out rigorously, that the procedures and processes of inquiry have minimized the possibility that the investigation was superficial, biased, or insubstantial. The reader should be able to see the rigor of the researcher in the narrative descriptions of the project design and implementation. Remember, in qualitative research, the researcher is the primary instrument; how you act and function as a research instrument cannot be minimized. Therefore, report any personal and professional information that may have affected data collection, analysis, and interpretation. Do not over- or underestimate your role. For example, if you are not adequately prepared to conduct an interview, then you as an instrument have affected data collection. If your participants respond to you in an unexpected or unfavorable way, then you will affect the project. If you have biases for or against some aspect of the project, then you will affect the project. And if you change your attitude, methods, or approach during the course of the project, then you will affect the project.

Booth, Colomb, and Williams describe this process as creating *ethos* when making an argument.

> This process of "thickening" an argument with other arguments is one way that writers gain the confidence of readers. Readers will judge you by how well you manage the elements of an argument so that you anticipate their concerns. In so doing, they are in effect judging the quality of your mind, even of your implied character— an image of yourself that you project through your argument, traditionally called your ethos. When you seem to be the sort of person who supports your claims thoroughly and who thoughtfully considers other points of view, you give readers reason to trust what you say and not to question what you don't. . . . The ethos you project in individual arguments settles into your reputation, something every researcher must care deeply about, because your reputation will be an invisible sixth element in every argument you write. It answers the unspoken question *Can I trust this person?* If the readers don't know you, you have to earn that trust n each argument. But if they do know you, you want the answer to their question to be *Yes.*[25]

As an author of your research, provide an analysis of the patterns of lived experienced by your observations and subsequent descriptions through the framing lenses of faith seeking understanding, faith relating to one another in community, and faith expressing itself in the church. Your structured analysis becomes a retrospective interpretation of what is most common, familiar, and self-evident from the actions, behaviors, intentions, and experiences found in the community. It is descriptive in that the analysis clarifies what is being expressed. It is interpretive in that the analysis is pointing to meaning concealed within the various discourses and data sets.[26]

Finally, as a co-authors and interpreters of the instructional patterns identified, your participants in the project produced theory and practice. The dialogic nature of qualitative research is most vividly seen as you enter the conversation and give voice to your theory and practice.

25. Booth, Colomb, and Williams, *Craft of Research*, 122–23.
26. Van Manen, *Researching Lived Experience*, 24–27.

SIGNIFICANCE AND IMPLICATIONS

I connect the terms *implication* and *significance*. There are both personal and public implications to your research. Some implications are more significant than others. As a pastor-leader, you may be asked to boldly state your implications in the form of recommendations. Implications are more tentative than recommendations and suit the stance of a researcher, yet as a pastor, your role is often that of an advocate, vision caster, and change agent. Likewise, the nature of action research calls for leading communal transformation. Depending on the nature of your context, you may choose to offer recommendations.[27]

Patton, qualifies significance by differentiating between *statistical significance* and *substantive significance*. He lists four questions readers will ask in determining substantive significance:

- How solid, coherent, and consistent is the evidence in support of the findings? (Triangulation, for example, can be used in determining the strength of evidence in support of a finding.)

- To what extent and in what ways do the findings increase and deepen understanding of the phenomenon studied (*Verstehen*)?

- To what extent are the findings consistent with other knowledge? (A finding supported by and supportive of other work has confirmatory significance. A finding that breaks new ground has discovered or innovative significance.)

- To what extent are the findings useful for some intended purpose (e.g., contributing to theory, informing policy, summative or formative evaluation, or problem solving in action research)?[28]

Below, I discuss significance and implications under the categories of sustainability, personal significance, ecclesial significance, and theological significance.

Sustainability

You pursued the project you did with the intent of affecting change. You implemented the intervention to address a specific problem in the life of the church. The intervention addressed one particular set of actions within a narrow context. However, systems are complex and interact with

27. Wolcott, *Writing Up*, 58, 61.
28. Patton, *Qualitative Research*, 467.

multiple contexts. For the change to sustain itself over time, it needs to be integrated into the life of the community. For, as Stringer reminds us,

> Unless research participants take systematic steps to incorporate changed procedures into the ongoing life of the organization, changes are likely to be short-lived and to have little impact. Systematic and principled action research has the potential to extend its influence to all sectors of activity that have an impact on the issue or problem originally investigated. Strategic thinking and acting enables research participants to engage in significant processes of change that improve the operation of the organization and incorporate sustainable change into its operation.[29]

Stringer continues, "Researchers are likely to disrupt practices that have long been institutionalized and that can have impacts on people's egos, dignity, power, status, and career opportunities. In almost all situations, some people will resist changes of any sort unless the processes are carefully defined and their interests taken into account."[30] This entails a discussion of how to create a normative climate that will reinforce the changes after the group has concluded its work. Therefore, ask, "What follow-up activities or action plans are needed to sustain the changes?" "What can the research group do to ensure that the changes last?" "What obstacles still remain or could develop that hinder the future success of the project?" "How has the change affected the lives of others within the larger system?" Finally, consider the various factors that contribute to success, for example, finances, human resources, and leadership support.

Personal Significance

Qualitative research itself is a pedagogical tool able to sensitize you to the dialogical interactive nature of cultural processes. It fosters listening to the multiple voices emanating from ever-emerging and developing contexts. Qualitative research facilitates and encourages interpretatively open processes of "becoming" through dialogical and interactive work and coordinates intersubjective processes. Consequently, it opens for you the possibility to construct, co-construct, and reconstruct coherently your identity, and to acknowledge your loyalties, traditions, and inherited roles.

29. Stringer, *Action Research*, 145.
30. Ibid., 147.

To avoid overlap, your section on personal significance could easily be integrated in the reflexivity segment above. I list personal significance separately because the standards of the DMin degree emphasize your personal growth. In that sense, personal significance differs from reflexivity. Therefore, concentrate on questions such as "How has your experience of conducting the research made an impact on your relationships with the persons in the study?" "What did you learn about yourself?" And "What will you do differently in the future?"

Since the theological reflection model below begins with your personal experience, the more you know yourself (your personal and professional identity), the better able you are to engage in the next stage of reflection. The process of personal reflection is common for ministers. Whether through Clinical Pastoral Education (CPE), contextual education, or a battery of assessments (e.g., NEO, MMPI, Profiles of Ministry, etc.), seminaries and ordination boards stress personal reflection. In the DMin project thesis, the emphasis is on exploring how your leadership in one concentrated pastoral intervention influenced you, your understanding of ministry, and your future attitudes and practices.

Ecclesial Significance

The options for exploring ecclesial significance abound. The choices you make should correlate directly with your problem and purpose statement. Some projects will call for an investigation of the relationship of ecclesiology and Christology or soteriology. The theological construct delineated in chapter 2 of your thesis provides the pathway for narrowing the options. Since the DMin degree aims to shape pastoral leadership, avoiding the questions relating to ecclesiology is not an option.

Specific questions you could ask yourself include the following: "What did you learn about the people involved in this study?" "What are the primary metaphors for the church that contribute to the church's self-understanding?" "How does the church's ecclesial understanding strengthen its role in its social location?" And, "What new activities or visions of the church's future emerged or can be anticipated at this time?"

What Stringer says about generic action research is true for churches as well:

> The payoffs for [action research] are potentially enormous. Not only do research participants acquire the individual capacity to engage in systematic research that they can apply to other issues

in other contexts, but they also build a supportive network of collaborative relationships that provides them with an ongoing resource. Solutions that emerge from the research process therefore become much more sustainable, enabling people to maintain the momentum of their activity over extended periods of time. Links established in one project may provide access to information and support that build the power of the people in many different ways.[31]

The DMin project provides congregations ways to meta-think their structures, activities, and goals. The project facilitates the acquisition of skills for churches to apply in their future. One of the primary serendipities of action research is communal empowerment. The congregation develops skills that enable it to influence its own future. The congregation is able to address future problems and opportunities with hope. Your leadership has equipped the church to function effectively.

In the introduction, I noted that theology is a communal activity. However, there are a variety of ways ecclesiology is understood in history and practice. For many parishioners, ecclesiology remains a tacit reality that they cannot verbalize. A new convert might associate with Church A and not Church B based on how the two view being church, yet neither the church nor the convert would explain it in those terms. While in graduate school, I was asked to compare and contrast my ecclesiology with my view of revelation and my homiletic. Did my understanding of scripture and the church agree with the sermons I preached? While illuminating, the exploration into my internal coherence was also painful. Naively, many assume that because we share the same denominational backgrounds, we automatically view the nature and work of the church the same. Tragic stories can be told when the congregation and the minister clash over petty issues, while the underlying concern is more substantial.

Kärkkäinen describes seven ecclesiological traditions and seven contemporary ecclesiologists that might prove useful when you explore the shape of the congregation's self-understanding and compare it with your own.[32] Likewise, how the congregation engages its cultural context influences how projects are implemented and completed. The classic

---

31. Stringer, *Action Research*, 21.

32. Kärkkäinen, *Introduction to Ecclesiology*.

work by Niebuhr, *Christ & Culture*, provides another ecclesial construct for examining how the project and the congregation interacted.[33]

Theological Significance

What are the pastoral or theological implications that your research suggests? What understandings of God's presence or activity in the community emerge? Intentionally recall chapter 2 by connecting what you learned in your research with the rationale you offered. Are there any shifts in your understanding that emerged along the way?

Everyone, whether consciously or not, does theology. Most DMin students, by this time in their career, have nestled down with a primary model for theological reflection. If not, a good place to begin the journey is to examine either Stone and Duke's *How to Think Theologically* or Kinast's *What are They Saying about Theological Reflection?*[34] Whatever your method, you need to make explicit how the reflection is taking place. You are "theorizing" about the implications of your research on practice; this step is an act of a practical theologian. My model below is a blending of various hermeneutical and contextual models that have shaped me through the years.

Figure 12: Theological Reflection Model

Interpretation is a process of theological reflection, a critical dialogue (labeled in the graphic above as "discernment" and illustrated as a circle/spiral) with experience, context, and theological resources. DMin students utilize their pastoral sensitivities in ways that help them recognize the grittiness of the congregation's lived experiences. So, you

33. Niebuhr, *Christ and Culture*. For a more current discussion of the church's potential to effect culture see Hunter, *To Change the World*.

34. Stone and Duke, *How to Think*, and Kinast, *What are They Saying*.

begin by identifying a practice or a situation that requires pastoral attention. Subsequently, a problem and purpose is developed. The inquiry of theological reflection will lead you to abductively propose a theological response. That response is formulated into a pastoral intervention. The data is gathered and analyzed in a way that allows the researcher to engage the results through critical correlation with culture and various theological resources. In the DMin thesis, the theological resources are explicated in chapter 2. The critical correlation or interpretation of data with theology is the primary subject of your final chapter. Your interpretation will not merely reflect upon your project but will also make pastoral proposals for the future life of the church. And the cycle progressively spirals (evolves) forward. A consistent pastoral practice of action-reflection-decision-action will transform people over time into a community of people who engage the life of God for the sake of the world. Mature practitioners whom others consider experts in the field have developed the skills of theological reflection. Becoming a reflective practitioner is a strenuous and ongoing journey, but that process can become a natural part of everyday thinking, deciding, and acting.[35]

What if your project and/or thesis is a failure? What if the theology you developed in chapter 2 is ill-informed? Or, what if the evaluation of your project shows that the intervention failed to address the problem and fulfill its purpose? Perhaps your advisors failed to guide you earlier in the process, or maybe your participants did not respond as you anticipated. Or, maybe you failed to implement your methodology correctly or the data produced was merely mundane and uninteresting. Never fear. Even though the intervention failed, the DMin process is still alive. All can be redeemed in the final chapter of the thesis; the outcome hinges on how you interpret and reflect theologically about the process. Sometimes the greatest growth comes through weakness and failure. That almost sounds theological.

FINAL CONSIDERATIONS

What Next? When the project is completed and the last "i" is dotted and the last "t" is crossed, you need to consider the next logical steps implicated for you, the minister, in your context. Do not put your work in a shoebox after graduation. Carefully consider the appropriate actions

---

35. Schön, *Reflective Practitioner.*

that will enhance the project's value, your growth as a minister, and the congregation's health. No one is in a better position than you to begin planning again for the next phase of work. I am not talking about your vacation plans. The DMin project thesis has positioned you to envision the next horizon and to lead the congregation over it. In this section of the thesis, expound upon several concrete possibilities.

Future Questions: You are also now in a position to pose future research questions. You can prompt your reader to consider future possibilities, new horizons, and probable obstacles that lie ahead. Often, the next questions are more mature and contain the potential for greater significance than the current thesis. The thesis cleared the underbrush, allowing you to conceptualize ministry that was not possible for you before. The project thesis process has given you the tools and perspectives to meta-think about ministry, no longer as a novice, but as an expert. Through your work on the DMin project and thesis, you have cultivated wisdom—the ability to ask the next question.

Sharing Your Results: Because DMin students are working with particular contexts to provide pastoral leadership and address specific problems, they will want to present their findings to both the participants in the project and the larger community. Prepare both an oral presentation and a written report. To present the whole project in all its diversity and complexity will often be counterproductive. Many will not find the details interesting or beneficial. Others will openly disagree with your conclusions. Finally, most groups will not want to take the amount of time necessary to understand the depth of your analysis. Therefore, it is imperative to find ways to communicate your research clearly and concisely, in a manner that will meaningfully advance the conversation and serve people. When presenting your findings to the church board or the whole congregation, you may find it less threatening if the entire project team joins you in the oral presentation. The rule of thumb of coherence, mentioned throughout this handbook, also governs your presentation. The problem and purpose statements define the focus and guide what is included and excluded from public presentations. In your presentation, include a clear delineation of the project's purpose, a concise description of your findings, gracious explanations of the implications and significance, and a faithful vision of the possible future. Finally, anticipate questions that folks may ask.

Appendices: Different DMin programs and individual primary advisors will have their own opinions and standards about what is or is not to be included in appendices. When I function as a primary advisor, I make recommendations to the student. However, I leave the final decision of what materials remain in the body of the thesis and what is relegated to an appendix to the student. Sometimes, if the material is easily displayed in the body of the thesis and does not interfere with the flow of the narrative, then I counsel against putting the item in an appendix. I prefer to refer to the material directly so that I do not have to flip to the end of the document. However, if the material is cumbersome and blocks the narrative flow, then an appendix is better. But in the end, it is a judgment call that should be made by you, the student. Items that I perceive to be best suited for an appendix include:

- Copies of signed consent forms (or an unsigned copy if confidentiality is a concern). Sometimes, only a representative copy is needed with a reference as to where the originals are stored.

- Copies of protocols, interview questions, surveys, questionnaires, etc., if otherwise not included in the thesis.

- Lesson plans, handouts, or other materials presented to the congregation, leadership, and participants during the intervention.

- Materials presented in any post-project sessions conducted for the participants, leadership, or congregation.

- Letters, descriptions, or other materials distributed for the purposes of informing people about the project.

- Written materials given to you by key informants or independent experts.

- Raw data if it is easily presented. Sometimes the raw data collected during the project is too extensive. In my PhD research, I collected several hundred pages of manuscripts from the participants' life stories. My primary advisor asked me to select one representative sample. In this way, a reader could discern how I handled and interpreted the raw data. Although I did not provide a comprehensive audit trail, within reason, I provided a slice of the data. The reader could decide whether it was reasonable that I similarly handled all the raw data.

The final chapter of your thesis answers the question, "So what?" Other practitioners and ministers will read your thesis to discover best practices in the field. Consequently, they will read your methodology section hoping to glean activities, projects, and programs they can emulate in their contexts. Some will prefer chapter 2 because of their interest in your theological constructs. However, the most valuable chapter for the practical theologian is the final one. Because the DMin degree is designed to enhance your ministerial leadership, the answers you provide to the question, "So what?" are the most important aspect of the entire DMin process. Do not dash off the last chapter during the crunch time of the last few weeks of your schedule. Take the same care and consideration for your final reflections as you did for the earlier chapters. Your ability to answer the "So what?" question is for you, your growth, and your appreciation of the significance of your work. Even if others do not value your project, you can know the value the difference the project has made in your personal and professional growth and identity. Here—the final chapter of your thesis—is where you intersect theology and practice for the sake of the church.

Appendices

APPENDIX 1

Sample Consent Form for Interviews[1]

Introduction: My name is _____, and I am a student at _____ conducting an ethnographic study for a course on ethnography and ministry. My telephone number is: _____. My professor (or research supervisor) is _____ and his/her phone number is _____. You may contact either of us at any time if you have questions about this study.

Purpose: The purpose of this research is to study the practice of _____ at (*name of congregation or agency*). I am trying to learn more about _____.

Procedure: If you consent, you will be asked several questions in an oral interview that will take place (*where*). I will make an audiotape recording of the interview.

Time required: The interview will take approximately 1–2 hours of your time.

Voluntary participation: Your participation in this study is completely voluntary. If you choose to participate, you may still refuse to answer any question that you do not wish to answer. You may also withdraw from the study at any time.

Risks: There are no known risks associated with this interview. However, it is possible that you might feel distress in the course of the conversation. If this happens, please inform me promptly.

1. Moschella, *Ethnography*, 96–97.

Benefits: While there is no guaranteed benefit, it is possible that you will enjoy sharing your answers to these questions or that you will find the conversation meaningful. This study is intended to benefit the congregation (or hospital, school, etc.) by enlivening our discourse on the theology and practice of _____.

Confidentiality/Anonymity: Your name will be kept confidential in all of the reporting and/or writing related to this study. I will be the only person present for the interview and the only person who listens to the tapes. When I write the ethnography, I will use pseudonyms—made up names—for all participants, unless you specify in writing that you wish to be identified by name.

> If you wish to choose your own pseudonym for the study, please indicate the first name you would like me to use for you here: _____.

Sharing the results: I plan to construct an ethnography—a written account of what I learn—based on these interviews together with my reading and historical research. This ethnography will be submitted to my professor (or research supervisor) at the end of the term.

I also plan to share what I learn from this study with the congregation (hospital or ecclesiastical board). Portions of the ethnography may be printed and made available to the members.

Publication: There is the possibility that I will publish this study or refer to it in published writing in the future. In this event, I will continue to use pseudonyms (as described above) and I may alter some identifying details in order to further protect your anonymity.

Before you sign: By signing below, you are agreeing to an audiotaped interview for this research study. Be sure that any questions you may have are answered to your satisfaction. If you agree to participate in this study, a copy of this document will be given to you.

Participant's signature: _____ **Date:** _____
    Print name: _____
Researcher's signature: _____ **Date:** _____
    Print name: _____

APPENDIX 2

Example of an Institutional Review Board Application: Research Protocol[2]

1. List your name, contact information, and the name of the institution, course, or project to which your research is related. List the names and contact information for your advisors to this project.

2. Explain the nature and purpose of this research. What do you hope to learn and why?

3. Describe your research methods and procedures. Be specific. Indicate the length of time involved and the place where you plan to conduct the interviews or observation. Explain how you will select or recruit participants, and how you plan to make and keep records of your research. Specify your intentions for the use of visual records, such as photographs and videotapes.

4. Attach a copy of the survey instrument or a list of the questions that you intend to ask potential participants. If these questions are not completely settled, submit your tentative plans.

5. Describe your relationship to the potential participants. Are you their pastor or rabbi? Are you their chaplain or a field education intern?

6. Discuss any potential benefits for the participants in your study. What is the good that you hope will result from this study? What benefits, if any, will accrue to the participants?

7. Discuss any potential risks to the participants in your study. Are any of your participants members of vulnerable groups (such as children, persons with stigmatizing illnesses, whistleblowers, prisoners, persons with physically or mentally disabling conditions, etc.)? Explain the measures that you will take to provide for their privacy. Explain how you will respond if a participant has adverse effects as a result of your study.

2. Ibid., 112.

8. Explain the policies and procedures that you will use to insure the confidentiality or anonymity of your participants Will you use pseudonyms or a numerical coding system? Are there any factors other than names that might identify your research subjects? If so, what will you do to insure anonymity? How will your data be stored? How long will the data be kept?

9. Include a copy of any consent forms that you are planning to use. The language used on these forms should be clear, simple, and straightforward, not laden with technical jargon.

10. What will happen to the final report of your research? Do you plan to share a summary with the community or congregation? What form will the representation take, and what media will you use? List any possible venues in which you might publish this work now or in the future.

APPENDIX 3

Preaching Response Questionnaire[3]

Instructions: Please read each statement carefully and respond by circling the response which describes your personal reaction to this statement. Please be completely open and honest in your responses to make the information useful for the speaker's preparation of sermons.

Name of Preacher:
Date:
Name of Listener:
Sermon Title:
Sermon Text:

1. Did the sermon have an organized structure that you could notice? (Please circle your choice.)

    a. No evident organization of structure (loose, informal collection of thoughts and points)

    b. Occasional evidences of organized structure (on occasion, a progression of points could be followed)

    c. Clearly evident organization of structure (structure obvious in evident progression of points)

2. How would you describe your involvement (participation) in arriving at the conclusion of this sermon?

    a. The conclusion was already made for me.

    b. I joined in forming the conclusion.

    c. No conclusion was offered, so I made my own.

3. Sensing, *The Testing.*

3. This sermon has a clear central idea (main point) which I could sense. (Please circle your choice.)

Strongly Agree	Agree	Undecided	Disagree	Strongly Disagree

4. I could easily follow the organization of this sermon.

Strongly Agree	Agree	Undecided	Disagree	Strongly Disagree

5. The speaker caught my attention by appealing to varied types of mental imagery and thought provoking illustrations.

Strongly Agree	Agree	Undecided	Disagree	Strongly Disagree

6. The speaker effectively held my attention.

Strongly Agree	Agree	Undecided	Disagree	Strongly Disagree

7. This sermon was interesting and easy to listen to.

Strongly Agree	Agree	Undecided	Disagree	Strongly Disagree

8. I felt the speaker properly explained and applied the biblical message.

Strongly Agree	Agree	Undecided	Disagree	Strongly Disagree

9. I felt I knew exactly what was expected of me through this sermon.

Strongly Agree	Agree	Undecided	Disagree	Strongly Disagree

10. In my judgment the speaker did not prove his point in this sermon.

Strongly Agree	Agree	Undecided	Disagree	Strongly Disagree

11. What is your impression of the speaker's opening remarks?

Strongly Agree	Agree	Undecided	Disagree	Strongly Disagree

12. To what degree did you find the speaker's line of thought clear?

Vivid	Clear-Cut	Intelligible	Confusing	Unintelligible

13. The logic of this sermon was:

Indisputable	Convincing	Acceptable	Doubtful	Fallacious

14. In my judgment, the speaker's concluding remarks in this sermon were:

Impressive	Effective	Relevant	Weak	Distracting

15. How would you rank this sermon in value to you?

Important	Worthwhile	Medium	Unimportant	Worthless

Circle the number that most nearly indicates the relative effectiveness of yourself as a listener to this sermon.

Attentive	1 2 3 4 5	Inattentive
Active	1 2 3 4 5	Passive
Sharp	1 2 3 4 5	Dull
Effective	1 2 3 4 5	Ineffective
Valuable	1 2 3 4 5	Worthless
Fast	1 2 3 4 5	Slow
Clear	1 2 3 4 5	Hazy
Stale	1 2 3 4 5	Fresh
Good	1 2 3 4 5	Bad
Abstract	1 2 3 4 5	Concrete
Dead	1 2 3 4 5	Alive

APPENDIX 4

Congregational Sermon Evaluation Form[4]

The following evaluation is an open-ended questionnaire used as a peer-evaluation tool.

> Name of Preacher:
> Date:
> Name of Listener:
> Sermon Title:
> Sermon Text:

1. What was the objective of this sermon? Was the objective met?

2. How was the biblical text employed in this sermon? (Was it confronted, avoided, distorted, transcended?)

3. Did the sermon address contemporary needs?

4. Did the sermon move smoothly from biblical text to the needs of people in today's world?

5. How was the liturgical occasion addressed? (Was it acknowledged, amplified, distorted, ignored, transcended?)

6. How did the text and liturgical occasion relate?

7. What did the preacher expect from you?

8. Outline the sermon's structure (plot the sermon's moves):

9. The strongest aspect of this sermon was?

---

4. Tim Sensing, "Class Notes Handout," Abilene Christian University, 1998.

Rate the following

1 = excellent; 2 = good; 3 = fair; 4 = needs attention; 5 = poor

Posture	Style	Voice
Language	Eye Contact	Force
Gestures	Introduction	Rate
Illustrations	Emotion	Pitch
Transitions	Logic	Articulation
Structure	Conclusion	

Suggestions and other Comments:

APPENDIX 5

Observation Protocol for Case Teaching[5]

Evaluating the Case Discussion

ENGAGEMENT CHART

Plot the level of engagement between facilitator and participants from Low (more reflective) to High (more interactive).

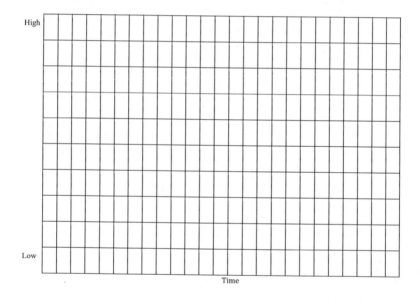

INTERACTION CHART

Diagram participants as situated in the room. Show interaction by drawing lines between participants as they interact with each other.

CASE EVALUATION

Rate each of the following on a scale of 1 to 5.
1 = needs improvement, 2 = fair, 3 = average, 4 = above average, 5 = excellent.

_____ Objectives for teaching the case

_____ Facilitator's body language

_____ Material assigned for presentation

_____ Facilitator's voice and inflection

_____ Teaching plan for case presentation

_____ Participants' involvement/interaction

_____ Opening for case presentation

_____ Participants' body language

_____ Facilitator/participant interaction

_____ Closing for case presentation

_____ Time management for presentation

_____ Overall effectiveness

On the back, comment on the following areas: areas of strength, areas of growth, and any additional comments you think would be helpful.

APPENDIX 6

Observation Tool for the Classroom[6]

Peer Coaching Guide: Inductive Thinking
Post-Conference

Name _____   Date _____

Topic _____

Observer _____

PHASE ONE: DATA COLLECTION/PRESENTATION

Did the teacher/students enumerate the data before attempting to categorize it? [yes/no]

PHASE TWO: CONCEPT FORMATION

1. In your opinion, did the students understand the criteria and procedures they were to employ during the categorizing activity? Did the teacher inadvertently give clues about what the "right" groups would be? [yes/no/partially]

2. Did the students work productively on the categorizing activity? [yes/no/partially]

3. If the teacher had the students work in pairs or small groups, did the students listen as other groups shared their categories? [yes/no/partially]

4. Were students able to explain the attributes on which they grouped items within categories? [yes/no/partially]

5. Were students able to provide names for their groups which reflected the attributes on which the groups were formed? [yes/no/partially]

PHASE THREE: INTERPRETATION OF DATA

1. Were the students able to discuss possible cause-effect relationships among the groups? [yes/no/partially]

6. Adapted from Joyce, Weil, and Showers, Models of Teaching, 445–50.

2. Did the teacher ask the students to go beyond the data and make inferences and conclusions regarding their data? [yes/no] If yes, were the students able to do so? [yes/no]. If students were unable to make inferences or conclusions, can you think of any ideas to share with your partner that might help them do so?

3. Were students able to make logical predictions based on the foregoing categorization and discussion? [yes/no]

4. Did the teacher ask the students to explain and support their predictions? [yes/no]

5. If students were unable to make logical predictions based on their previous work with their categories, can you think of questions or examples that might assist students in doing so?

COMMENTS ON STUDENT TRAINING NEEDS

Please comment on the skills with which the students engaged in the activities and suggest any areas where you believe training might be useful. Think especially of their ability to group by attributes, to provide labels for groups that accurately described the groups or synthesized attributes characteristic of a given group, their understanding of possible cause-effect relationships among groups, and their ability to make inferences or conclusions regarding their categories.

Bibliography

Abilene Christian University. "Academic Integrity and Honesty." http://www.acu
.edu/campusoffices/studentlife/judicialDocuments/Acad_Integ_Policy_20.pdf
(accessed December 14, 2010).

———. "ACU Institutional Review Board Policy." http://www.acu.edu/academics/orsp
/irb_policy.html (accessed December 14, 2010).

Allen, Ronald J. "Why Preach from Passages in the Bible?" In *Preaching as a Theological
Task: World, Gospel, Scripture*, edited by T. G. Long and E. Farley, 176–88. Louisville:
Westminster John Knox, 1996.

Altheide, David L., and John M. Johnson. "Criteria for Assessing Interpretive Validity in
Qualitative Research." In Denzin and Lincoln, *Handbook of Qualitative Research*.
Thousand Oaks, CA: Sage, 1994, 485–99.

American Anthropological Association. "Code of Ethics of the American Anthropological
Association." http://www.aaanet.org/committees/ethics/ethcode.htm (accessed October
22, 2009).

———. "Statement on Ethnography and Institutional Review Boards." http://aaanet.org
/stmts/irb.htm (accessed October 22, 2009).

American Sociological Association. "American Sociological Association Code of
Ethics." http://asanet.org/cs/root/leftnav/ethics/code_of_ethics_table_of_contents
(accessed October 22, 2009).

American Theological Library Association. "ATLA Catalog: Research in Ministry."
American Theological Library Association. http://www.atla.com/products/catalogs
/catalogs_rim.html (accessed October 28, 2009).

Ammerman, Nancy T., Jackson W. Carroll, Carl S. Dudley, and William McKinney, eds.
Studying Congregations: A New Handbook. Nashville: Abingdon, 1998.

Ammons, R. B. "Effects of Knowledge of Performance: A Survey and Tentative Theoretical
Formulation." *Journal of General Psychology* 54 (1956): 279–99.

Anderson, Herbert, and Edward Foley. *Mighty Stories, Dangerous Rituals: Weaving
Together the Human and the Divine*. San Francisco: Jossey-Bass, 1998.

APA Style Manual. "Supplemental Materials." http://www.apastyle.org/manual/supple
ment/index.aspx (accessed December 14, 2010).

Association of Case Teaching. *Case Teaching Institute*. Unpublished manual. Wesley
Theological Seminary, 2001.

———. *Case Teaching Institute*. Unpublished manual. Abilene Christian University,
2006.

Association of Theological Schools. "Degree Program Standards: Section F—Advanced
Programs Oriented Toward Ministerial Leadership." http://www.ats.edu/Accrediting
/Documents/08DegreeStandards.pdf (accessed October 22, 2009).

Atkinson, Paul, Amanda Coffey, Sara Delamont, John Lofland, and Lyn Lofland, eds.
Handbook of Ethnography. Los Angeles: Sage, 2008.

Avery, W. O., and R. A. Gobbel. "The Word of God and the Words of the Preacher." *Review of Religious Research* 22 (Sept 1980): 41–53.

Babbie, Earl. *The Practice of Social Research*. Belmont, CA: Wadsworth, 2009.

Bain, Alexander. *The Emotions and the Will*. London: J. W. Parker & Son, 1859.

Bakhtin, Mikhail. *The Dialogic Imagination*. Edited by Michael Holquist. Translated by Caryl Emerson and Michael Holquist. Minneapolis: University of Minnesota Press, 1981.

Bandura, A. "Perceived Self-Efficacy in Cognitive Development and Functioning." *Educational Psychologist* 28 (1993): 117–48.

———. "Self-efficacy: Toward a Unifying Theory of Behavioral Change." *Psychological Review* 84 (1977): 191–215.

Bass, Diana Butler. *Christianity for the Rest of Us: How the Neighborhood Church is Transforming the Faith*. New York: Harper One, 2006.

Beckelhymer, Hunter. "I Look Like I Belong Up There." *The Christian Century* 95 (1978): 123–8.

Bell, Judith. *Doing Your Research Project: A Guide for First-Time Researchers in Education and Social Science*. 3rd ed. Philadelphia: Open University Press, 1999.

Berg, Bruce L. *Qualitative Research Methods for the Social Sciences*. 3rd ed. Boston: Allyn and Bacon, 1998.

Bevans, Stephen B. *Models of Contextual Theology*. Maryknoll, NY: Orbis, 2006.

Bischoping, Katherine. "Quote, Unquote: From Transcript to Text in Ethnographic Research." In *Doing Ethnography: Studying Everyday Life*, edited by Dorothy Pawluch, William Shaffir, and Charlene Miall, 141–56. Toronto: Canadian Scholars' Press, 2005.

Bodey, R. A. "Graduated Sermon Critique Forms for use in the Preaching Labs at Trinity Evangelical Divinity School." DMin diss., Trinity Evangelical Divinity School, 1984.

Bolker, Joan. *Writing Your Dissertation in Fifteen Minutes a Day: A Guide to Starting, Revising, and Finishing Your Doctoral Thesis*. New York: Henry Holt, 1998.

Booth, Wayne C., Gregory G. Colomb, and Joseph M. Williams. *The Craft of Research*. 2nd ed. Chicago: University of Chicago Press, 2003.

Bradley, B. E. "An Experimental Study of the Effectiveness of the Video-recorder in Teaching a Basic Speech Course." *The Speech Teacher* 19 (1970): 166–84.

Branson, Mark Lau. *Memories, Hopes, and Conversations: Appreciative Inquiry and Congregational Change*. Herndon, VA: Alban, 2004.

Brooks, K. "Some Basic Considerations in Rating Scale Development: A Descriptive Bibliography." *Central States Speech Journal* 9 (December 1952): 27–31.

Browning, Donald S. *Practical Theology*. San Francisco: Harper & Row, 1983.

Bryan, I., and W. H. Wilke. "Audience Tendencies in Rating Public Speakers." *Journal of Applied Psychology* 26 (1942): 371–81.

———. "A Technique for Rating Public Speeches." *Journal of Consulting Psychology* 5 (Mar 1941): 80–90.

Bullough, R. V., and D. K. Stokes. "Analyzing Personal Teaching Metaphors in Preservice Teacher Education as a Means for Encouraging Professional Development." *American Educational Research Journal* 31, no. 1 (1994): 197–224.

Burke, Kenneth. *A Grammar of Motives*. New York: Prentice-Hall, 1945.

———. *A Rhetoric of Motives*. New York: Prentice-Hall, 1950.

———. *Permanence and Change*. New York: New Republic, 1935.

Buros Institute of Mental Measurements. *The Tenth Mental Measurements Yearbook*. Lincoln, NE: Buros Institute of Mental Measurements, 1989.

Burris, Allen. "Sermon Preparation for Hearers: A Collaborative Approach to Preaching in the Mitchell Church of Christ." DMin thesis, Abilene Christian University, 2006.

Camp, Jonathan W. "Bridging the Generation Gap at the Church of Christ at White Station." DMin project thesis, Abilene Christian University, 2007.

Carter, Kathy. "The Place of Story in the Study of Teaching and Teacher Education." *Educational Researcher* 22, no. 1 (1993): 5–12.

Casey, K. "Class Notes." UNCG, 1996.

———. *I Answer With My Life: Life Histories of Women Practical Theologians Working for Social Change.* New York: Routledge, 1993.

———. "The New Narrative Research in Education." *Review of Research in Education* 21 (1995): 1–43.

Cathcart, R. S. "An Experimental Study of the Relative Effectiveness of Four Methods of Presenting Evidence." *Speech Monographs* (Aug 1955): 227–33.

Christian, Jeff M. "Preaching as Character-forming Discourse." DMin project thesis, Abilene Christian University, 2007.

Clevenger, Theodore Jr. "Retest Reliabilities of Ten Scales of Public Speaking Performance." *Central States Speech Journal* 14 (November 1963): 285–91.

———. "Retest Reliability of Judgments of General Effectiveness in Public Speaking." *Western Speech* 26 (Fall 1962): 216–9.

Conniry, Charles J. "Reducing the Identity Crisis in Doctor of Ministry Education." *Theological Education* 40, no. 1 (2004): 147.

Cooperrider, David L., and Suresh Srivastva. "Appreciative Inquiry in Organizational Life." In *Research in Organizational Change and Development*, vol. 1, edited by W. Pasmore and R. Woodman, 129–69. Greenwich, CT: JAI Press, 1987.

Cooperrider, David L., and Diana Whitney. *Appreciative Inquiry: Collaborating for Change.* Edited by Peggy Holman and Tom Devane. San Francisco: Berrett-Koehler, 1999.

Corbin, Juliet, and Anselm Strauss. *Basics of Qualitative Research: Techniques and Procedures for Developing Grounded Theory.* Los Angeles: Sage, 2008.

Cortazzi, Martin. "Narrative Analysis in Ethnography." In *Handbook of Ethnography*, edited by Paul Atkinson, Amanda Coffey, Sara Delamont, John Lofland, and Lyn Lofland, 384–94. Los Angeles: Sage, 2008.

Creswell, John W. *Research Design: Qualitative, Quantitative, & Mixed Methods Approaches.* 2nd ed. Thousand Oaks, CA: Sage, 2003.

Crites, Stephen D. "The Narrative Quality of Experience." *Journal of the American Academy of Religion* 39 (September 1971).

Deihl, E. R., M. P. Breen, and C. V. Larson. "The Effects of Teacher Comment and Television Video Tape Playback on the Frequency of Nonfluency in Beginning Speech Students." *The Speech Teacher* 19 (1970): 185–9.

Denzin, Norman. *The Research Act.* Chicago: Aldine, 1978.

Denzin, Norman K., and Yvonna S. Lincoln, eds. *Handbook of Qualitative Research.* Thousand Oaks, CA: Sage, 1994.

———. *Handbook of Qualitative Research.* 2nd ed. Thousand Oaks, CA: Sage, 2000.

———. *Handbook of Qualitative Research.* 3rd ed. Thousand Oaks, CA: Sage, 2005.

Dewey, John. "The Pragmatism of Peirce." In *Chance, Love and Logic: Philosophical Essays*, edited by M. R. Cohen, 301–2. International Library of Psychology, Philosophy and Scientific Method. London: Kegan Paul, Trench, Trubner, 1923.

Draper, Stephen W. "The Hawthorne Effect and Other Expectancy Effects: A Note." http://www.psy.gla.ac.uk/~steve/hawth.html (accessed October 28, 2009).

Edwards, O. C., and D. J. Schlafer. "Learning to Preach—and How Short Conferences Can Help." *Homiletic* 20 (Summer 1995): 1.

Eisner, E. W. *The Enlightened Eye: Qualitative Inquiry and the Enhancement of Educational Practice.* New York: Macmillan, 1991.

Emerson, Robert M., Rachel I. Fretz, and Linda L. Shaw, "Participant Observation and Fieldnotes." In *Handbook of Ethnography,* edited by Paul Atkinson, Amanda Coffey, Sara Delamont, John Lofland, and Lyn Lofland, 352–68. Los Angeles: Sage, 2008.

Engel, J. *How Can I Get Them to Listen?* Grand Rapids, MI: Zondervan Publishing House, 1977.

Erlandson, David A., Edward L. Harris, Barbara L. Skipper, and Steve D. Allen. *Doing Naturalistic Inquiry: A Guide to Methods.* Newbury Park, CA: Sage, 1993.

Fackre, Gabriel J. *The Christian Story: A Narrative Interpretation of Basic Christian Doctrine.* Grand Rapids: Eerdmans, 1978.

Family Health International "Research Ethics Training Curriculum." http://fhi.org /training/en/RETC/ (accessed October 22, 2009).

Farnham-Diggory, S. "Paradigms of Knowledge and Instruction." *Review of Educational Research* 64 (1994): 463–77.

Fielding, Nigel G. "Computer Applications in Qualitative Research." In *Handbook of Ethnography,* edited by Paul Atkinson, Amanda Coffey, Sara Delamont, John Lofland, and Lyn Lofland, 453–67. Los Angeles: Sage, 2008.

Fielding, Nigel G., and Jane L. Fielding. *Linking Data.* Beverley Hills, CA: Sage, 1986.

Flick, Uwe. *An Introduction to Qualitative Research.* Thousand Oaks, CA: Sage, 1998.

Florida Institute for Human and Machine Cognition. "Cmap Tools." http://cmap.ihmc.us/conceptmap.html (accessed October 22, 2009).

Fontana, Andrea, and James H. Frey. "Interviewing: The Art of Science." In Denzin and Lincoln, *Handbook of Qualitative Research.* Thousand Oaks, CA: Sage, 1994, 361–76.

Frei, Hans W. *The Eclipse of Biblical Narrative: A Study in Eighteenth and Nineteenth Century Hermeneutics.* New Haven, CT: Yale University Press, 1980.

Friedman, Paul G., and Elaine A. Yarbrough. *Training Strategies from Start to Finish.* Indianapolis: Prentice Hall, 1985.

Frye, Northrop. *The Great Code: The Bible and Literature.* San Diego: Harcourt Brace Jovanovich, 2002.

Geertz, Clifford. *The Interpretation of Cultures.* New York: Basic Books, 2000.

Gilkinson, H., and D. K. Smith. "Measurement in Speech." In *An Introduction to Graduate Study in Speech and Theater,* edited by C. W. Dow, 276–311. East Lansing: Michigan State University Press, 1961.

Gilkinson, Howard. "Experimental and Statistical Research in General Speech: II. Speakers, Speeches, and Audiences." *Quarterly Journal of Speech* 30, no. 2 (1944): 180–6.

———. "Indexes of Change in Attitude Behavior Among Students Enrolled in General Speech Courses." *Speech Monographs* 8 (1941): 23–33.

Gillespie, Richard. *Manufacturing Knowledge: A History of the Hawthorne Experiments.* Cambridge: Cambridge University Press, 1991.

Gillis, F. R. "The Role of Feedback in Preaching: Some Methods for Acquiring Feedback from the Congregation." DMin diss., Lancaster Theological Seminary, 1983.

Glasser, Barney, and William Strauss. *The Discovery of Grounded Theory*. Chicago: Aldine, 1967.

Gobo, Giampietro. *Doing Ethnography*. Translated by Adrian Belton. Los Angeles: Sage, 2008.

Godelier, Maurice. *Perspectives in Marxist Anthropology*. Cambridge: Cambridge University Press, 1989.

Greenwood, Davydd J., and Morten Levin. *Introduction to Action Research: Social Research for Social Change*. 2nd ed. Thousand Oaks, CA: Sage, 2006.

Guthrie, Clifton F. "Quantitative Empirical Studies of Preaching: A Review of Methods and Findings." *Journal of Communication and Religion* 30 (March 2007): 65–117.

Hammersley, Martyn, and Paul Atkinson. *Ethnography: Principles and Practice*. 3rd ed. New York: Routledge, 2007.

Hammond, Sue Annis. *The Thin Book of Appreciative Inquiry*. 2nd ed. Plano, TX: The Thin Book Publishing Co, 1998.

Harré, Rom, and Grant Gillet. *The Discursive Mind*. London: Sage, 1995.

Hays, Richard. *The Moral Vision of the New Testament: Community, Cross, New Creation*. San Francisco: Harper Collins, 1996.

Holman, Peggy, and Tom Devange, eds. *The Change Handbook: Group Methods for Shaping the Future*. San Francisco: Berrett-Koehler, 1999.

Howe, Kenneth, and Margaret Eisenhart. "Standards for Qualitative (and Quantitative) Research: A Prolegomenon." *Educational Researcher* 19, no. 4 (1990): 2–9.

Hunter, James Davison. *To Change the World: The Irony, Tragedy, & Possibility of Christianity in the Late Modern World*. Oxford: Oxford University Press, 2010.

Ilgen, D. R., C. D. Fisher, and M. S. Taylor. "Consequences of Individual Feedback on Behavior in Organizations." *Journal of Applied Psychology* 64 (Aug 1979): 349–71.

Jackson, D. E. "Feedback in Preaching Communication." PhD diss., University of Southern Mississippi, 1988.

Jaeger, Richard M., ed. *Complementary Methods for Research in Education*. Washington, DC: American Educational Research Association, 1988.

Johnson, Stephen C. "A Narrative Model for Forming Pastoral Leaders at the Edgemere Church of Christ." DMin project thesis, Abilene Christian University, 2000.

Joyce, Bruce, Marsha Weil, and Beverly Showers. Models of Teaching. Boston: Allyn and Bacon, 1992.

Kärkkäinen, Veli-Matti. *An Introduction to Ecclesiology: Ecumenical, Historical & Global Perspectives*. Downers Grove, IL: InterVarsity, 2002.

Karl, K. A., and J. M. Kopf. "Guidelines for Using Videotaped Feedback Effectively." *Human Resource Development Quarterly* 4 (1993): 303–10.

Kelm, Jackie. "Introducing the AI Philosophy." In *Lessons From the Field: Applying Appreciative Inquiry*, edited by Sue Annis Hammond and Cathy Royal, 161–72. Plano, TX: Practical Press, 1998.

Kinast, Robert L. *What are They Saying about Theological Reflection?* New York: Paulist Press, 2000.

Kleinman, Sherryl. "Field-Workers' Feelings: What We Feel, Who We Are, How We Analyze." In *Experiencing Fieldwork: An Inside View of Qualitative Research*, edited by William B. Shaffir and Robert A. Stebbins, 184–5. Newbury Park, CA: Sage, 1991.

Kleinman, Sherryl, and Martha A. Copp. *Emotions and Fieldwork*. Qualitative Research Methods Series 28. Thousand Oaks, CA: Sage, 1993.

Knower, F. H. "A Suggestive Study of Public-Speaking Rating-Scale Values." *Quarterly Journal of Speech* 15 (Feb 1929): 30–41.

Krueger, Richard A. *Analyzing and Reporting Focus Group Results*. Focus Group Kit 6. Thousand Oaks, CA: Sage, 1998.

Lather, P. "Research as Praxis." *Harvard Educational Review* 56 (1986): 257–77.

Lazear, David. *Seven Ways of Teaching: The Artistry of Teaching with Multiple Intelligences*. Palatine, IL: Skylight, 1991.

Lee, Thomas W. *Using Qualitative Methods in Organizational Research*. Thousand Oaks, CA: Sage, 1999.

Lewins, Ann, and Christina Silver, *Using Software in Qualitative Research: A Step-by-Step Guide*. Los Angeles: Sage, 2007.

Lincoln, Yvonna S., and Egon G. Guba. *Naturalistic Inquiry*. Beverly Hills, CA: Sage, 1985.

———. "Paradigmatic Controversies, Contradictions, and Emerging Confluences." In *Handbook of Qualitative Research,* edited by Denzin and Lincoln, 163-88, Thousand Oaks, CA: Sage, 2000.

Lindbeck, George A. *The Church in a Postliberal Age*. Edited by James J. Buckley. Grand Rapids: Eerdmans, 2002.

———. *The Nature of Doctrine: Religion and Theology in a Postliberal Age*. Philadelphia: Westminster, 1984.

Lipman, Matthew. "Thinking in Education." In *Philosophical Documents in Education*, edited by R. F. Reed and T. W. Johnson, 259–71. White Plains, NY: Longman, 1996.

Long, Thomas G., and Leonora Tubbs Tisdale, eds. *Teaching Preaching as Christian Practice: A New Approach to Homiletic Pedagogy*. Louisville: Westminster John Knox, 2004.

MacIntyre, Alasdair. *After Virtue: A Study in Moral Theory*. Notre Dame, IN: University of Notre Dame Press, 1981.

Mack, Natasha, Cynthia Woodsong, Kathleen M. MacQueen, Greg Guest, and Emily Namey. *Qualitative Research Methods: A Data Collector's Field Guide*. Research Triangle Park, NC: Family Health International, 2005.

Madison, D. Soyini. *Critical Ethnography: Methods, Ethics, and Performance*. Thousand Oaks, CA: Sage, 2005.

MaGuire, J. T. "A Scale on Preaching Style: Hortatory vs. Interactive Preaching." *Review of Religious Research* 22 (Sept 1980): 60–65.

Martin, Steve D. "Envisioning Self-emptying Practices for the Union Hill Church of Christ." DMin project thesis, Abilene Christian University, 2008.

Marutzky, Gregg L. "Transforming Leadership Model for the Denver Church of Christ." DMin project thesis, Abilene Christian University, 2007.

Mason, Jennifer. *Qualitative Researching*. 2nd ed. London: Sage, 2002.

McDaniel, J., and A. Watson. "A Study of Post-Sermon Discussion Groups: Group's Self Evaluation." Guided Research, Harding Graduate School of Religion, 1977.

McEwan, Hunter, and Kieran Egan. *Narrative in Teaching, Learning and Research*. New York: Teachers College Press, 1995.

Merriam, Sharan B. *Qualitative Research and Case Study Applications in Education*. 2nd ed. San Francisco: Jossey Bass, 1998.

Miles, Matthew B., and A. Michael Huberman, *Qualitative Data Analysis: An Expanded Sourcebook*. 2nd ed. Newbury Park, CA: Sage, 1994.

Miller-McLemore, Bonnie J., and William Myers. "The Doctorate of Ministry as an Exercise in Practical Theology: Qualitative Research with Living Human Documents." *Journal of Supervision and Training in Ministry* 11 (1989): 5–24.

Millson, W. A. D. "Experimental Work in Audience Reaction," *Quarterly Journal of Speech* 18 (Feb 1932): 24–25.

———. "Problems in Measuring Audience Reaction." *Quarterly Journal of Speech* 18 (Nov 1932): 621–37.

Monroe, A. H., H. H. Remmers, and E. Venemann-Lyle. "Measuring the Effectiveness of Public Speech in a Beginning Course." *Studies in Higher Education* 29 (Sept 1936): 5–29.

Morgan, David L., ed. *Successful Focus Groups: Advancing the State of the Art.* Newbury Park, CA: Sage, 1993.

———. *Focus Groups as Qualitative Research.* 2nd ed. Qualitative Research Methods Series 16. Thousand Oaks, CA: Sage, 1997.

Moschella, Mary Clark. *Ethnography as a Pastoral Practice: An Introduction.* Cleveland: Pilgrim Press, 2008.

Munby, Hugh. "Gazing in the Mirror: Asking Questions About Validity in Self-study Research." Annual Meeting of the American Educational Research Association, San Francisco, CA, ERIC Document Reproduction Service No. ED 389 726, 1995.

Murphy, Elizabeth, and Robert Dingwall. "The Ethics of Ethnography." In *Handbook of Ethnography*, edited by Paul Atkinson, Amanda Coffey, Sara Delamont, John Lofland, and Lyn Lofland, 339–51. Los Angeles: Sage, 2008.

Murphy, Nancey C. *Reasoning and Rhetoric in Religion.* Eugene, OR: Wipf and Stock, 2001.

Mutch, Barbara Horkoff. "Assessing a Doctor of Ministry Program." *Theological Education* 39, no. 2 (2003): 87–88.

Myers, William R. *Research in Ministry: A Primer for the Doctor of Ministry Program.* Rev. ed. Chicago: Exploration, 1997.

National Commission for the Protection of Human Subjects of Biomedical and Behavioral Research. "The Belmont Report: Ethical Principles and Guidelines for Protection of Human Subjects of Research." Office of Human Subjects Research. http://ohsr.od.nih.gov/guidelines/belmont.html (accessed October 22, 2009).

National Council of Teachers of English. "Guidelines for Gender-Fair Use of Language." http://www.ncte.org/positions/statements/genderfairuseoflang (accessed December 14, 2010).

Nelson, Dwight K. "A Comparison of Receptivity to the Deductive and Inductive Methods of Preaching in the Pioneer Memorial Church." DMin diss., Andrews University, 1986.

Newman, W. M., and S. A. Wright. "The Effects of Sermons Among Lay Catholics: An Exploratory Study." *Review of Religious Research* 22 (Sept 1980): 54–59.

Niebuhr, H. Richard. *Christ and Culture.* San Francisco: HarperCollins, 1951.

———. *The Meaning of Revelation.* New York: Macmillan, 1941.

Nieman, James R. *Knowing the Context.* Elements of Preaching Series, edited by O. Wesley Allen. Minneapolis: Fortress, 2008.

Norvelle, L. "Development and Application of a Method for Measuring the Effectiveness of Instruction in a Basic Speech Course." *Speech Monographs* 1 (Sept 1934): 41–65.

Novak, Joseph D., and Alberto J. Cañas. "The Theory Underlying Concept Maps and How to Construct and Use Them: Technical Report IHMC CmapTools 2006–01

Rev 01–2008." Florida Institute for Human and Machine Cognition. http://cmap
.ihmc.us/Publications/ResearchPapers/TheoryUnderlyingConceptMaps.pdf
(accessed October 22, 2009).

O'Conner, Patricia T. *Woe Is I: The Grammarphobe's Guide to Better English in Plain
English*. New York: Riverhead, 1996.

——. *Words Fail Me: What Everyone Who Writes Should Know about Writing*. New
York: Harcourt Brace, 1999.

Ogren, John Albert. "Discerning Missional Criteria for the Practice of Church Planting
by the South MacArthur Church of Christ." DMin project thesis, Abilene Christian
University, 2006.

Olson, M. R. "Conceptualizing Narrative Authority: Implications for Teacher Education."
Teaching & Teacher Education 11, no. 2 (1995): 119–35.

Ornstein, A. C. "Teacher Effectiveness: A Look at What Works." *Peabody Journal of
Education* 70, no. 2 (1995): 2–23.

Pargament, K. I., and D. V. DeRosa. "What was that Sermon About? Predicting Memory
for Religious Messages From Cognitive Psychology Theory." *Journal for the Scientific
Study of Religion* 24 (1985): 180–93.

Pargament, K. I., and W. H. Silverman. "Exploring Some Correlates of Sermon Impact
on Catholic Parishioners." *Review of Religious Research* 24 (1982): 33–39.

Parsons, H. M. "What Happened at Hawthorne?" *Science* 183 (1974): 922–32.

Patton, Michael Quinn. *How to Use Qualitative Methods in Evaluation*. Thousand Oaks,
CA: Sage, 1987.

——. *Qualitative Evaluation Methods*. Thousand Oaks, CA: Sage, 1990.

——. *Qualitative Research & Evaluation Methods*. 3rd ed. Thousand Oaks, CA: Sage,
2002.

Pawluch, Dorothy, William Shaffir, and Charlene Miall, eds. *Doing Ethnography: Studying
Everyday Life*. Toronto: Canadian Scholars' Press, 2005.

Peirce, Charles S., Nathan Houser, and Christian J. W. Kloesel. *The Essential Peirce:
Selected Philosophical Writings*. 2 vols. Bloomington: Indiana University Press,
1992–1998.

Peshkin, Alan. "In Search of Subjectivity: One's Own." *Educational Researcher* 17 (1988):
17–21.

Porter, D. T., and G. W. King. "The Use of Video-tape Equipment in Improving Oral
Interpretation Performance." *The Speech Teacher* 21 (1972): 99–106.

Postman, Neil. *The End of Education: Redefining the Value of School*. New York: Alfred
A. Knopf, 1995.

Poulakos, J. "Toward a Sophistic Definition of Rhetoric." *Philosophy and Rhetoric* 16
(1983): 35–48.

Price, D. L., R. W. Terry and B. C. Johnston. "The Measurement of the Effect of Preaching
and Preaching Plus Small Group Dialogue in One Baptist Church." *Journal for the
Scientific Study of Religion* 19 (June 1980): 186–97.

Quantz, Richard A. "Interpretive Method in Historical Research: Ethnohistory
Reconsidered." In *The Teacher's Voice*, edited by R. Altenbaugh, 174–90. Washington,
DC: Falmer, 1992.

Quigley, B. L., and J. D. Nyquist. "Using Video Technology to Provide Feedback to
Students in Performance Courses." *Communication Education* 41 (1992): 324–34.

Ragsdale, D. J., and K. R. Durham. "Audience Response to Religious Fear Appeals."
Review of Religious Research 28 (Sept 1986): 40–50.

Reason, Peter. "Three Approaches to Participative Inquiry." In *Handbook of Qualitative Research*, edited by Denzin and Lincoln, 324–39. Thousand Oaks, CA, 2000.

Reese, Jeanene, ed. *A Case Method Approach to Teaching and Learning: Exploring Applications for Teaching in Academic and Community Contexts.* Abilene, TX: Association for Case Teaching, 2006.

Reid, Robert. *Four Voices of Preaching.* Grand Rapids: Brazos, 2006.

Rendle, Gil, and Alice Mann. *Holy Conversations: Strategic Planning as a Spiritual Practice for Congregations.* Herndon, VA: Alban, 2003.

Reynolds, Bert. "Deep Calls to Deep: Equipping Teachers for Facilitating Classes on Spiritual Disciplines in the Chenal Valley Church of Christ." DMin project thesis, Abilene Christian University, 2006.

Riessman, Catherine Kohler. *Narrative Analysis.* Qualitative Research Methods Series 30. Newbury Park, CA: Sage, 1993.

Rife, C. B. "The Understanding and Utilization of Feedback in the Preaching Situation." DMin diss., Wesley Theological Seminary, 1973.

Savage, Carl, and William Presnell. *Narrative Research in Ministry: A Postmodern Research Approach for Faith Communities.* Louisville: Wayne E. Oates Institute, 2008.

Schön, Donald A. *The Reflective Practitioner: How Professionals Think in Action.* Burlington, VT: Ashgate, 1995.

Scriven, Michael. "Philosophical Inquiry Methods in Education." In *Complementary Methods for Research in Education*, edited by Richard M. Jaeger, 131–48. Washington, DC: American Educational Research Association, 1988.

Sensing, Tim. *African American Preaching in Churches of Christ.* DVD presentation and interviews. Cullen Grant 2002–2003. Archived at the Abilene Christian University Library.

———. "Pedagogies of Preaching." PhD diss., University of North Carolina Greensboro, 1998.

———. *The Testing of the Validity of Buttrick's Homiletic: Preaching from Matthew 13.* DMin thesis, Harding Graduate School of Religion, 1992.

Shadish, William R. "The Logic of Generalization: Five Principles Common to Experiments and Ethnographies." *American Journal of Community Psychology* 23.3 (1995): 424–6.

Shaffir, William B., and Robert A. Stebbins, eds. *Experiencing Fieldwork: An Inside View of Qualitative Research.* Newbury Park, CA: Sage, 1991.

Shulman, Lee S. "Disciplines of Inquiry in Education: An Overview." In *Complementary Methods for Research in Education*, edited by Richard M. Jaeger, 3–17. Washington, DC: American Educational Research Association, 1988.

Siburt, John B. "Crossing the Threshold: Catechesis as a Means for Discerning Relevant Christian Virtues for Members of the Richardson East Church of Christ." DMin project thesis, Abilene Christian University, 2005.

Sikkink, D. E. "An Experimental Study of the Effects on the Listener of Anticlimax Order and Authority in an Argumentative Speech." *Southern Speech Journal* 22 (Winter 1956): 73–78.

Smiley, Tavis. "Tavis Smiley: How to Get More from Your Subjects—PBS." Public Broadcasting Service. YouTube video. http://www.youtube.com/watch?v=loPmtnx I12o (accessed September 1, 2009).

Smith, R. G. "Development of a Semantic Differential for use with Speech Related Concepts." *Speech Monographs* 26 (Nov 1959): 263–72.

———. "Validation of a Semantic Differential." *Speech Monographs* 30 (Mar 1963): 50–55.

Snow, Luther K. *The Power of Asset Mapping: How Your Congregation Can Act on Its Gifts.* Herndon, VA: Alban, 2004.

Social Research Association. "Ethical Guidelines." http://www.the-sra.org.uk /documents/pdfs/ethics03.pdf (accessed October 22, 2009).

Spradley, James P. *The Ethnographic Interview.* Developmental Research Sequence. New York: Holt, Rinehart and Winston, 1979.

———. *Participant Observation.* Developmental Research Sequence. New York: Holt, Rinehart and Winston, 1980.

Stake, Robert E. "Case Studies." In *Handbook of Qualitative Research*, edited by Denzin and Lincoln, 236–47. Thousand Oaks, CA: Sage, 1994.

Stevens, W. E. "A Rating Scale for Public Speakers." *Quarterly Journal of Speech* 14 (April 1928): 223–32.

Stone, Howard W., and James O. Duke. *How to Think Theologically.* 2nd ed. Minneapolis: Fortress, 2006.

Stringer, Ernest T. *Action Research.* 2nd ed. Thousand Oaks, CA: Sage, 1999.

———. *Action Research.* 3rd ed. Thousand Oaks, CA: Sage, 2007.

Swinton, John, and Harriet Mowat. *Practical Theology and Qualitative Research.* London: SCM Press, 2006.

Szala-Meneok, Karen, and Lynne Lohfeld. "The Charms and Challenges of an Academic Qualitative Researcher Doing Participatory Action Research (PAR)." In *Doing Ethnography: Studying Everyday Life*, edited by Dorothy Pawluch, William Shaffir, and Charlene Miall, 52–56. Toronto: Canadian Scholars' Press, 2005.

Thelen, M. H., R. A. Fry, P. A. Fehrenbach, and N. M. Frautschi. "Therapeutic Videotape and Film Modeling: A Review." *Psychological Bulletin* 86 (1979): 701–20.

Thiemann, R. "The Scholarly Vocation: Its Future Challenges and Threats." *Theological Education* 24 (1987): 86–101.

Thomas, David. "Putting Nature to the Rack: Narrative Studies as Research." Practical theologians' Stories of Life and Work Conference, Liverpool, ERIC Document Reproduction Service No. ED 346 451, 1992.

Thompson, W. N. "An Experimental Study of the Accuracy of Typical Speech Rating Techniques." *Speech Monographs* 11 (1944): 65–79.

Thumma, Scott L. "Methods for Congregational Study." In *Studying Congregations: A New Handbook*, edited by Nancy T. Ammerman, Jackson W. Carroll, Carl S. Dudley, and William McKinney, 199–226. Nashville: Abingdon, 1998.

Tillich, Paul. *Systematic Theology.* Vol. 1. London: SCM Press, 1951.

Tisdale, Leonora Tubbs. *Preaching as Local Theology and Folk Art.* Minneapolis: Fortress, 1997.

Tracy, David. *Blessed Rage of Order.* New York: Seabury, 1975.

UCLA Health Sciences. "CTRL Training." UCLA Health Sciences, David Geffen School of Medicine. http://training.arc.ucla.edu/ (accessed October 22, 2009).

University of Wales Institute. "UWIC Student Services." http://www.uwic.ac.uk /studentservices/useofinclusivelanguage/ (accessed October 22, 2009).

U.S. Copyright Office. "Fair Use." http://www.copyright.gov/fls/fl102.html (accessed October 22, 2009).

U.S. Department of Health and Human Services. "Code of Federal Regulations: Title 45, Public Welfare, Part 46, Protection of Human Subjects." http://www.hhs.gov/ohrp /humansubjects/guidance/45cfr46.htm (accessed October 22, 2009).

U.S. National Institutes of Health. "Educational Materials About Clinical Trials." National Cancer Institute. http://cme.nci.nih.gov (accessed October 22, 2009).

Utterback, W.E. "Measuring the Reaction of an Audience to an Argumentative Speech." *Quarterly Journal of Speech Education* 8 (April 1922): 180–3.

Van Manen, Max. *Researching Lived Experience: Human Science for an Action Sensitive Pedagogy*. New York: State University of New York Press, 1990.

Vyhmeister, Nancy Jean. *Quality Research Papers for Students of Religion and Theology*. Grand Rapids: Zondervan, 2001.

Wardlaw, Don. M., ed. *Learning Ministry: Understanding and Participating in the Process*. Lincoln, IL: The Academy of Homiletics, 1989.

Weijer, Charles, Gary Goldsand, and Ezekiel J. Emanuel. "Protecting Communities in Research: Current Guidelines and Limits of Extrapolation." *Nature Genetics* 23, no. 3 (1999): 275–80.

West, Cornel. *The American Evasion of Philosophy: A Genealogy of Pragmatism*. Madison: University of Wisconsin Press, 1989.

Whitney, Diana, and David L. Cooperrider. "The Appreciative Inquiry Summit: Overview and Applications." *Employment Relations Today* (Summer 1998): 17–28.

Whitney, Diana, and Amanda Trosten-Bloom. *The Power of Appreciative Inquiry: A Practical Guide to Positive Change*. San Francisco: Barrett-Koehler, 2003.

Wilke, W. H. "A Speech Profile." *Quarterly Journal of Speech* 26 (Dec 1940): 625–30.

Wilson, P. S. *The Practice of Ministry*. Nashville: Abingdon, 1995.

Wilson, R. "Video Technology Revisited in Teacher Training." *Educational Media and Technology Yearbook* 17 (1991): 54–62.

Witherell, Carol, and Nel Noddings. *Stories Lives Tell: Narrative and Dialogue in Education*. New York: Teachers College Press, 1991.

Wolcott, Harry F. *Writing Up Qualitative Research*. 3rd ed. Qualitative Research Methods Series 20. Newbury Park, CA: Sage, 2009.

Woodward, H.S. "Measurement and Analysis of Audience Opinion." *Quarterly Journal of Speech* 14 (Feb 1928): 94–111.

Yin, Robert K. *Case Study Research: Design and Methods*. Thousand Oaks, CA: Sage, 2003.

Subject Index

A

abduction, 181
academic integrity, 37–38
action-reflection, xii, xix, xv, xxvii, 8, 231
action research, xv, xx, 13, 16, 42, 52, 54, 55n, 56, 59, 61, 63–64, 144, 157, 168, 216, 226, 229
analysis,
    case, 148–49
    computer-assisted, 176
    congregational, 14n
    content, 62
    contextual, 141
    Criss-Cross, 128–29
    document, 125, 181, 196–09, 211
    heuristic, 181
    inter-textual, 167
    intra-textual, 167
    narrative, 165, 167
    pattern, 225
    secondary, 157, 202
    statistical, 74, 83, 85, 90, 106, 114, 116–17
    structural, 163, 225
    theme, 162
    theological, 192
analytical framework, 210
angle
    insider, 74–75, 78, 90, 168
    of interpretation, 74, 76–77, 125, 171, 191, 195, 197
    of evaluation, 29, 77, 116, 128, 144, 168, 180–81, 202, 221
    of vision, 43n, 76, 90, 179
    outsider, 75, 77–78, 90, 223
    reflexive, 184
    researcher, 75–78, 90

triangulation, 73–74, 115, 209, 221
anonymity, 32, 36–37, 236, 238
appendices, 30, 233
applicability, 29, 214–16, 219
appreciative inquiry, 69, 168–79
    4–D Cycle, 170–71, 173
artifacts, 14, 19, 57, 100, 124–25, 134, 136–38, 176, 194
asset mapping, 172, 175
Association for Theological Schools, xvii, 2, 16, 109
assumptions, xxi, 5, 11, 19–20, 23, 28, 44, 198, 224
auditor, 219, 223
audit trail, 181, 186, 206–07, 219, 234

B

biases, 41, 45–46, 85n, 89, 94–95, 104, 110, 134–35, 138, 149, 161, 197, 224–25
bracketing, 46–47, 149
bricoleur, 52n

C

case,
    analysis, 148–49
    deviant or disconfirming, 84, 200, 202, 222
    method, 51, 57, 62, 147
    presenting, 153–54
    resources, 156
    study, 140–44, 179–80, 190, 204, 222, 244–45
    teaching, 154–56
    writing, 149–53